Penguin Handbooks
Spanish Regional Cookery

Anna MacMiadhacháin was born in Hampstead, London,
and went to school in Watford, where she later attended
the art college. She then worked for several years for the
British Baking Industries at their research station at
Chorley Wood.

In 1960 she met and married the painter poet
Pádraig MacMiadhacháin and took up painting again.
Since then, she has travelled widely with him and has
exhibited some of her paintings at Studio 7, which she
shares with her husband near their home in Swanage,
Dorset. She has also exhibited at Liberty's and Heal's
art galleries in London and written the Iberian section for
Mitchell Beazley's *World Atlas of Food* (1974).

She has two children and her main interests are
painting and the food of the countries she visits with her
husband – especially Spain.

GW00375118

Anna MacMiadhacháin

Spanish Regional Cookery

With illustrations by the author

Penguin Books

Penguin Books Ltd,
Harmondsworth, Middlesex, England
Penguin Books Inc.,
7110 Ambassador Road, Baltimore, Maryland 21207, U.S.A.
Penguin Books Australia Ltd,
Ringwood, Victoria, Australia
Penguin Books Canada Ltd,
41 Steelcase Road West, Markham, Ontario, Canada
Penguin Books (N.Z.) Ltd,
182–190 Wairau Road, Auckland 10, New Zealand

First published 1976
Copyright © Anna MacMiadhacháin, 1976

Made and printed in Great Britain by
Richard Clay (The Chaucer Press) Ltd,
Bungay, Suffolk
Set in Monotype Ehrhardt

For Sasha, Penny, Shane and Jill

Contents

Introduction

If my husband had not become interested in Spanish food when he was living on the island of Ibiza in 1954 this book would probably never have been written. Everywhere he travelled in Spain he searched out local recipes, culling them from every source, friends, restaurants, books and newspapers. When we met in 1960 a liking for good food was one of the things which brought us together. I had been an admirer of Elizabeth David for some years and to my collection of recipes my husband added his large exercise book filled with over a hundred Spanish recipes, many of the sources long since forgotten. From 1960 we travelled together on many painting trips to remote parts of Spain, and our collection of Spanish recipes grew larger year by year, until it filled three large exercise books.

The very first time we went to live in Spain I knew virtually nothing of Spanish food apart from the rather stodgy *paella* eaten at a friend's house, and an abortive attempt of my own at making *gazpacho*. We went to paint, but we also had to eat, and eat well on a very small budget – the 'starving artist' image was not for us. This involved finding out what the local people bought in the markets and how they prepared their meals and how to make the best use of what fresh foods were cheap and readily available. Kind friends would give us recipes their mothers taught them, and whenever we ate out in one of the excellent and cheap local restaurants (there is nothing in England which stands comparison) we would ask the owners how certain dishes were prepared. This way I gradually learnt about Spanish cooking and in the process collected many recipes.

Luckily we were both addicted to garlic and olive oil and ate great quantities of the local bread which contained *anis* seeds and was crusty and delicious. I also made lots of vegetable soups using the Mouli provided by our landlord, a charming and kind priest called Don Pablo Artilles who lived below us. We lived in a small flat on the first floor of a little house overlooking the sea on the Paseo de las Canteras in Las Palmas. At that time Las Canteras beach had not yet become the crowded mass of humanity that it is now. It was one of our delights to walk along the deserted beach in the early morning to buy fish from the local boatmen as they brought in their catch. This was always a new experience as nearly every day there was some creature unknown to us caught up in the nets, often brilliant in colour and exotic in shape. The smaller ones I would often rescue and throw back into the sea, much to the amusement of the boatmen. The boats themselves were also rather beautiful, brightly painted in blue, white and yellow, with both bow and stern rising in a graceful curve. The fishermen were delighted to weigh us out the fish of our choice, and we would wander happily home bearing a plastic bag containing either a fair-sized *sama* (a beautiful pinkish-grey fish of the bream family), a kilo of sardines, or a mass of tiny *boquerones* (fry of the anchovy). I made great use of these local fish, especially the fresh sardines, which we ate covered in sea salt, grilled and washed down with red wine.

Fruits and vegetables were plentiful and cheap – in those days tomatoes were three pesetas (about two pence) a kilo – and altogether we lived pretty well. Things have changed considerably since then, but it is still possible to live well on comparatively little and enjoy the zest and piquancy of Spanish food.

One evening a couple of years ago, sitting in the warm winter air of the Canary Islands after a good meal, my husband had the idea of putting all our recipes together into a cook book of classic Spanish food, and so follows a collection, started in Ibiza in 1954 and ending in Las Palmas in 1974, but still only an introduction to Spanish food.

*

Though many of the sources of the early recipes are forgotten, I would like to thank the following, as without them this collection would not have been possible: Dr and Señora Tomas Erice Cano, Sr Luis F. Monreal, Sr Carlos Brown, Sr Antonio Amado, Rhoda Wheeler, Louise and Gerry Forte, Señora Olga Villardaga Martin, Dr Manuel Romero, the late Sr A. Llobet, Don Pablo Artilles, Sr Benito Artilles, Señora Isabel Mas de Salter, Mrs B. Engels, Mr and Mrs Tony Valenti, Sr Toledo (the Alcalde of the most beautiful island in the Canaries, La Graciosa), Sr Miguel-Angel Pujol, Sr Antonio Navarro of the Spanish embassy, the chef we met on the *Monte Umbe* (Aznar Line), and a Spanish chef we met on the Southern Ferries ship *Eagle*. He was a passenger on the ship (it is a very pleasant way of reaching Spain via Portugal) and he spent two evenings giving us recipes; our great disappointment is that we wrote down everything but his name. Also thanks to my mother for her patient typing and our long-suffering editor Jill Norman.

ANNA MacMIADHACHÁIN

SANTIAGO

GALICIA

ASTURIAS

BASQUE

NAVARRE

OLD CASTILE

LEÓN

SEGOVIA MADRID

PORTUGAL

NEW CASTILE

ESTREMADURA

MURCIA

CORDOBA

SEVILLE

ANDALUSIA

JEREZ DE LA FRONTERA

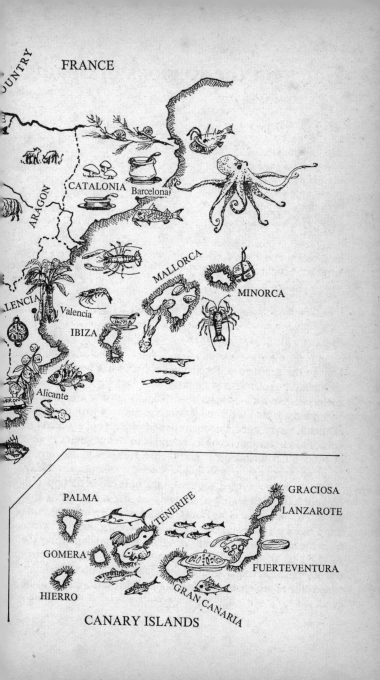

FRANCE

BASQUE COUNTRY

ARAGON

CATALONIA

Barcelona

MALLORCA

MINORCA

VALENCIA

Valencia

IBIZA

Alicante

PALMA

GRACIOSA

LANZAROTE

TENERIFE

GOMERA

FUERTEVENTURA

HIERRO

GRAN CANARIA

CANARY ISLANDS

Notes on the Regions of Spain

The soul of all the winds
sweeps the sky and plains
of Old Castile
giving an historic death
to Gothic castles
churches
walled cities
dignity to thin standing men
ice winter on their shoulders
burnt grass as summer shoes

death washes blue
the cotton shrouds
of Spain.

Pádraig MacMiadhacháin

During the past two or three decades Spain has become an in-creasingly popular tourist country, and many people have be-come familiar with Spanish food. Inevitably much of this has been food adapted for foreign tastes, sometimes with disastrous results. Richard Ford, that unsurpassed observer of Spanish life, wrote 'whenever their cookery attempts to be foreign it . . . ends in being a flavourless copy' and though this was written over a hundred years ago it still holds good to some extent today. Travellers have returned home with the impression that Spanish cookery has little identity of its own and that it is in fact rather poor. This of course is far from true as anyone with an inquiring mind will soon discover. One has only to venture a small distance from the main tourist centres to find the cafés and bars where the real Spanish food is served, and where the Spaniards themselves eat. Even so, having found these places it is helpful to know which dishes are special to the region and therefore sure to be good.

Until the fifteenth century, and the reign of Ferdinand and Isabella, the Iberian peninsular, which includes Portugal, was divided into many small kingdoms and principalities, each fiercely independent, defending itself against the others. The regions of Spain are based on these ancient kingdoms and though no frontiers exist now they still retain to a great extent their individuality in their way of life, their architecture and, especially, their food. These regions are distinct from the provinces of Spain. Modern Spain is subdivided into forty-eight such provinces, and each region may consist of several. For example, the Spanish Basque country contains the three provinces of Viscaya, Guipuizcoa and Álava, whereas Navarre is both a province and a region. Geographically, too, Spain is divided and sectioned off by jagged chains of mountains, arid plateaux and deep gorges, which until less than a century ago made communications extremely difficult. People tended to stay in their own towns and villages, often for their entire lifetime, and it is therefore not surprising that a feeling of belonging to a certain region is deeply entrenched in every Spaniard.

Perhaps of all the regions of Spain the Basque country is one of the richest from the culinary point of view. It has the best of both worlds, being blest on the one hand with a rugged coastline along the Bay of Biscay, offering an abundant supply of all the best that the cold northern sea has to offer – dozens of different kinds of shellfish, sardines, anchovies, bream, hake and tuna, all of the finest quality and flavour; and, on the other hand, away from the coast, the many small farms, which produce some of the finest cattle, sheep and dairy foods in Spain. The big four-square Basque farmhouses provide shelter for animals and humans alike and with their huge shallow-pitched red-tiled roofs spreading protectively out over the metre-thick stone walls they give a feeling of solid security.

The Basques have prodigious appetites which befit their colder climate, but this in no way affects their appreciation of the finer points of good cooking. There exist in the Basque towns gastronomic societies – esoteric groups of men (and only men) devoted to the art of producing ever better and more refined dishes. Needless to say, I have never penetrated such a gathering, but I have tasted much Basque food, which is without doubt excellent.

Further inland from the Basque country the landscape changes from green to pale ochres and browns and here the villages crowd on to the tops of small hills and are the same colour as the earth. This is Navarre, where the rivers, swollen with the melting snows of the Pyrenees, are famous for their trout. The carefully tended vineyards of the Rioja wine-growing district begin to appear in Navarre, and from there they stretch south into Old Castile, and surround Logroño, the centre of the Rioja wine-growing area. But following the road further east and then north and upwards into the Pyrenees one comes into Aragon, a hilly and then mountainous country of birch and pine forests, and the long-haired lacha sheep, good for both their milk and meat. In a remote village near the French border we were offered a delicacy savoured by the local inhabitants. These were lamb's heads, split in two but otherwise intact, and simply roasted. Laced with plenty of garlic, which is used heavily in this region, and served sizzling hot they were absolutely delicious. The lambs reared on the mountain slopes have a close-textured, sweet-tasting meat unlike any other, and a good *cordero en chilindrón* (an Aragonese dish of lamb and red peppers) is hard to beat.

Travelling down from the Pyrenees, but still in Aragon, and following the broad valley of the River Ebro, one eventually reaches Catalonia, and the first smell of the Mediterranean. At one time Catalonia was a kingdom which stretched across the border and included a sizeable piece of France. The French–Mediterranean influence is quite noticeable in Catalan cooking, which is rich in the use of aromatic herbs, garlic and fragrant olive oil. Snails are relished here and French omelettes too are popular, often filled with the delicate tips of wild asparagus or tiny button mushrooms. This is the region of interesting sauces, not by any means all French. That pungent Catalan garlic sauce *all-i-oli* is said to have originated in Roman times, and the hot red sauce *romesco* or *romescu*, made with tiny red peppers from a special valley in the region, is a Catalan invention. *All-i-oli* and *romesco* sauces are often served at the same time in separate small bowls, one complementing the other. *Romesco* sauce can be extremely hot and should be eaten with caution; a little *all-i-oli* taken with it can soften the impact.

The Balearic Islands, and in particular Mallorca, are similar in many respects to Catalonia – snails are eaten here too and are cultivated in some places, and both Mallorca and Catalonia produce excellent sausages, *butifarra* and *sobresada*, though *sobresada* is traditionally Mallorquin in origin. These are used in many local dishes, such as *butifarra con rovellons* (red pine mushrooms), *butifarra* with broad beans and potatoes with *sobresada*. *Sobresada* is also used as a basic flavouring in many soups and stews.

Mallorca is an extremely beautiful island once away from the tourist areas, and has to my mind a great deal to offer as well as excellent food. In summer the wooded hillsides are sweetly scented with wild thyme, rosemary and lavender, and a hundred other warm intangible perfumes of the Mediterranean soil, and in the winter the smell of burning olive wood hangs like incense over the villages. The people are gentle and friendly and life here has an ease about it and a sense of quiet sophistication.

Ibiza too is intensely beautiful, though here the Moorish influence is more obvious and the white villages begin to take on the aspect of Southern Spain, with their small square flat-roofed houses and blue painted shutters.

Menorca is different again in character, and perhaps less touched by tourism than the others. It is windy and fairly flat and has a wild beauty of its own. It used to be a favourite resting-place for the migrating quails, once trapped here in their thousands. Quails are still a popular dish here as elsewhere in Spain, which may account for the fact that there are not so many left now. Menorca produces an excellent cheese – called *queso de Mahón* which is fashioned in a large flat rectangular shape with rounded corners, and is usually sold with a bit of grass rope round it, the rope from which it was suspended while maturing. Unfortunately, like so many other good Spanish cheeses, it is not exported to Britain.

To return to the mainland you take a boat to Barcelona. This is often a rough trip, and before the airstrips were built it was the only method of travelling between the islands and the mainland.

Once in Barcelona it is not a very long drive southward through the vineyards of Tarragona into the lush region of Valencia, which contains the three provinces of Castellón, Valencia and Alicante.

The city of Valencia itself is a huge port and also one of Spain's major agricultural towns. It lies in the centre of the bowl-shaped area of the old kingdom of Valencia. Originally developed by the Moors it has become one of the most densely populated and richest agricultural districts in Europe, and the Moors' intricate systems of irrigation and terracing exist to this day, though much was allowed to fall into decay after their final defeat by the Christians in 1492. The huge groves of sweet oranges, and almonds, the *huertas* (vegetable gardens) and the great rice fields of the Albufera lagoon were all laid down by the Moors, who during their seven-hundred-year-long occupation of Spain radically changed the face of the country. These Muslim invaders from Africa were a mixture of Berbers, Arabs and Syrians, collectively called Moros (Moors) by the Spaniards. They were a cultured people who brought a rich infusion of new blood into Spanish life. Spain blossomed culturally and economically under their rule and parts which had been arid deserts before burst into green life and productivity. New spices, exotic fruits and strange foods from the East became a part of everyday life, and it is in Valencia, and all around the southern coasts of Spain and up into the fertile river valleys that the legacy of the Moorish occupation is most in evidence.

Because of the plentiful rice, vegetables and seafood it is not surprising that Valencia became the birthplace of one of Spain's national dishes – the *paella*. The Spanish have always been expert at combining local resources to make a perfect dish, and the *paella* is a prime example. It is often difficult to get a really good *paella* outside Valencia, and the purists say that it has to be cooked over a wood fire, and preferably in the open air to be just right. This, they say, is because the flames have to lick round the sides of the pan to cook the rice properly. Perhaps this is why Spanish families are so fond of picnics. Often whole parties set off on a Sunday morning with a huge *paëllera*, bags of rice and an assortment of the ingredients of their choice, to find a favourite spot, light a fire and make a giant paella, which gives off delicious smells in the warm air.

Just south of this delectable place lies the region of Murcia with its jumble of white houses lying along the coast, and the beginning of the great plain of La Mancha behind. This region includes the two provinces of Murcia and Albacete (*Al-basiti* – the plain – of Moorish times), and is quite a contrast to the lush vegetation of Valencia. It is a region of spices and strongly flavoured dishes, and strong wines to go with them – some of the red wines of Jumilla and Bleda reach a dizzy nineteen degrees proof. A delicious variation of *sangría* is made here in which the red wine is diluted with a little carbonated water, peach juice and fresh peaches – it is called *cuerva*, and is drunk from shallow earthenware bowls of ancient design.

Andalusia, the next region following the road south, is the largest in Spain, and stretches across the whole of the southern part of the country. This is the Spain of popular imagination – the land of fiesta, flamenco, romantic gipsies and the sound of guitars being played behind closed shutters. It is the traditional land of *sombre y sol* – with the contrasts of brilliant sunshine and the deep shadows of shaded patios – where the centre of the house is the cool tinkle of water instead of a crackling fire. Less romantically it is known as the region of the frying-pan, for here are the ingredients for perfect frying – olive oil in abundance and small fish in their multitudes from the sea. Andalusians have a light touch with the frying-pan. Perfectly dry, crisp and sizzling hot fish emerge from the pan, cooked for exactly the right length of time and at exactly the right temperature. This is quite a difficult feat as most cooks will know. Heavy food is not suitable for this climate and the people tend to be slim, with the darker skin and hotter temperament of their Moorish ancestry.

The region is cut across by the majestic ranges of the Sierra Nevada and backed by the Sierra Morena, from where the vast high central tableland of Spain stretches out northward to Madrid and beyond. These are the ancient kingdoms of old and new Castile, and Leon, a brown and dusty landscape where the villages often look more like heaps of rubble than human habitations, and great medieval cities such as Avila, Salamanca and

Segovia rise like mirages out of the plain. It has a wild majestic quality which totally captures you once experienced. The climate here runs to extremes with short bitterly cold winters and long burning summers; the rainfall is sparse and erratic which makes the growing of crops difficult. Sheep roam in vast flocks on La Mancha, the south-eastern part of the plain, and these produce that other very fine cheese of Spain – Manchego. This is eaten either fairly young and soft, when it has the consistency of Cheddar, or later when it gets crumbly and hard, not unlike the Italian Parmesan. Either way it has a unique flavour, and the softer kind is often eaten with a knife and fork as a separate course. *Pisto manchego* is another speciality from La Mancha, rather like *ratatouille*, but often with pieces of chicken, ham or bacon mixed with it. However, the central plains of Spain are generally thought of as the regions of the roasts, especially the baby lambs and piglets so rightly prized by the Spaniards. Segovia in particular specializes in roast suckling pigs, and the famous restaurant of Casa Candida, which has a magnificent view of the great Roman viaduct, will serve you this succulent dish perfectly cooked.

Madrid is, of course, the hub of Spain, and once all roads spanned out like a spider's web from the city. Now Spanish roads are many and excellent, and modern Madrid is expanding at a tremendous rate. Here you will find restaurants from all over the world, and, especially interesting, from all the regions of Spain. If you want to sample regional dishes to perfection it is only necessary to spend a little time in Madrid, if your gastronomic staying power can stand it.

To the west of the plains of Castile lies that rather desolate part of Spain, Extremadura. The great armies of the Conquistadores were largely made up of men from Extremadura, as they were tough and brave, hardy countrymen used to the rigours of life in this wild place. The old dishes from Extremadura were designed to make the best use of everything nourishing available and even lizards were eaten. Some of the best dishes, however, use the partridges and hares which thrive in this kind of terrain.

There are some beautiful old towns in Extremadura – Caceres, for example, where the storks make their ragged nests on every high building – and everywhere there are the busts of local heroes, and monuments to the glory of Spain's past.

Galicia, too, in the north-west corner of Spain, has an important place in history for here is the ancient city of Santiago de Compostela, for centuries a place of pilgrimage for Christians from all over Europe. The old road – the Camino de Santiago – that winds down across the Somport Pass in the Pyrenees and continues for 800 kilometres over the plains and hills of northern Spain, is still signposted. The people of Galicia are Celtic in origin and their food tends to reflect this. The climate is comparatively cold and wet and good for growing the greens and potatoes which form an important part of their diet. Their best-known dish is probably *lacón con grelos*, hand of pork boiled with green turnip tops and served with potatoes and corn bread. Galicia is also a wonderful place for shellfish, and the shellfish *tapas* served in the coastal towns are some of the best in Spain. Small red crabs called *necoras* are a speciality in La Coruña and the scallop, which is the symbol of St James, is a speciality of Santiago de Compostela.

The green hills of Galicia gradually give way eastwards to the more mountainous region of Asturias whose jagged granite rocks run right down to the sea in some places. Asturias produces that very special black smoked sausage used in *fabada asturiana*, the regional stew which is so well loved all over Spain.

Lastly there are those faraway and delightful islands, the Canaries, known to ancient travellers as the Fortunate Isles. Their climate has been called an everlasting spring, which is much appreciated the year round, and especially in winter, by the sun-starved northern Europeans and Scandinavians. The Canary Islands consist of two provinces – Gran Canary and Tenerife – and between them there exists a friendly rivalry. There are seven principal islands, and each one is different from the others in character and customs. The food of all the islands has a bias towards fish, most of which is caught off the African banks, and to fruit and vegetables, which grow in a rich variety according to altitude. The islands are volcanic in origin and are quite high in places – the volcano of Tiede on Tenerife reaches 12,000 feet. Though tourism is very important, the old Spanish way of life still goes on much as before in most places, and there are even traces of the Guanches (the indigenous people of the islands), mostly in place-names and in traditional foods such as *gofio*.

The strange thing is that this whole great nation, peninsula and islands, with its diversities of race, language and climate, has running through the heart of it something special that unifies it, so that wherever you set foot upon the land you know at once that it is unmistakably Spanish.

The river had died
and its dry stone bones were hard
with a golden onion hanging above
burning our skin with its sting
sharp edged
as the swords of Toledo.

PADRAIG MacMIADHACHÁIN

Weights and Measures

Metric measurements have been used throughout this book and the following table of comparative weights and volumes of common items used in cooking may be useful.

	Level tablespoons	Grammes
Black olives with stones	5	100
Brown lentils	5	100
Chickpeas	5	100
Chopped green beans	5	75
Dried beans	5	100
Flour	5	75
Fresh breadcrumbs	5	25
Ground almonds	5	50
Minced meat	5	100
Raisins	5	125
Rice	5	100
Soft brown sugar	5	75
White sugar	5	125
Whole unpeeled almonds	5	100

Tomatoes. Medium can is 14 oz. (397 g) size; small can is 8 oz. (227 g) size.

When a **tablespoonful** is referred to the British *level* tablespoon is intended. (The American equivalent is $1\frac{1}{2}$ level tablespoons.) The **cup** referred to holds 10 fluid oz. (equivalent to $1\frac{1}{4}$ American cups).

Standard Weights and Measures

Liquid Measures

British

1 quart	= 2 pints	= 40 fluid oz.
1 pint	= 4 gills	= 20 fl. oz.
½ pint	= 2 gills	
	or one cup	= 10 fl. oz.
¼ pint	= 8 tablespoons	= 5 fl. oz.
	1 tablespoon	= just over ½ fl. oz.
	1 dessertspoon	= ⅓ fl. oz.
	1 teaspoon	= ⅙ fl. oz.

Metric

1 litre = 10 decilitres (dl) = 100 centilitres (cl) = 1,000 milli-litres (ml)

American

1 quart	= 2 pints	= 32 fl. oz.
1 pint	= 2 cups	= 16 fl. oz.
	1 cup	= 8 fl. oz.
	1 tablespoon	= ⅓ fl. oz.
	1 teaspoon	= ⅙ fl. oz.

Approx. equivalents

British	Metric	American
1 quart	1·1 litre	2½ pints
1 pint	6 dl	1¼ pints
½ pint	3 dl	10 fl. oz. (1¼ cups)
¼ pint (1 gill)	1·5 dl	5 fl. oz.
1 tablespoon	15 ml	1½ tablespoons
1 dessertspoon	10 ml	1 tablespoon
1 teaspoon	5 ml	⅙ fl. oz.

Metric	British and American
1 litre	35 fl. oz.
½ litre (5 dl)	18 fl. oz.
¼ litre (2·5 dl)	9 fl. oz.
1 dl	3½ fl. oz.

American	British		Metric
1 quart	1½ pints + 3 tbs. (32 fl. oz.)		9·5 dl
1 pint	¾ pint + 2 tbs. (16 fl. oz.)		4·7 dl
1 cup	½ pint — 3 tbs. (8 fl. oz.)		2·4 dl

Solid Measures

Approx. equivalents

British	Metric
1 lb. (16 oz.)	450 g
½ lb. (8 oz.)	225 g
¼ lb. (4 oz.)	110 g
1 oz.	25 g

Metric	British
1 kg (1,000 g)	2 lb. 3 oz.
½ kg (500 g)	1 lb. 2 oz.
¼ kg (250 g)	9 oz.
100 g	3½ oz.

Oven Temperatures

Fahrenheit	Gas Mark	Centigrade	Heat of Oven
225° F	¼	110° C	Very cool
250° F	½	130° C	Very cool
275° F	1	140° C	Cool
300° F	2	150° C	Cool
325° F	3	170° C	Moderate
350° F	4	180° C	Moderate
375° F	5	190° C	Fairly hot
400° F	6	200° C	Fairly hot
425° F	7	220° C	Hot
450° F	8	230° C	Very hot
475° F	9	240° C	Very hot

Special Equipment

It is not absolutely essential to have any special equipment for Spanish cookery – except perhaps a large pestle and mortar. But there are one or two things that help a lot. One gadget I would hate to be without is my garlic press, which is French, although bought in Spain; these are usually obtainable in kitchen shops in this country. It is neat, easy to clean, and makes what was a messy chore into one simple operation. You can crush quite a big clove of garlic with one squeeze of the fingers. You really have to like garlic to enjoy Spanish cooking to the full, though it is rarely as overpowering as in some French and Italian dishes since it is usually used sparingly and combined with other strong flavours. The smell of fresh young garlic gently heating in olive oil is quite aromatic – almost like crushing wild garlic under your feet in an English water meadow – although not everyone shares this view.

A pestle and mortar, as I have said, are essential. Ideally two are needed, a small one for crushing cumin seeds and the like, and a larger one for making sauces. These are sold cheaply everywhere in Spain, and can usually be found in craft or kitchen shops in England. Wooden ones are nice, and we have an old pewter one that we like a lot. The porcelain or ceramic ones are best in the larger sizes.

A soup and vegetable mill is almost essential, too, but don't buy a plastic one. These have a nasty habit of springing apart at a crucial moment, and flicking lumps of half puréed vegetable over your face, the walls and the ceiling. Of course an electric blender will save you a lot of time and trouble.

The Spanish earthenware dishes so often mentioned in these recipes may be bought at Ortega Bros. in Soho, or similar ones may be bought at Habitat or at craft or kitchen shops throughout the country. They hold the flavour of the food and certainly look delightful on any table. Their great advantage is that they may be used both on top of the stove and in the oven (it is probably best to use an asbestos mat if you are cooking on gas) and of course they make the perfect traditional serving dish for Spanish food. It is worth the effort to carry some genuine ones home from a holiday in Spain if you can, as they are very cheap and come in all shapes and sizes. Some of them are made with a rounded bottom for cooking over a charcoal or wood fire – a design which has hardly changed since Roman times – but they are quite stable enough for use on a gas or electric cooker, though obviously on an electric cooker the flat-bottomed ones are more efficient. They are glazed only in the inside and are rather brittle, but we have some which have been used for many years with great success.

It is usually necessary to prime these *ollas*, *cazuelas de barra* or *greixoneras* (an old Balearic name) as they are variously known, before using them for the first time, as there may be some seepage of liquid through the porous earthenware. This is quite simply done by rubbing the entire outer unglazed surface with a juicy cut clove of garlic. Fill the pot to about one inch below the brim with cold water and set it to boil on a medium heat. When the water boils turn off the heat and allow it to cool a little. Throw the water away and your pot is ready to use. Strangely enough these pots are rarely if ever made with a lid, and the usual Spanish way of covering them is with an earthenware plate, sometimes filled with water. A typical Mallorcan method of sealing a dish is to cover the contents with a thick layer of the coarse outside leaves from a lettuce, either whole or finely shredded. Sometimes spinach is used in this way too and adds to the flavour of the food being cooked.

If you like *paellas* and enjoy cooking them it is well worth investing in a *paëllera*, the two-handled iron frying-pan made especially for the purpose. These may be bought in a wide range of sizes at Ortega Bros. in Soho, from Habitat and from kitchen shops in the larger towns. They should be kept oiled when not in use. Earthenware dishes are also made in a large flat shape especially for *paellas*.

Do get an *aceitera* if you get the chance. This is a tin object rather like an oil can in shape, and is especially good for making mayonnaise. Its long thin spout allows the oil to drip out at just the right speed and it has a nice little hinged lid. Spanish cooks use them for sprinkling oil on the *plancha* (see below) or over any dish that requires just a little oil. It is worth looking round the old-fashioned *ferreterias* (hardware shops) in any Spanish town or village to find one, or on the tinware stall in the local market. Something similar in glass is sold at Elizabeth David Ltd, 46 Bourne Street, Pimlico, London, SW1.

Lastly, that much loved object in Spanish kitchens – the *plancha*. This as its name implies (*plancha* is plate in Spanish) is an iron plate, often an integral part of the older cooking stoves. Separate *planchas* made of heavy aluminium are especially made for use with the butane gas cookers which are now almost universal throughout Spain. Many things are cooked *a la plancha*: steak, chops, seafood, and even eggs are quickly and efficiently cooked directly on the hot oiled plate. Most of the dishes in this book have been cooked both on a butane gas cooker with a *plancha* in Spain, and later re-tested in this country on an electric cooker, which has no *plancha*, but is otherwise satisfactory. Personally I think the ideal cooker for Spanish food is a solid fuel one, such as an Aga, which seems to be the nearest thing to the great black stoves used in older Spanish kitchens. Many dishes which need long gentle cooking may be left in the slow oven overnight; also you have a built-in *plancha* and a permanent source of heat for such things as pots of chickpeas and beans, which need to boil for a long time.

Special Ingredients

CHORIZO

A spiced coarsely textured red sausage, eaten in great quantities throughout Spain, either thinly sliced as a *tapa* or in a fresh crusty roll with olive oil (a *bocadillo*), or cooked in stews and soups to give a characteristic flavour and colour. It is made primarily with pork, pork fat, paprika and garlic. There are specific varieties; the finest and most expensive – such as the Rioja, Especial de Lomo, Cantimpalos and Pamplona (which is a more finely textured sausage) – are for eating raw; others more suitable for cooking are often made locally. Spanish *chorizo* may be bought in this country (there is an English-made substitute, which should be avoided) and many delicatessen and continental food shops sell it.

MORCILLA

A smoked blood sausage principally made in Asturias (an essential ingredient for *fabada*) but also found in other regions, and still prepared at home in country districts when the family pig is killed. Basic ingredients are pig's blood, fat, spices and onions. There are two kinds – ordinary *morcilla*, which is used most often, has a strong smoky flavour, and *morcilla dulce*, which is sweet and spicy and tastes not unlike Christmas pudding, and is eaten as a *tapa*. These sausages are usually stocked by specialists in Spanish foods.

BUTIFARRA or BUTIFARRONES

This sausage is also made from the pig and comes from Catalonia and the Balearic Islands, mainly Mallorca. It is made either in a large fat shape, which is a *butifarra*, or small and thin rather like chipolatas – these are called *butifarrones*. Pine-nuts, almonds, cumin seed and cinnamon give it its special taste, and there are two varieties – *negra* (black) and *blanca* (white). They are used for soups and stews and go particularly well with broad beans, which are grown extensively in Catalonia and Mallorca. These sausages are hard to find in England so if you know someone who is going to Mallorca get them to bring some back. The market in the centre of the old district of Palma de Mallorca is one of the finest in Spain, and the upper floor is filled with row upon row of stalls richly stocked with all kinds of sausages, including *butifarra*, *sobresada* and *chorizo*. Quite a good way of making imitation *butifarrones* is to pound two teaspoons of cumin seed and one of cinnamon together in a mortar and poke the resulting mixture into small incisions in an ordinary English black pudding. Use the best-quality black pudding you can find.

SOBRESADA

A typical Mallorcan sausage. It is quite different from other sausages – large in diameter, soft and smooth in texture, suitable for spreading on bread and of an orangey-red colour. The ingredients include pork, pork tripe, paprika and cayenne pepper and plenty of salt. This sausage is only made of the finest ingredients and it should keep well for months if hung in a cool airy place. Used for breakfast or as a flavouring for other dishes, it is a very common item in most Spanish kitchens.

LONGANIZAS

These are a type of *sobresada*, suitable for cooking only. They are sold in strings and are about the same size as English sausages. *Longaniza* is a rather general term and includes other kinds of sausage of about this size, varying from region to region.

SALCHICHÓN

Very similar to salami, this sausage (*salchicha* means sausage) is never used in cooking. It includes finely chopped pork, pork fat and whole white peppercorns, but no paprika, and is generally eaten as a *tapa*.

JAMÓN SERRANO

A highly esteemed delicacy. This famous ham, which is eaten raw, comes from the province of Huelva and is cured in the cold dry air and the sunshine of the Sierra Morena mountains. There are several other places in Spain which produce similar ham but the one from Huelva is reputed to be the best.

TOCINO

Salted pork fat, similar to central European *speck*. Bacon fat may sometimes be substituted.

BACALAO

Dried salt cod. (See also the chapter on fish.) This is very popular in Spain, France and especially Portugal, and used to be fairly common in England during the winter when fresh fish could be scarce. Even today housewives in the Shetlands salt their cod and hang it to dry in the sun and wind. In England it is only available from the larger fish shops or continental food shops.

OLIVE OIL

It is cheaper and more convenient to buy Spanish olive oil in bulk, either in two or four kilo cans. Torre del Oro, made in Seville, is an excellent brand available in this country. It is sold in two grades, 'extra virgin' which is made from the first pressing of the olives and tends to be rather heavy and strong in flavour, although personally I like it very much, and the standard grade which is a lighter more refined oil, simply called pure olive oil. This grade is more suitable for use with delicately flavoured foods such as lobster and other shellfish. There are many brands of olive oil made in Spain, and they vary from region to region. One I can highly recommend is Sabater, especially the 'extra virgin' quality which is delicious without being too strong. This comes from Reus in Catalonia. Boots' olive oil is one of the cheapest and best of the British brands.

PIMENTÓN

This is dried powdered red pepper, either hot (*picante*), which is cayenne, or sweet (*dulce*), which is paprika.

HERBS

All the herbs mentioned in this book can readily be obtained in Britain. If possible herbs grown at home are best, either in the garden or in pots or boxes, but if you haven't time for this the next best thing is either to buy, or beg from friends, bunches of fresh herbs such as rosemary, thyme, sage, basil and mint and hang them in a cool airy larder to dry. Ideally they should be cut just as they come into flower when their aromatic quality is at its peak. When the leaves are quite dry, crumble them into airtight jars for storage. Many brands of packet herbs are excellent – continental brands are usually the best. We always bring a good supply of little bags of herbs and spices back from a trip to Spain. Parsley is the one herb which you need in constant fresh supply. If washed and dried and put in a screw-topped jar in the fridge it will keep well for a week.

SAFFRON

Made from the stamens of the pale mauve autumn crocus, saffron is expensive. In Spain it is sold in tiny envelopes for a few pesetas apiece, each one containing about two pinches of red saffron stamens. Powdered saffron is easier and possibly more economical to use and can be bought in this country, though it doesn't always have the same pungency as the stamens as it sometimes contains additives. When using saffron stamens you can either gently toast and then crush them, or soak them in a little hot water or stock, crushing them with the back of a teaspoon till their brilliant yellow colour infuses into the liquid. Saffron gives the yellow colour to *paella* and other dishes, and has a subtle warm bitter flavour.

GARBANZOS

Chickpeas. These are used in many Spanish dishes and have a unique flavour, rather like chestnuts.

PINE-NUTS

Pine-nuts grow round the Mediterranean coasts and are used a lot in Catalan cooking. They are sometimes available in health food shops and continental food shops in this country.

VINEGAR

Wine vinegar is always used in Spanish cookery, but one need not be too dogmatic about this and in many cases malt vinegar will do just as well.

To sum up – if you enjoy Spanish cooking you can stock your kitchen and larder with all kinds of *comestibles* (groceries) so that you can have everything to hand. A piece of *bacalao* hanging up, a *chorizo*, a few strings of onions and garlic, a big can of olive oil and you are well on your way to a Spanish kitchen. (An alternative way of storing *bacalao* is to cut or saw it into fairly large pieces and to put approximately enough for each meal into a polythene bag and seal it tightly.) Keep as many herbs as you can and always have some paprika and cayenne pepper in the cupboard. Pulses, such as brown lentils, chickpeas and white and red beans should be stored in jars. If you also have some cans of tomatoes, tomato paste and asparagus tips in the cupboard you have the basis for many of the dishes in this book.

List of Suppliers

Most health food stores and delicatessen shops stock chickpeas and brown lentils, and many delicatessens, continental food shops, the food sections of large department stores, and even some chains of supermarkets sell *chorizo* and *tocino* or *speck*. *Morcilla* and *serrano* ham are usually only sold in shops that specialize in Spanish products, and so are pine-nuts, though these can also be found in Greek and Middle Eastern shops. The following is a list of shops throughout the country which sell most of the Spanish products mentioned in this book, subject to fluctuations in supplies.

Centro Español: A. Gomez Ortega Ltd,
74–6 Old Compton Street, Soho, London, W 1.
(They have a catalogue and postal service.)

L. Palm Ltd, Delicatessen,
84, The Market, Oxford.

Sargeson Food Shops Ltd,
48 White Ladies Road, Clifton, Bristol, and
22 Portland Street, Old Clifton, Bristol.

Continental Food Centre,
148 Cornwall Street, Plymouth.

The Delicatessen,
Christchurch Road, Bournemouth.

Langford's Larder Ltd,
89c Church Road, Hove.

Dossetts Delicatessen,
36 The Market Place, Cirencester.

Gourmet,
6 The Forum, Bell Walk, Gloucester.

'Concetta', Continental Foods,
13 Henry Street, Swindon.

Cullens,
The Quay, Dartmouth.

Forsyth's Food Hall and Wine Gallery,
3 St Andrew Square, Edinburgh.
(Postal service.)

C. & A. Bain,
47 Station Road, Newcastle-upon-Tyne.
(Will obtain *chorizo* to order.)

Rowntrees,
10 The Pavement, York.

Beatties of Wolverhampton.

Cambridge Continental Store,
9 The Broadway, Cambridge.

Continental & Delicatessen Food Stores,
Fish Hall, Leicester Retail Market, Leics.

The Delicatesserie,
146 High Street, Stourbridge, Worcs.

Owen Owen Ltd,
Broadgate, Coventry.

Manchester Delicatessen,
58 Wilmslow Road, Manchester 14.

C. de Paolo,
2 Rippinghams Road, Manchester 20.

Schofields,
The Headrow, Leeds.

Walsh's of Sheffield,
50 High Street, Sheffield.

Spanish Wines

Spain is the third largest wine-producing country in the world, with France and Italy taking first and second place. Although thousands of square miles of vineyards flourish throughout the country, less wine per acre is produced than in either France or Italy, because of the unreliable and sporadic rainfall. This also accounts for the variation in the quality of the wine from year to year.

The areas which produce the best wines are, first the Rioja district in the north of Spain, which possibly produces the best wines of all, and includes the region of Navarre in the upland valleys of the Pyrenees, and part of Old Castile. Vineyards have been established here since pre-Roman times and the wine industry is centred on the ancient town of Logroño. Second comes the district of Valdepeñas in the central southern part of Spain, surrounding the town of that name. This area roughly takes in the plains of La Mancha and most of New Castile south of Madrid. Here fairly strong dry red wines of excellent quality are produced. Alella is another good wine-making area, though a relatively small one, lying just north of Barcelona and reaching up towards the French frontier. Here very good white wines are made, notably the Panadés wines.

There is only one region in Spain where wine is not the principal drink, and this is the rocky province of Asturias on the north Atlantic seaboard. Excellent apples are grown here and they make very good cider. In the Basque provinces lying north of Asturias and reaching up across the Pyrenees it is the custom to drink *chacolí*, a green wine or a *vino verde* – a young wine, very sharp and acid, and best drunk in its own climate and with the foods of the region. Another rather extraordinary wine from the north of Spain is El Ribiero from Galicia, also a green wine; it tastes almost like cider and is often opaque. In the bars and tavernas it is drunk from shallow white porcelain bowls instead of glasses and is quite unlike any other wine I have ever tasted.

It is the custom for everybody to drink wine with meals in Spain and locally produced wines are on sale everywhere, many of them excellent. The most popular are the reds, then the whites. Rosé is not drunk widely in Spain – probably because it is too light a wine to accompany many Spanish dishes.

Wine may either be bought *corriente*, or loose, from the *bodegas*, in which case you take your own bottle or carafe to be filled from the cask, or ready bottled in one-litre bottles from good stores, supermarkets and also from the *bodegas*. Though Spanish wines may lack the delicacy of some of the French wines, they are none the less of fine quality and are usually aromatic and full-bodied and go well with the robust Spanish food. No great importance is to be given to the drinking of red wine with meat and white with fish or fowl; for example a white wine would be lost in competition with many Spanish fish dishes, particularly those made with *bacalao*.

Unfortunately Spanish table wines have acquired rather a poor reputation in this country. This is probably because of the large-scale bulk shipments of the cheaper blended wines, bottled in this country by the shipper and sold under various brand names. Though many of these wines are quite pleasant, inexpensive and certainly drinkable, the quality is not at all consistent. This is a pity, as it gives the impression that Spanish wines are generally rather poor, which is untrue. These wines bear little relation to most of the excellent table wines which are produced and sold throughout Spain, though not exported to this country.

However, there are a few very good Spanish wines which are bottled by the grower and exported to Britain – one of these is the Marques de Riscal, produced both as a red and a rosé. It is a light, dry wine and is justly highly esteemed in Spain, particularly the rosé. Another very fine wine which is bottled and exported by the grower is the Marques de Murrieta. This estate produces both a red and a rosé, and an extremely good white wine – one of the finest from the Rioja district. All these wines should be available throughout Britain from the better wine merchants.

Two other good Spanish table wines available in Britain are Tarragona and Malaga. Tarragona is the general name given to a low-priced sweet red table wine made from grapes grown in the district surrounding Tarragona. Malaga is a rather strong heavy dessert wine, produced in a variety of types, some of which may be fortified. It is made from the same grapes as some of the sherries, for example the Pedro Ximenez, and the moscatel, and these are grown in the hills surrounding Malaga in the south of Spain, near the sherry-producing district.

SHERRY

Sherry is a fortified and blended wine made from the grapes grown only in the thirty square miles of chalky soil surrounding the small town of Jerez de la Frontera in Andalusia, from which the wine takes its name. Here the combination of soil and a reliable climate produces grapes of a unique and consistent quality – these include the Pedro Ximenez grape, the moscatel and the white palomino. The production of sherry is a skilled and complex process which has been developed to a fine degree of perfection over the years.

Britain has been bound up with Spain in the sherry industry for centuries and imports the finest selection of sherries available anywhere – in fact more sherry is drunk in the U.K. than in Spain itself. Briefly, sherry is produced as *fino* – pale and dry; *amontillado* – slightly darker and less dry; and *oloroso* – a full-bodied sweeter darker wine, but there is an infinite variety of qualities and types of sherries in and around these broad definitions to suit all individual tastes.

Manzanilla is the name given to a special kind of sherry produced around San Lúcar de Barrameda, a small town situated at the mouth of the river Guadalquivir, still inside the sherry-producing area. Experts say it has the salty tang of the estuary about it, and it has a light fresh flavour not unlike camomile – which in Spanish is called *manzanilla*.

SPANISH BRANDY

Spanish brandy is also produced in and around Jerez de la Frontera, and is made from grape spirit, which is often supplied from distilleries in other parts of Spain. It is aged in old sherry butts and has a distinctive flavour of its own and is not at all like French cognac. In Spain it is an inexpensive and popular drink and there are many brands on sale. It may also be bought *corriente* from the *bodegas*. Fundador and Soberano are both good rather dry inexpensive brandies; Carlos Primero is a more expensive, smoother, sweeter brandy perhaps closer to French cognac. It may occasionally be possible to buy these brandies in Britain.

AGUADIENTE

A white colourless spirit of high alcohol content, made from the residue of pips and skins left from the last wine pressing. Possibly an acquired taste, it used to be the traditional drink of the muleteers who travelled the length and breadth of Spain in the days before proper roads were built. It is not exported.

SANGRÍA

This delightfully refreshing Spanish invention is made by mixing a bottle of ordinary red wine with a glass of Spanish brandy (it must be Spanish brandy – Fundador is a good one to use, and may be bought in this country) and adding plenty of ice cubes, some carbonated water, and slices of lemon and orange. Other fruits may also be added, such as sliced fresh peaches, apricots or strawberries, and a sprig of mint or a teaspoon of powdered cinnamon may be put in.

It should be served in a large glass jug.

Tapas, Entremeses and Salads

Tapas, those appetizing little dishes offered with a glass of wine in the bars and tavernas are some of the most delicious things to eat in Spain. They may vary from fresh shellfish, simply cooked *a la plancha*, to various kinds of croquettes or elaborate spicy stews consisting of tripe or beef or a mixture of finely chopped meats and offal. Why are they called *tapas*? I don't think anyone really knows, but one feasible theory is as follows. When a Spaniard ordered a drink in a bar, the barman also gave him a small slice of bread, and this was used to cover his glass of wine to keep the flies out (*tapa* is the Spanish for top or lid). From this custom developed small plates instead of a slice of bread on which, to encourage trade, the barman placed a titbit, such as a few olives, a slice of *chorizo*, or perhaps some crisply fried fresh anchovies or grilled prawns. Another theory suggests a legacy of the Moorish occupation when the Muslim religion forbade alcohol except possibly when accompanied by food. But whatever their origin, *tapas* are certainly one of Spain's most delightful customs.

Tapas are not usually served in a Spanish home except perhaps the more simple ones as canapés at a cocktail party. As I have said, many *tapas* are quite complicated and take a long time to cook, and since it is usual to present several different kinds this is hardly practical for the average housewife. However, I have included some recipes for simply prepared *tapas* which would make a pleasant alternative to the usual offerings of peanuts and crisps to serve with pre-dinner drinks.

The difference between *tapas* and *entremeses* (hors-d'œuvre) is not clearly defined, as the ingredients may be almost the same, but as a general rule *entremeses* are eaten as a prelude to a meal and are served in somewhat larger quantities.

There are only two main meals in Spain, the first a large lunch consisting of either a substantial soup or *entremeses* (although Sunday lunch often starts with a *paella*) followed by a meat or fish dish, then a salad and perhaps cheese, accompanied by copious quantities of fresh crusty bread and suitable wines. This meal is usually taken at about two o'clock in the afternoon and is frequently followed by a siesta. Everything comes to life again at about four o'clock and continues until quite late in the evening without anything like our afternoon tea. Though *tapas* are served freshly made at all hours of the day or night, this is the time when they are really appreciated, since the second large meal of the day does not appear until nine o'clock at the earliest and usually much later. This meal may be similar to lunch but is more elaborate and usually ends with a dessert.

Spanish housewives are conscientious cooks and the standard of food served at home is extremely high. Home-made sauces and soups are taken for granted and most women seem to have a great appreciation for natural foods, together with an inborn talent for presenting them attractively, and it is perhaps to making interesting *entremeses* and salads that they devote their special attention.

Calamares Fritos
Fried Squid Rings

To serve 4

About ½ kg of very tiny squid, ¼ litre light batter, oil for deep frying, a lemon.

Wash the squid and remove the ink bags and tentacles. Cut the bodies into thin rings, dry them thoroughly and dip into the batter. Deep fry them until crisp and serve hot with quarters of lemon.

Gambas a la Plancha
Prawns a la Plancha

Cooking *a la plancha* means literally cooking 'on the plate', i.e. directly on an oiled hotplate or griddle. It is a favourite Spanish way of cooking fish or meat. For this recipe you could use a large iron frying-pan, or a grill over charcoal.

To serve 2

About ½ kg of freshly caught prawns, 1 clove garlic, 3 tablespoons olive oil, juice of one lemon, salt and pepper.

Crush the garlic and stir it into a mixture of oil and lemon juice seasoned with pepper and salt. Brush the prawns with this and put them onto the hotplate or pan. Turn them over and over as they cook and sprinkle them with more oil and lemon. They will soon turn bright red and should be cooked in about 15–20 minutes. Eat with the fingers.

The prawns should, like all shellfish, be bought live, and you may feel it kinder to kill them by immersing in rapidly boiling water before dropping them onto the hotplate.

Chiperones a la Plancha
Baby Squid a la Plancha

This is a favourite *tapa* in most coastal regions of Spain. Abso-

lutely fresh fish are best, preferably only a few hours out of the
sea, and not more than two or three inches in length.

To serve 4

8–12 baby squid (cuttlefish may be used instead), olive oil, 2 tablespoons
finely chopped parsley, 1 teaspoon finely chopped garlic, 1 teaspoon paprika
and salt to taste.

Wash the squid and remove the transparent central bone and the
ink bags. Sprinkle some oil on a heated *plancha*, hotplate, or large
iron frying-pan and set the fish on it side by side. Place a little of
the parsley, garlic, paprika, salt mixture on each one, keeping
some in reserve, and sprinkle liberally with olive oil – an *aceitera*
is used for this in Spain. If you have a large flat saucepan lid
press it down on top of the squid – it will speed the cooking and
keep in the flavour. After a few minutes turn the squid over and
scatter the rest of the parsley mixture over them. Cook for a little
longer, about 6 minutes in all, and serve at once. They should be
golden brown and sizzling.

Almejas en Salsa de Ajo *Valencia*
Clams in Garlic Sauce

This is a *tapa* which is simple to prepare at home. Mussels may
be used with equal success.

To serve 4

About two dozen clams or mussels, olive oil, a few spring onions, 3 cloves
garlic, a handful of finely chopped parsley.

Rinse the clams or mussels under running water and scrape off
any weed or barnacles with a knife. Scrub them thoroughly. Put
them into a large saucepan and just cover with cold water. Put a
lid on the pan and bring it to the boil. The shellfish will then
open, and any which do not should be discarded. Drain off the
water, and when cool enough to handle detach the clams or
mussels from their shells, reserving one half of each shell. Heat
some olive oil in a small frying-pan and put in the spring onions
chopped very finely. Peel and crush the garlic and add it to the

onions, stir in the parsley and a little salt and cook gently for 5–6 minutes to make a sauce.

To serve put the clams or mussels back into their half shells and arrange them in small earthenware bowls, one for each person. Pour the sauce over them and eat with the fingers.

Dátiles con Jamón
Dates with Ham

Simply roll a small piece of tasty fat ham, ideally *jamón serrano*, but ordinary English ham could be used, round each date and secure with a toothpick.

Pan con Tomate y Jamón   *Catalonia*
Bread with Ham and Tomato

To serve 4

4 slices of bread, 4 thick slices of *jamón serrano* (no substitute), 1 sweet ripe tomato, oil and salt.

Cut thick slices of bread and toast them on both sides. Rub one side with a cut tomato, sprinkle well with olive oil and salt and put a slice of *jamón serrano* on each slice.

Albondigas
Meat Balls

To serve 4

¼ kg first-quality lean minced beef (best to buy steak and mince it yourself), a 2-inch piece of cooking quality *chorizo* also minced, ½ teaspoon salt, 1 clove garlic, crushed, pinch grated nutmeg, 1 tablespoon finely chopped or minced parsley, 1 egg, a little sherry or brandy, 2 tablespoons flour, 3 tablespoons olive oil.

Blend the minced meat and *chorizo* with the salt, garlic, spices and parsley. Bind it together with beaten egg and a dash of

sherry or brandy. Form into small balls and roll them in flour.
Fry them in hot olive oil until well browned all over. Serve hot
with toothpicks.

Almendras Tostadas   *Andalusia*
Toasted Almonds

These are very good with sherry.

To serve 4

About 250 g blanched almonds split in half, a little salted butter.

Put the almonds in the grill-pan with a few knobs of butter and
toast for a few minutes, turning once. Watch them all the time,
as they burn quickly. Drain on kitchen paper and serve in small
bowls.

Olivas en Ajo
Garlic Olives

Drain half the brine from a jar of green stuffed olives. Crush a
clove of garlic, mix it with a small cup of olive oil, a little wine
vinegar and a pinch of oregano and pour it into the olive jar.
Leave to marinate for 24 hours before use.

In the Canary Islands large black olives are pickled in Mojo
sauce (see page 220). This may be made at home by replacing the
brine in a jar of black olives (these may be bought loose in some
delicatessen shops) with red or green Mojo sauce and keeping for
a few days. Serve the olives in a little of the sauce.

Migas Andaluzas   *Andalusia*
Spiced Fried Bread Cubes

To serve 4

2 or 3 thick slices of stale white bread, 3 teaspoons paprika, 1 teaspoon ground
cloves, 1 teaspoon crushed cumin seed, salt, olive oil.

Remove the crusts from the bread and cut it into cubes, dust evenly with paprika. Mix the rest of the spices and the salt with a little water and sprinkle over the bread. Heat some oil in a frying-pan and when really hot quickly fry the cubes, turning them over and over to ensure they are evenly cooked on all sides. They should be nicely coloured with the paprika. Drain thoroughly and serve hot in little bowls either as a *tapa*, or with soup.

Entremeses

Cargols o Caracoles
Snails

Catalonia and the Balearic Islands

The wild snails of the Mediterranean are much more attractive to look at than our grey glutinous English ones. They have delicate sandy or tabby markings on their shells like tiny cats, and their slender bodies are often of the palest coral pink. But, however pretty they may be, they are still eaten with great relish by the local inhabitants. The best way to collect snails is to go out after dark with a lamp, preferably after rain when the snails are at their most active. When a satisfyingly large bag of snails has been gathered they should be either sewn up in muslin or put into a covered basket – don't use anything else or they won't be able to breathe.

The preparation of the snails from then on is rather lengthy and unpleasant as every trace of slime and grit must be removed. Leave the snails in their basket overnight, or preferably longer – up to three days. Then put them in a colander and wash them in cold running water two or three times, rubbing them with your hands to remove as much slime as possible. Sprinkle them with a little salt and tip them into a bowl of fresh cold water. The water must be absolutely cold or the snails will die. Leave them in this for two or three hours, then wash them again thoroughly under the tap. By this time all the slime and any grit should have gone. Now put the snails into a large pan of lukewarm water. (If they are plunged straight into boiling water they retreat into their shells and are hard to extract.) Add plenty of fennel and a smaller amount of thyme and about a tablespoon of salt. Fennel goes particularly well with snails – possibly as it is one of their favourite food plants. Bring the pot slowly to the boil. The snails quickly appear to become unconscious and as far as one can tell it seems to be a fairly humane way of killing them. Simmer the snails for about 1½ hours, or until they are tender, and drain thoroughly. They may then be eaten with a variety of sauces as an hors-d'œuvre, or put into a *paella* (see page 77). In England ordinary garden snails may be used, or French snails may be bought in jars or cans in most delicatessen shops.

Caracoles en Salsa   *Catalonia*
Snails in Sauce

This is a good way of preparing snails as none of the flavour is lost in the cooking.

To serve 4

About 24 snails, olive oil, 1 large onion finely chopped, 2 or 3 cloves of chopped garlic, 4 tomatoes peeled and chopped, or a small can of tomatoes, a pinch of cayenne pepper, salt, about 2 tablespoons of chopped fennel, a glass of dry white wine.

Prepare the snails as described, but remove them from the tepid water as soon as they are dead – do not boil them. Drain thoroughly.

Heat a little olive oil in a heavy pan and sauté the onion, garlic and tomatoes for a few minutes. Add the snails, still in their shells, then the cayenne pepper, salt and the chopped fennel. Pour in the glass of wine, cover the pan and cook very gently on the lowest possible heat for about 1½ hours, stirring occasionally. If it becomes dry, add a little more wine or water. When the time is up, taste a snail and if it is tender they are ready; if still rather rubbery, cook for another ½ hour or so. Serve the snails in their own sauce, which should be quite thick.

Caracoles Rellenos
Stuffed Snails

Balearic Islands

For these you need fairly large snails. On the Balearic Islands there is a type of large snail called *viudes* and smaller ones which are called *bovers*. If a mixture of large and small snails is used, reserve only the larger shells for stuffing. Ordinary English snails may be used.

To serve 4
About 24 large snails, olive oil, 1 onion, 6 cloves of garlic, 4 tomatoes, 2 tablespoons of chopped parsley, 1 tablespoon of chopped herbs such as fennel, thyme or oregano, salt and pepper, a little dry white wine, 2 tablespoons of fresh breadcrumbs.

Prepare the snails as described and remove them from their shells. Chop the snail meat finely, discarding the dark bit at the very end of each snail. Reserve the shells. In a frying-pan heat a little olive oil and prepare a *sofrito* (see page 215) with the finely chopped onion, the peeled and chopped tomatoes and 4 cloves of crushed garlic. Add 1 tablespoon of chopped parsley and the herbs of your choice, season with salt and pepper and simmer gently for about 20 minutes, stirring occasionally until a thick sauce is formed. Stir in the chopped snails and cook for a few minutes. Spoon enough of this mixture into each shell to fill it to the brim. Oil a shallow ovenproof dish and fit the stuffed shells in fairly tightly, mouth side up. If they do not fit well they will fall over and the stuffing may come out, or four small individual *escargot* dishes may be used if preferred.

Finally sprinkle the snails with the following mixture – 2 cloves of garlic peeled and crushed, a tablespoon of olive oil, salt, 2 tablespoons of breadcrumbs, a little dry white wine and 1 tablespoon of chopped parsley. Put the snails into a hot oven for about 10 minutes, or under the grill to lightly crisp the tops.

Chiperones Rellenos
Stuffed Baby Squid

*Catalonia and the
Balearic Islands*

The best time to catch squid (or cuttlefish) in the Mediterranean is at sundown on a calm warm evening. The fisherman use a ring-shaped device set with unbarbed hooks which they slowly raise and lower, catching the squid as they swim past a few feet below the surface. The squid become entangled on the hooks which, being without barbs, are easily removed without tearing the flesh. Later when darkness falls big carbide lamps are lowered over the side and squid and other fish are caught as they rise to investigate the light. For the following recipe only very small squid are suitable. It is equally good either as an hors-d'œuvre or served as a main course accompanied by saffron-flavoured rice and a salad.

To serve 4

8–12 tiny squid, 8 rashers of streaky bacon, 2 cloves garlic, 1 tablespoon chopped parsley, 1 tablespoon chopped fennel, salt and pepper, olive oil, 2 tomatoes (optional), about ¼ litre white wine.

Wash the squid, remove the small bone in the centre and the ink bags. Cut off the tentacles and chop them finely. Chop the bacon and fry it to a crisp, remove and fry the chopped tentacles in the bacon fat. Add the garlic, herbs and seasoning to the pan and put back the bacon, mix well and use this mixture to stuff the bodies of the squid; fasten each one with a toothpick. Take four small earthenware dishes, brush them with oil and put 2 or 3 stuffed squid in each. A few slices of tomato may be added if this is to be a main course. Pour in a little white wine and put the dishes into a moderate oven, 350° F, gas 4, and bake for about 30 minutes, or until the fish are tender.

Angulas
Basque Country
Baby Eels

For each person

150 g *angulas* (baby eels),* 1 tablespoon olive oil, 1 clove garlic, small piece of hot red pepper.

Heat the oil in a small earthenware dish with the whole garlic clove and a piece of hot red pepper. Wash and dry the eels.

* You may not be able to find baby eels in this country, but you could substitute whitebait.

When the oil is quite hot put in the eels and stir them round quickly with a fork, cook for only a few seconds and serve immediately in the same dish. Use wooden forks for eating them, as the oil is still sizzling.

Emparedado de Mejillones   *Galicia*
Mussel Sandwich

For each person

2 thick slices of bread, 1 tablespoon of olive oil, ½ teaspoon paprika, pepper, salt, 1 onion cut into rings, 4 canned mussels (or if fresh ones are used, first cook and remove from their shells).

Sprinkle the slices of bread liberally with oil, and then with paprika, salt and pepper. Allow to soak for a few minutes. Put a layer of onion rings on to one piece of the bread, more salt, then the mussels. Cover with the other piece of bread.

Langostinos a la Vinagreta   *Murcia*
Prawns in Vinaigrette Sauce

To serve 4

12 large live prawns or ready cooked prawns, olive oil, wine vinegar, a pinch of cayenne pepper, a pinch of crushed saffron, salt to taste, ¼ of an onion, 1 hard-boiled egg, 1 small glass brandy.

Cook the prawns, if live, in boiling salted water for 10 minutes. Remove the heads and shells and cut into pieces. Prepare a vinaigrette sauce with a small cup of olive oil, a tablespoon of wine vinegar, salt, cayenne pepper and crushed saffron. Add the onion, cut up finely, the chopped hard-boiled egg and a glass of brandy, and put in the prawns. Leave to stand for at least an hour before serving.

Arenques en Adobo   *Galicia*
Marinated Herrings

To serve 4

4 small herrings, or fillets of any firm fresh white fish, 1 onion, 1 carrot, 2 cups
wine vinegar, or 1 cup vinegar to 1 cup dry white wine, bay leaf,
4 peppercorns, sprig thyme, ½ teaspoon salt, 1 sprig parsley.

Thoroughly clean and wash the herrings and open them out flat.
Remove the backbone. Arrange them in a shallow ovenproof
dish. Cut the onion and carrot into rings and simmer them in
wine and vinegar, together with the bay leaf, thyme, finely
chopped parsley, peppercorns and salt. After 10 minutes pour
the hot liquid over the herrings and cover the dish, use foil or
greaseproof paper if it has no lid. Bake in a moderate oven, 350°
F, gas 4, for 20 minutes. Allow to cool completely before serving.
This dish is best made the day before it is needed.

Vieras Guisadas   *Galicia*
Baked Scallops

A speciality of Santiago de Compostela.

To serve 4

4 scallops, a handful of chopped parsley, 2 cloves of garlic, ground black
pepper, salt to taste, pinch of ground clove, a little nutmeg, 3 small onions,
olive oil, fresh breadcrumbs.

Choose large scallops the size of the palm of the hand. Remove
the meat from the shell, which is easily done if you put them in a
warm oven for a few minutes first. Chop the meat small and mix
with finely chopped parsley and garlic, the ground clove and
nutmeg, a little ground black pepper, salt, and the onions minced
or very finely chopped. Fill the shells with this mixture and pour
a tablespoon of olive oil on top of each. Sprinkle with breadcrumbs and bake in a hot oven for 15–20 minutes. This is a
substantial delicacy and very highly appreciated in Galicia.

Alcachofas con Vinagreta
Artichokes with Vinaigrette Dressing

To serve 4

4 globe artichokes, salt, a lemon, vinaigrette dressing.

Prepare the artichokes as described on pages 202–3. Drain thoroughly, cut into quarters and allow to cool. Serve chilled with vinaigrette dressing and slices of lemon.

Patatas con Sobresada *Catalonia*
Potatoes with Sobresada

To serve 4

4 large long-shaped potatoes, *sobresada* sausage, butter, 1 small can red peppers, olives.

Boil the potatoes in their jackets and allow them to cool. Remove the skins and cut them into thick rounds. Spread each piece with a mixture of *sobresada* and butter, decorate with strips of red pepper and olives.

Huevos Rellenos
Stuffed Hard-boiled Eggs

To serve 4

8 hard-boiled eggs, $\frac{1}{4}$ litre mayonnaise, $\frac{1}{2}$ teaspoon dry mustard, 2 tablespoons tomato paste.

Cut the eggs in half lengthwise and take out the yolks. Mix the crumbled yolks with the mayonnaise (which should be thick and made with lemon juice and plenty of seasoning). Blend the mustard and tomato paste together, add to the mayonnaise mixture and fill the halves of egg with it.

See also the more substantial stuffed egg recipe from Asturias on page 98.

Tomates Rellenos   *Canary Islands*
Stuffed Tomatoes

To serve 4

1 large ripe tomato per person, vinaigrette dressing, 1 can anchovy fillets,
12 stoned olives, 2 thick slices of cooked ham, a hard-boiled egg, watercress.

Cut each tomato in half and remove the seeds, sprinkle with
vinaigrette dressing and fill each half with a mixture of chopped
olives, anchovies and ham, sprinkle with the finely chopped hard-
boiled egg and some more dressing. Serve on a bed of watercress.

Flanes de Tomate
Tomato Moulds

To serve 6

2 tablespoons butter, 12 tomatoes, salt, 1 teaspoon sugar, pinch tarragon,
3 eggs.

Butter as many individual moulds as you need, or one large ring
mould. Chop the tomatoes roughly and simmer them with very
little water for 10 minutes. Melt the butter in a saucepan and
sieve the tomatoes into it, add salt and the sugar and tarragon and
simmer gently for a few minutes. Remove from the heat and add
the well-beaten eggs. Fill the moulds with this mixture and cook
in a moderate oven, 350° F, gas 4, in a bain-marie for 20 minutes,
or until they are set. Cool and turn out. These may also be eaten
as an accompaniment to a cold fish or meat dish.

Flanes de Queso   *Old Castile*
Cheese Moulds

To serve 4

4 eggs, 1 breakfast-cup milk, 4 tablespoons finely grated cheese, salt and white
pepper, dried breadcrumbs, some finely diced ham and/or cooked chopped
mushrooms.

Beat the eggs thoroughly, bring the milk to the boil and allow it
to cool. Add the eggs and the cheese, the ham and/or mushrooms

and plenty of seasoning. Pour the mixture into small buttered and breadcrumbed moulds, or into one large ring mould, and bake in a bain-marie in a moderate oven, 350° F, gas 4, for 20 minutes until set. Cool in the moulds and turn out when ready to serve.

Bolets amb Pernil   *Catalonia*
Mushrooms and Ham

Bolets and *pernil* are the Catalan words for mushrooms and ham. In Catalonia large red pine mushrooms would be used.

To serve 4
½ kg fresh mushrooms, 200 g ham (cooked shoulder of ham is good for this), olive oil, 1 tablespoon white breadcrumbs, 1 tablespoon chopped parsley, 3 cloves garlic, glass of sherry, black pepper.

Cut the ham into thick cubes and fry in oil. Peel the mushrooms but do not cut them up unless they are very large. Add to the ham and cook for 10 minutes, or until they start to become dry. Add the breadcrumbs mixed with finely chopped parsley and garlic and cook a little longer without stirring. Then add a small glass of sherry and some freshly ground black pepper. Cook for 15 minutes and serve hot.

Melon con Jamón Serrano   *Andalusia*
Melon with Ham

To serve 4
1 medium-sized ripe melon, 8 thin slices of *serrano* ham.

Serve slices of chilled melon on individual plates with 2 thin pieces of ham per person.

Sesos con Mahonesa
Calves' Brains with Mayonnaise

To serve 4

2 calves' brains, lemon juice or vinegar, a sprig each of thyme, mint and parsley, salt, 1 lettuce, olive oil, 2 or 3 tablespoons mayonnaise, 1 tablespoon capers, chopped parsley or tarragon.

Wash the brains, removing any bits of skin or membrane, and soak them for at least an hour in cold water. Put them in a saucepan with fresh water, a little lemon juice or vinegar, the herbs tied in a bunch, and some salt. Bring to the boil, skim and simmer for 10 minutes. Drain and allow to cool. Wash and cut up the lettuce and sprinkle with oil and vinegar or lemon juice, arrange it in a salad bowl and put the brains cut into thin slices on top. Mix the capers with 2 or 3 tablespoonfuls of mayonnaise and pour over the brains. Sprinkle with finely chopped parsley or tarragon.

Magras   *Aragon*
Lean Pork, Cubed

To serve 4

½ kg fresh lean pork or raw smoked ham, flour, olive oil, 3 cups tomato sauce (see pages 224–5, no. 2 or 3), pinch of brown sugar.

Cut the pork or ham into cubes, coat with flour and fry in olive oil. Pour in the tomato sauce and simmer for ½ hour. Add a pinch of sugar and a little salt if fresh pork is used. Serve very hot in individual bowls to start a meal.

Pringadas Extremeñas   *Extremadura*
Spicy Fried Bread

To serve 4

4 rashers fat bacon, olive oil, 4 slices of white bread (not pre-sliced), 4 slices good *chorizo* (Pamplona or Rioja).

Heat the oil in a frying-pan and lightly fry the bacon and *chorizo*. Remove and keep hot. Fry the pieces of bread in the same oil, which will have become very red. Serve each slice piping hot with a piece of *chorizo* and bacon.

A Few Salads

Ensalada de Tomate
Tomato Salad

Canary Islands

To serve 4

12 small firm bright red tomatoes, 2 medium-sized Spanish onions, vinaigrette dressing.

This salad relies on the flavour of the tomatoes, so there is no point in making it unless you can find good ones. The best tomatoes I have ever tasted come from the island of Fuerteventura in the Canaries; they are small, deep red and very sweet, presumably because there is little rainfall and lots of sun. You may be lucky enough to find some in the shops, otherwise use home-grown ones. Sometimes late-season Channel Island tomatoes are excellent.

You simply wash and dry the tomatoes and slice them in thin rounds, or in quarters if they are very tiny, mix them with thin rings of onion and serve in individual earthenware bowls with plenty of garlicky vinaigrette dressing.

Tomatoes are also very pleasant served in the same way but substituting lots of chopped fresh mint for onion. Sprinkle each serving with a little castor sugar.

Both these salads are superb with a juicy cold tortilla (see page 89) on a picnic.

Ensalada Rusa   *Canary Islands*
Russian Salad

As far as I know this salad has nothing to do with Russia – it is often served as a *tapa*, and it is delicious either on its own or with cold meats or fish.

To serve 4

4 large potatoes, ¼ litre mayonnaise, 1 can red peppers, 1 tablespoon capers, 1 onion, 4 small pickled gherkins, 1 fresh green pepper, 2 tablespoons cooked peas, 8 chopped olives.

Boil the potatoes in their skins, drain them, peel them and mash them thoroughly. Stir in the mayonnaise and then add all the other ingredients finely chopped, reserving some strips of red pepper and some peas for decoration. Make a smooth mound of the mixture on a plate and arrange the strips of red pepper and the peas all over it. Serve when completely cold.

Alcachofas con Atun
Artichokes with Tuna

To serve 4

4 large artichokes, 1 small tin tuna fish, ¼ litre mayonnaise, 1 carrot, 1 cooked beetroot, 1 green pepper.

Prepare the artichokes as described on pages 202–3. Allow to cool. Mix the tuna fish with a few spoonfuls of mayonnaise and fill the artichokes. Put a little mayonnaise into a glass or porcelain serving dish and arrange the artichokes on it. Scrape and grate the carrot and chop the beetroot into tiny cubes, de-seed the green pepper and cut it into fine strips, mix these together and make a decorative border round the artichokes. Spoon mayonnaise over each artichoke and around the border and serve the remainder in a separate bowl.

Ensalada de Arroz   *Valencia*
Rice Salad

To serve 4

1 cup long-grain rice, 8 tomatoes, 1 green pepper, 1 teaspoon made mustard, small cup vinaigrette dressing.

Put the rice into boiling water and boil for 20 minutes. Drain thoroughly – it should be as dry as possible. Scald and peel the tomatoes, chop them up and remove the seeds, wash and de-seed the pepper and cut it into thin strips. Mix the mustard with the vinaigrette dressing and pour it over the tomatoes and peppers. Mix well and blend thoroughly with the rice. Serve absolutely cold.

Ensalada Valenciana   *Valencia*
Salad Valenciana

To serve 4

1 small onion thinly sliced, 2 oranges peeled and thinly sliced, 4 tablespoons olive oil, 2 tablespoons red wine vinegar, $\frac{1}{4}$ teaspoon salt, freshly ground black pepper, 1 crisp lettuce, black olives.

Marinate the sliced onions and oranges in the olive oil, vinegar, salt and pepper for an hour. Wash and cut up the lettuce. Toss all together and add a few black olives.

Ensalada Sevillana   *Andalusia*
Salad Sevillana

To serve 4

1 small can of red peppers, 3 small onions, 4 tomatoes, 100 g Seville olives,
100 g cold cooked rice, 1 clove garlic, salt, oil and vinegar.

Cut the peppers into strips and the onions into fine rings, chop
the tomatoes into segments. Rinse the olives. Make a bed of cold
cooked rice in an earthenware serving dish and arrange the prepared ingredients on top. Make a dressing using 3 parts of olive
oil to 1 of vinegar, the crushed clove of garlic, and a good pinch
of salt. Pour this over the salad – the garlic may be strained out if
preferred.

Amanida   *Catalonia*
Catalan Salad

To serve 4

4 small chicory heads, 4 stalks of celery, 6 spring onions or shallots,
100 g ham, 12 anchovy fillets, 1 cup mayonnaise, 1 clove garlic, 1 hard-boiled
egg, 100 g white *butifarra* sausage (or substitute salami).

Wash and chop the chicory, celery and onions, and mix them
together in a bowl. Add the ham cut into small dice and the
drained and chopped anchovies. Have ready a cupful of good
mayonnaise made with a little extra vinegar. Press the oil from
the clove of garlic (a garlic press is essential for this, otherwise
use garlic oil if available), and blend it into the mayonnaise. Pour
the mayonnaise over the vegetables in the bowl, and decorate
with slices of hard-boiled egg and *butifarra* sausage.

This salad may be eaten with an oil, vinegar and salt dressing
if preferred.

Soups

Spanish soups generally tend to be a nourishing blend of whatever foods are plentiful in each particular region, and it is sometimes difficult to draw the line between a soup and a stew. For example, nearly every coastal region and certainly the islands have their own version of a fish soup, and these are very often stew-like in character, containing a mixture of different fish and shellfish in something approaching a bouillabaisse.

Since vegetables, both dried and fresh, are abundant nearly everywhere in Spain, various kinds of vegetable soups are also eaten widely as an everyday family meal, always accompanied by plenty of bread, either served in the soup or separately. Spanish bread is excellent, especially the hand-made bread produced in the smaller bakeries. It is bought freshly made, usually in the form of small oval-shaped rolls, at least once a day.

The best known of all Spanish soups, *gazpacho*, originated as a peasant dish for those who could afford no better. Consisting as it does of raw salad vegetables served cold, it must have been a welcome though somewhat frugal meal after the burning heat of an Andalusian summer day.

Sopa Mallorquina de Pescado   *Balearic Islands*
Mallorcan Fish Soup

To serve 4

2 tablespoons olive oil, 1 onion, 2 cloves garlic, 4 tomatoes, parsley, 2 glasses
white wine, 1 litre good fish stock made from fresh heads and bones, salt,
pepper, 4 thin slices of brown bread.

Using a deep pan, fry the chopped onion in oil until golden, add
the chopped garlic and peeled chopped tomatoes and the
chopped parsley. Season well. Pour in the white wine and cook
for a few minutes, letting it bubble and stirring constantly. Then
put in the strained fish stock. Add a slice of brown bread for each
person and cook for 15 minutes.

Sopa de Cadiz   *Andalusia*
Fish and Rice Soup from Cadiz

To serve 4

One large head of hake or cod, 1 litre water, salt, bay leaf, olive oil, 1 onion,
3 cloves of garlic, parsley, 4 tablespoons rice, juice of one lemon.

Simmer the fish head in the water with salt and the bay leaf.
After about ½ hour remove the head and allow it to cool. Strain
the stock. Cook the rice separately in water. In a frying-pan heat
some oil and fry the chopped onion, garlic and parsley until soft.
Add this mixture to the fish stock and boil for 10 minutes, then
put in the cooked rice, the fish from the fish head and the lemon
juice. Reheat and serve with chunks of crusty bread.

Caldo de Pescado   *Galicia*
Fish Soup

To serve 4–6

2 kg of assorted fish (hake, bass, cod or any other fresh fish available but not
oily fish such as mackerel or sardines), 4 onions, 3 cloves garlic, parsley, bay
leaf, 1 tablespoon wine vinegar, 1 coffee-cup olive oil, 1½ litres water, salt,
black pepper, 50 g flour, crusty bread.

Clean the fish discarding the heads, and cut them into big pieces. Take a deep earthenware dish and make a marinade with the oil, vinegar, chopped onion and garlic, parsley and bay leaf. Leave the fish to stand in this for 2 hours. Now pour in 1½ litres of cold water, season with salt and freshly ground black pepper and bring to the boil, skim if necessary and simmer for 20 minutes. Five minutes before it is ready thicken the soup with the flour mixed with a little cold water. Pour the soup into a large tureen in which 8 slices of oven-crisped bread have been placed, remove the pieces of fish and serve them in a separate dish.

Sopa de Muscos del Litoral Catala   *Catalonia*
Catalan Mussel Soup

To serve 4

8 mussels per person, 1 onion, 2 tablespoons olive oil, 4 peeled tomatoes, 4 slices dry toast (crushed either with a rolling-pin or in an electric mixer), a small glass brandy, 2 cloves garlic, 2 sprigs parsley, black pepper, ½ teaspoon cinnamon, salt.

Scrub the mussels and put them into cold water, bring them to the boil and remove from the water as soon as they open. Heat some olive oil in an earthenware casserole and fry the finely chopped onion. When it is golden, add the peeled and chopped tomatoes, fry for a few minutes, and then add sufficient strained stock from the mussels to make enough soup for 4 people (you may need to add water). When it starts to boil add the crushed toast and glass of brandy. Make a *picada* as follows: put the peeled garlic in a mortar with chopped parsley, cinnamon, salt and black pepper and pound into a paste. Add this to the soup. Finally put in the mussels, removed from their shells. Sprinkle with grated cheese if you like.

Porru-Saldo
Salt Cod Soup

Basque Country

To serve 4

250 g salt cod, 4 tablespoons olive oil, 2 small cloves of garlic, 4 leeks, ½ litre vegetable stock, 4 potatoes, pepper and chopped parsley.

Soak the cod overnight and next day poach it for 5 minutes in fresh water. Allow it to cool sufficiently to handle, then remove the skin and bones, and shred it as finely as possible, keeping the water in which it was cooked. In a deep pan heat the oil and fry the chopped garlic till it takes colour, then remove it and put in the leeks, cleaned and sliced into rounds. Fry them for a few minutes on each side, then pour in the stock and the water in which the cod was cooked. Peel and dice the potatoes and add these, together with the shredded fish, to the soup. Season with pepper, add the chopped parsley, and cook gently with the lid on for 1 hour. If you want a smooth consistency, put it through an electric blender, a food mill, or sieve.

Gazpacho (1)
Iced Vegetable Soup

Andalusia

Although experts past and present have been unable to agree on the origin of the word *gazpacho*, it seems likely that it has been derived from a pre-Roman word *caspa* meaning remains, or bits and pieces. The suffix *acho* has a derogatory sense, and was probably added by those who could afford better. *Gazpacho* is eaten throughout the hotter regions of Spain and there are many ways of preparing it.

It may be accompanied by small bowls of finely chopped salad vegetables and hard-boiled eggs as a garnish.

To serve 4

2 tablespoons of stale breadcrumbs, 2 cloves of garlic, crushed, 1 tablespoon wine vinegar, 1 tablespoon olive oil, 1 green pepper, de-seeded and chopped, 1 onion chopped, 4 tomatoes and half a cucumber peeled, de-seeded and chopped, 8 almonds peeled and crushed, white pepper and salt.

For the garnish: cucumber, onion, red and green peppers, tomato and hard-boiled egg, all cut into tiny cubes and served in separate bowls.

Soak the breadcrumbs and garlic in the vinegar and olive oil for about an hour. Put the prepared vegetables through a vegetable mill or an electric blender and reduce to a smooth purée. Add the crushed almonds, season with pepper and salt, and dilute with water to the required consistency. Chill for several hours before serving. Ice cubes may be added at the last minute.

Gazpacho (2) *Catalonia*

The ingredients for *gazpacho* are fairly elastic and may vary slightly from region to region. For example in Andalusia almonds are added whereas in Catalonia pine-nuts or hazelnuts would be used, while in Extremadura small pieces of rabbit or game are put in.

Personally I like *gazpacho* without tomatoes and using mint as a flavouring. It has an appetizing cool green colour and is especially good garnished with chopped green olives. The following recipe is a simple and quick way to make *gazpacho* in an electric blender with or without tomatoes.

To serve 4

1 large onion chopped, 1 green pepper de-seeded and chopped, 2 cloves garlic chopped, 1 cucumber peeled and chopped, 8 tomatoes peeled and chopped or 1 can of tomatoes (optional), a tablespoon of chopped parsley,

2 or 3 sprigs of fresh mint, a few pine-nuts or hazelnuts if available,
2 tablespoons of olive oil, 1 tablespoon of wine vinegar, salt and pepper, about
1 litre water.

For the garnish: finely diced raw onion, cucumber and green pepper or a few
stoned green olives if preferred.

Put all the ingredients excluding the water into the blender and
blend at minimum speed for a few minutes or until you have a
smooth purée. Turn into a large bowl and dilute with the water.
Cover the bowl and chill it thoroughly for several hours, or better
still overnight. When ready to serve add a few ice cubes. The
garnishes should be handed round in small bowls.

Gazpacho (3) *Extremadura*

To serve 4

Half a day-old loaf, ½ cucumber, ½ kg ripe tomatoes or one large can of
tomatoes, ½ a sweet red pepper, 1 large clove garlic, salt, pepper, 1 tablespoon
wine vinegar, ¼ kg finely chopped cooked chicken or game, ice cubes.

Soak the bread in cold water. Peel and chop the cucumber and
tomatoes, de-seed and chop the red pepper and the garlic. Put
everything except the chopped meat into an electric blender if
you have one, including the squeezed-out bread. Otherwise put
it through a vegetable mill or pound together in a large mortar.
Add about a litre of cold water, season with pepper, salt and
vinegar and mix together thoroughly and add the cooked meat.
Chill, and serve with ice cubes.

Sopa de Almendras *Andalusia and general*
Almond Soup

This cold soup is sometimes served with a red rose petal floating
on it, or, less romantically, sprinkled with ground cinnamon. It
should look milky white.

To serve 4

100 g blanched almonds, 2 cloves garlic, 2 tablespoons mild olive oil, salt to

taste, 4 cups of cold water, 2 teaspoons wine vinegar, about 24 white grapes (optional).

Crush the almonds and garlic together with the olive oil and salt. Gradually add the water. (This may all be done quickly and easily in an electric blender.) When you have a smooth milky consistency your soup is ready. Add some lumps of ice for immediate use or chill the soup in a refrigerator. Just before serving stir in the vinegar and add the peeled and stoned grapes, or sprinkle on the cinnamon, or float a red rose petal on each person's dish, as you like.

Sopa de Nueces   *Catalonia*
Nut Soup

To serve 4

4 slices of bread, 2 tablespoons olive oil, 2 cloves garlic, pinch of saffron stamens (toasted) or saffron powder, ½ cup blanched hazelnuts, ½ cup blanched almonds, 1 litre of light chicken or ham stock or water, salt.

Fry the bread in oil with the chopped garlic. When it is crisp remove it and drain off any surplus oil. Pound it together with the garlic, saffron and the nuts in a large mortar (or use an electric blender). Heat the stock in a saucepan and when it is boiling put in the pounded nuts and stir briskly to make a thick soup. Season with salt and simmer for ½ hour.

Sopa de Galets   *Catalonia*
Pasta Soup

To serve 4

200 g minced lean pork, a handful of fresh breadcrumbs, 1 clove garlic, 2 sprigs parsley, pinch ground cinnamon, salt, 1 egg, flour, olive oil, 1 onion, 2 stalks celery with leaves, 2 cups *galets* (shell-shaped pasta often used for soups in Catalonia), a little saffron, grated cheese.

Make small balls about the size of a marble with the meat, bread-crumbs, garlic and finely chopped parsley, salt and cinnamon, bound with beaten egg. Roll them in flour. Heat some oil in a saucepan and gently fry the finely chopped onion until it is transparent, then add the meatballs and fry them as evenly as possible. Pour in about a litre of water and add the cut-up celery. Simmer for ½ hour, then add the *galets* and saffron and continue to cook for another ½ hour.

Serve with grated cheese on top.

Sopa de Calabaza   *Canary Islands*
Pumpkin Soup

Big pumpkins or calabashes are grown in the Canary Islands and are much used in cooking. This soup is light and may be eaten hot or cold.

To serve 4–6
1 kg pumpkin, peeled and diced, 2 tablespoons olive oil, 1 onion, 1 small red or green pepper, 2 cloves garlic, 2 tablespoons chopped parsley, 2 tomatoes, 1 pinch saffron, 2 teaspoons paprika, ½ teaspoon crushed cumin seed, ½ teaspoon brown sugar, 2 teaspoons vinegar, salt and pepper.

Put the prepared pumpkin into about a litre of water and bring it to the boil, cover and simmer for about ½ hour. Meanwhile, chop the onion and garlic and green or red pepper fairly small and fry them in olive oil. When they are half cooked add the chopped tomato and parsley and the spices and cook a few minutes more, then add it all to the pumpkin. Season with salt, pepper, sugar and vinegar and simmer for another 30 minutes, adding more water if necessary. When it is ready put the soup through a mill and serve.

Potaje de Berros   *Canary Islands*
Watercress Soup

To serve 4
¼ kg dried white or red beans or chickpeas, 2 chicken stock cubes or some pieces of boiling fowl, 2 tablespoons olive oil, 2 cloves garlic, 1 onion, 4 large handfuls of watercress.

The dried beans or chickpeas should be soaked overnight. Next day put them to boil in about 2 litres of cold salted water with the stock cubes or pieces of chicken. Simmer for 2 hours or until the peas or beans are tender. Meanwhile heat the oil in a separate pan and sauté the finely chopped onion and garlic till tender. Wash and finely chop the watercress. When the peas or beans are tender remove any chicken bones and then put through a food mill or electric blender to make a thickish soup. Add the fried onions and the watercress and cook gently for another 30 minutes. Like other thick soups this improves with standing for a few hours, or overnight.

Sopa de Vainas   *Basque Country*
Green Bean Soup

To serve 4

½ kg green beans, 4 potatoes, oil, 4 cloves garlic, salt, 1 slice of bread per person, grated cheese, a few stoned olives.

Wash the beans, string them and cut into small pieces. Peel and cut up the potatoes. Fry the garlic and crush it in a mortar. Put all the above ingredients into about a litre of salted water with a little oil and boil until the potatoes break up to make a thick soup. Cut each slice of bread in half, fry, and cover with grated cheese. Place them in a large soup tureen and pour in the hot soup. Decorate with the olives cut into rings.

Sopa de Coliflor
Cauliflower Soup

To serve 4

1 large cauliflower, a little flour, olive oil, 1 onion, 2 cloves garlic, 2 potatoes, a little butter, chopped parsley, salt.

Break up the cauliflower and wash it. Cook for 15 minutes in salted water, using some of the leaves. Drain the cauliflower and coat it with flour, discard the leaves, but keep the water. Fry the pieces of cauliflower in 2 tablespoons hot oil in a deep pan together with the very finely chopped onion and the chopped garlic. Gradually add the water from the cauliflower and put in the potatoes peeled and diced. Simmer for ½ hour. Put the soup through a mill, blend in some tiny knobs of butter and serve sprinkled with parsley.

Sopa de Ajo Asturiana   *Asturias*
Asturian Garlic Soup

To serve 4

About ½ a stale loaf, or the equivalent amount of crusts, 4 or 5 large cloves of garlic, a coffee-cup of olive oil, ½ teaspoon salt, 2 or 3 ripe tomatoes, 1 litre of water.

Heat the oil gently in a large saucepan, chop up the garlic and allow it to stew in the oil. Break up the bread into walnut-size pieces and gradually add it to the oil and garlic, stirring well. Do not allow it to brown. Add about 1 litre of water and the salt. Throw in the peeled and chopped tomatoes. (These may be omitted if not available.) Allow to simmer gently until the bread is very soft but not completely disintegrated – about 15 minutes.

This recipe may sound dull, but in fact if served piping hot, and if you like garlic, it is very good indeed. It was taught to me by a family from Asturias but there are many other variations from different parts of Spain, in which hot red pepper, or sweet pepper, or a beaten egg may be added just before serving.

Sopa Escaldada   *Mallorca*
Mallorcan Vegetable Soup

Brown bread, very thinly sliced, is sold in Mallorcan shops especially for use in soup. Use ordinary brown bread, preferably a day old and in thin slices.

To serve 4–6

¼ kg brown lentils, salt, a mixture of any or all of the following vegetables –

artichokes, broad beans, green beans, cabbage, peas and spinach, to make approximately 1 kg in all, a little *sobresada* if available, 100 g of *tocino* or fat bacon cut into tiny dice, 4–6 slices of brown bread.

Pick over the lentils, wash and boil them in salted water until tender. Meanwhile wash and chop all the vegetables quite small and boil them in a large saucepan with the *sobresada* and diced *tocino*. Use just enough water to cover. When the lentils are soft put them through a soup mill or sieve and add the resulting purée to the vegetables. Continue to cook gently, adding more water or stock until a thick soup is obtained. Put a slice of bread into each person's plate and pour the soup over it.

This is an old country dish traditionally cooked in a *greixonera* over an olive-wood fire in the open. The older houses in Mallorca still have their cooking fires outside, usually under a vine-covered trellis attached to the house, and in many cases they are still in everyday use. The sweet smell of olive-wood smoke is to me one of the most evocative memories of this very beautiful island.

Sopa a la Valenciana   *Valencia*
Valencian Rice Soup

To serve 4

100 g cooking *chorizo*, parsley, thyme, 1 bay leaf, salt, 1 litre of water, 1 onion, 50 g lard, 50 g smoked ham, 2½ cups rice.

Make stock by boiling the *chorizo* and herbs in salted water for about ½ hour. Fry the finely chopped onion in the lard in a deep pan until it is golden, then put in the ham cut into small cubes and the *chorizo* cut in slices. Add the rice and stir till it begins to colour, then pour in all the stock, first taking out the bay leaf. Cover the pot and cook for 15 minutes, add more water if necessary. Leave to stand a few minutes before serving. It should be quite thick.

Caldo Gallego
Galician Soup

Galicia

To serve 4–6

¼ kg white beans, a 6-inch piece of cooking *chorizo*, one meaty ham bone, ¼ kg smoked fat bacon, ½ kg potatoes, ½ kg greens (cabbage or spring greens), an onion, a tablespoonful of flour, 2 tablespoons of olive oil, 1 teaspoon of paprika.

Soak the beans overnight, put them in a large pot of cold salted water and bring it to the boil. When it boils add the whole *chorizo*, the bacon cut up, and the ham bone. Simmer for 1 hour and then add the peeled chopped potatoes, the washed and shredded greens, and the onion roughly cut up. Cover the pot and continue to cook slowly for as long as possible, at least 2 hours, so that all the vegetables disintegrate.

Just before serving add a tablespoon of flour mixed with 2 tablespoons of olive oil and one teaspoon of paprika and cook for a further 10 minutes. Remove the ham bone. The meat and sausage are removed from the soup and served as a side dish.

Sopa de Mandonghuilles a la Casolana
Catalan Soup

Catalonia

To serve 4

1 chicken carcass or breast of chicken, ½ clove garlic, 250 g minced beef, parsley, salt, black pepper, flour, oil or lard for frying, 1 slice of toast per person, a *picada catalana* (see page 221).

Make chicken stock with the carcass, or chicken breast, (the meat may afterwards be used for croquettes). Crush ½ clove garlic and mix it with the minced beef, chopped parsley, pepper and salt. Make this into tiny balls and cover them with flour. Heat a little oil or lard in a frying-pan and brown them lightly all over. Add a slice of toast per person to the boiling stock and let it disintegrate, then add the meat balls and the *picada* and cook gently for 15–20 minutes.

Sopa de Lentejas Madrileña   *New Castile*
Lentil Soup Madrileña

To serve 4

1 onion, 1 green or red pepper, 2 or 3 tablespoons olive oil, 1 tablespoon flour, ½ kg brown lentils, small can tomatoes, 2 carrots, 1 teaspoon salt, ground black pepper, 1 litre water.

Stew the chopped onions and the green pepper in oil, using a deep pan with the lid on. When they are soft stir in the flour and cook for a few minutes without burning, then add the lentils, which should not have been previously soaked, the tomatoes, cut-up carrots, salt and pepper and the water. Cover the pan and simmer very gently for 2 hours.

Serve as it is, or put through a food mill or electric blender.

Potaje Canariense   *Canary Islands*
Thick Canary Island Soup

To serve 4–6

250 g chickpeas, 4 potatoes, 4 carrots, 4 tomatoes, 250 g green beans, 2 courgettes, 250 g diced pumpkin, 2 tablespoons olive oil, 1 onion, 2 cloves garlic, 1 teaspoon paprika, 1 teaspoon crushed cumin seeds, 1 pinch saffron, salt and pepper to taste, 1 tablespoon *gofio* (see page 241) or substitute wholemeal flour.

Soak the chickpeas overnight. Next day put them in a big saucepan with about 2 litres of cold water and bring them to the boil, lower the heat and simmer for 2 hours. Be careful that the water does not boil away; add more hot water if necessary. Meanwhile prepare the vegetables – peel and roughly chop the potatoes and carrots, scald, peel and chop the tomatoes, wash and slice the courgettes and green beans and peel and finely chop the onion and garlic. When the chickpeas are softening add the potatoes, carrots, green beans, courgettes and pumpkin, and continue to cook gently. Heat the olive oil in a skillet and sauté the finely chopped onion, garlic and tomato, adding the spices and pepper and salt. When the onion is tender blend in the *gofio* or flour and add it to the soup. Stir well and cook for a further 15 minutes or so. If it is allowed to stand for a few hours before being reheated and served the flavours will be improved. It is even better the following day.

Rice, Pasta and Eggs

Rice Dishes

In Spain rice is a staple food – it is probably eaten every day in most homes and often as a main dish. Round or medium grain rice is most often used, and it is quite difficult to cook well because it easily becomes sticky. It should be washed thoroughly under a running tap before use to remove excess starch, and – although everyone has their own theory about cooking rice – if you remember to use double the volume of cooking liquid to rice you should get good results. Avoid stirring the rice while cooking, keep the lid on and let the pot simmer very gently till all the liquid is absorbed; it usually takes about 15–20 minutes to dry the rice out completely. If you use long-grain rice it is easier to achieve good results – each grain dry, separate and just cooked through.

Paella a la Valenciana   *Valencia*

The ingredients for a *paella* are fairly elastic and may include all kinds of seafood, including squid, prawns, lobster, mussels, clams, snails and pieces of white fish. Chicken, rabbit and pork are the meats used, though other things have been known to find their way in. The methods of preparation differ too – in the following recipe the rice is added before the stock, others suggest putting in the stock first.

To serve 4–6

1 coffee-cup olive oil, 3 cloves garlic peeled and chopped, 1 onion chopped, 3 tomatoes peeled and chopped, 1 red pepper de-seeded and cut into strips, 1 chicken cut into small pieces, 1 teaspoon paprika, 2 pinches of saffron toasted and crushed, 2 cups rice, 4 cups well-seasoned chicken stock (the bones from the chicken may be used to make this, or use a bouillon cube), salt and pepper, 100 g shelled peas, 12 cooked shelled prawns, 1 tablespoon sherry (optional) 12 cleaned and scrubbed mussels.

Heat the oil in a *paëllera* of suitable size (or use an ordinary frying-pan) and put in the garlic, cook for a few minutes to flavour the oil and remove. Add the onion, tomatoes and strips of red pepper and the pieces of chicken. Turn them over in the oil and sprinkle with paprika as you do so. Continue to cook gently for 10 minutes, stirring often. Stir in the rice and cook on a slightly higher flame for 2–3 minutes, add the saffron and, removing the pan from the heat, pour in the stock. Stir well and bring to the boil, season with salt and pepper if necessary. Stir in the peas and the prawns and cook very gently for about 15 minutes, or until most of the liquid has been absorbed. Sprinkle with sherry and put the mussels on top of the rice, cover the pan with a large saucepan lid and the mussels will open in the steam. (Reject those that do not open.) Cook for 1–2 minutes and the *paella* is ready to serve. Some of the red pepper strips, peas and prawns may be removed to make a decorative pattern on top, also quarters of lemon may be slit and wedged onto the rim of the *paëllera*.

Paella Catalana   *Catalonia*

Here is a recipe from eastern Spain, which does not mix meat and fish.

To serve 4–6

1 tender chicken, 1 coffee-cup or more olive oil, 3 cloves garlic, ½ onion,
2 tomatoes, 1 litre chicken stock, 400 g short-grain rice, a handful sliced green
beans, 250 g peas, 12 cleaned snails (optional), see pages 46–7, 2 artichokes,
½ teaspoon cayenne pepper, 2 small envelopes saffron (approximately
4 pinches), salt.

Clean the chicken and cut it into 6 or 8 pieces. Heat the oil in a
paëllera and throw in two peeled cloves of garlic to give flavour.
Remove it before it burns. Put in the chopped onion and peeled
and chopped tomatoes and move them around well, then add the
chicken pieces and brown them lightly. Add the last clove of
garlic, chopped, then pour in the hot chicken stock (lower the
heat first) and when it starts to boil add the rice in handfuls,
spreading it evenly over the surface. Put in the peas, beans and
snails, and the artichokes cut in quarters, the cayenne pepper,
salt and saffron. Boil fast for 5 minutes, then lower the heat and
cook without stirring until the rice is tender and has absorbed all
the liquid – about 20 minutes. It should be loose and fairly dry.
Serve in the *paëllera*.

Paella con Alcachofas   *Valencia*
Paella with Artichokes

This is a *paella* using no meat or fish.

To serve 4–6

Olive oil, 4 fresh sweet red peppers, 4 cloves garlic, 1 tomato, 100 g cooked
peas or frozen ones, 4 fresh artichokes or 1 can, 400 g rice, a little saffron,
2 teaspoons paprika, 1 litre ham or chicken stock (a bouillon cube may be
used).

Having removed the seeds, cut the red peppers into strips and
fry them in a coffee-cup of olive oil in a *paëllera*, or large shallow
ovenproof dish. Cook for 5 minutes only – remove and keep hot.

Into the same oil put the chopped garlic, the peeled and chopped tomato, the peas and the artichokes, cleaned and cut up. Stir everything round in the oil for 2–3 minutes, add the rice in handfuls and then the boiling stock. Add the saffron and paprika, season well with salt and cook rapidly for 5 minutes. Put the fried strips of red pepper on top, lower the heat and cook for a further 15 minutes or until the rice has absorbed all the liquid. When the rice is cooked, put the dish in a warm oven for 5 minutes and serve piping hot.

Paella con Caracoles
Paella with Snails

Catalonia and the Balearic Islands

For the preparation of snails see pages 46–7.
The quantities of ingredients need not be too precise, except for the proportion of liquid to rice.

To serve 4–6

1 coffee-cup olive oil, 1 large chicken leg or half a small chicken, 250 g lean pork, 250 g of eel, squid or young octopus cleaned and cut up (substitute any firm white fish if none of these are available), ½ onion, 1 clove garlic, 1 sweet red pepper, 2 tomatoes, 150 g peas, 150 g sliced green beans, 1 tablespoon chopped parsley, a little grated nutmeg, a pinch of thyme, one bay leaf, saffron, salt and pepper, 450 g rice, about 18 snails, 12 cooked prawns, 12 well-scrubbed mussels or clams.

Heat the oil in a *paëllera* or a large shallow casserole and fry the chicken, pork and fish, all cut into one-inch cubes. When golden on all sides add the onion and garlic very finely chopped, and the sweet pepper cut into strips. Cook gently for a few minutes then add the tomatoes, peeled and chopped, the peas, the green beans and all the herbs and spices except the saffron. Pour in about ½ litre of water, season well with salt and pepper and simmer until most of the liquid has evaporated. Now stir in the rice, and then the saffron and the snails. Carefully pour in a litre of water, bring to the boil and simmer for about 15–20 minutes without stirring, by which time the rice should be cooked and have absorbed most of the liquid. Arrange the prawns and mussels or clams on top and either cover the pan and leave on a low flame or transfer it to the oven for about 5 minutes, when the prawns will heat through and the mussels will open. Serve in the same dish. In general Spaniards are not too keen to eat their food piping hot, but personally I think a *paella* is nicest eaten as hot as possible.

Paella Alicantina   *Valencia*

To serve 4–6

400 g short-grain rice, 1 chicken or rabbit, salt, pepper and olive oil, 2 pinches saffron, one large clove garlic, about 20 mussels, a few whole cooked prawns or shrimps, one can of red peppers.

Use a *paëllera* to cook this in if you have one, otherwise any round shallow fireproof dish of suitable size. Cut up the chicken or rabbit into fairly small pieces and season with salt and pepper. Fry in hot oil until nearly cooked and well browned. Meanwhile put about 4 cups of salted water to boil with the saffron. Remove the pieces of meat and keep them hot, and put the whole peeled garlic clove into the hot oil, tilting the pan to let the flavour permeate the oil. Remove after a few minutes. Lower the heat a little and spread the uncooked rice evenly over the base of the pan. Cook for 2 minutes, then turn up the heat and carefully pour in enough of the boiling water to just cover the rice completely (about 1 litre). Cover the pan, lower the heat and simmer gently for about 20 minutes, when the rice should be tender and form a crust on the bottom. Now stir in the pieces of meat and put the shellfish on top, arranging the red peppers in strips to make a pattern. Cover the dish again, allowing the mussels to open and cook for a few minutes in the steam. Ideally the *paella* should be firm enough to be cut in wedges like a cake and should be served in the pan in which it was cooked. This is a very simple and delicious dish.

Arroz a la Marinera *Valencia*
Sailor's Rice or Rice with Sea Food

This is traditionally served to the sailors in the waterfront cafés of the Levante, where a whole head of young garlic is put into the centre of the rice. Here we use only two cloves.

To serve 4–6

1 hake or cod's head, ¼ kg each of any three of the following fish: angler-fish, hake, turbot, halibut, fresh haddock or squid; 12 cooked prawns (in shell), 12 mussels, a bay leaf, a sprig of thyme, salt, a coffee-cup olive oil, 1 onion, 1 tablespoon paprika, 1 envelope (2 pinches) saffron, 2 cloves garlic, 400 g rice.

Clean and wash the fish and cut it up. Scrub the mussels. Make fish stock with water and the hake or cod's head and any trimmings from the fish. Add the bay leaf and thyme and season with salt. Heat the oil in a large shallow ovenproof dish or a *paëllera* and gently fry the chopped onion and brown the pieces of fish. Stir in the paprika. Next add the rice and spread it evenly over the dish. Let it cook in the oil for just 1 minute. Then add twice its volume of strained fish stock – about a litre – and bring to the boil. Crush the garlic and saffron together in a mortar and stir in. Now arrange the cleaned mussels and the prawns in their shells on top of the *paella*. Cook on a fairly high flame for about 15 minutes or until all the liquid is absorbed, covering it with a lid for the last 5 minutes, and then transfer the dish to a fairly hot oven. Allow about 5 minutes to give a slightly crusty, dry surface to the rice. Serve in the same dish.

Arroz a la Mallorquina *Balearic Islands*
Mallorcan Rice

To serve 4–6

1 pigeon, olive oil, 2 onions, 2 red or green peppers, 2 cloves garlic, 4 tomatoes, 400 g round grain rice, 12 mussels, salt, pepper, pinch saffron, parsley, ¼ kilo white fish, 1 cup cooked peas, 1 cup cooked green beans, about 100 g *sobresada*.

Clean and wash the pigeon and joint it. Heat some oil in a large casserole and brown the pieces of pigeon, and the onion and peppers, cut up. Then add the chopped garlic and chopped peeled tomatoes. Cover the casserole and cook slowly for about 1 hour. Put in the rice and the well-scrubbed mussels. Pour in 1 litre of boiling water, season with salt, pepper and saffron and boil gently for 10 minutes. Put in the white fish cut into pieces, the peas and beans and some chopped parsley. Cover the rice with slices of *sobresada* and cook in a moderate oven for 20 minutes. Serve in the same dish.

Mejillones con Arroz   *Valencia*
Rice with Mussels

To serve 4

About 3 dozen mussels, 1 large onion, olive oil, 1 tablespoon chopped parsley, 400 g rice, salt, pepper, a little saffron, 1 small can red peppers.

Thoroughly scrub the mussels, cover them with cold water and bring them to the boil. Simmer them until they open, and throw away any that do not. Meanwhile fry the onion in oil in a deep saucepan, or better, an earthenware pot for 10 minutes, then stir in the rice. Cook for a few minutes, then add 1 litre of water from the mussels (strain it to remove any grit) adding plain water if there is not enough. Season well and bring it to the boil. Add the saffron, the red peppers cut into strips and the parsley, and cook on a low flame for 20 minutes. Take the mussels out of their shells and mix them with the rice. Allow them to heat through.

If you have used an earthenware pot take it straight to the table from the stove.

Arroz con Bacalao   *Basque Country*
Rice with Salt Cod

To serve 4–6

250 g dried salt cod, 1 onion, 1 green pepper, olive oil, 6 tomatoes or one

medium can of tomatoes, 250 g peas, 12 mussels, ½ kg rice, 4 cloves garlic, chopped parsley, salt, saffron.

Soak the cod overnight in the usual way. Wash well, remove the skin and bones and break it into small pieces. Chop the onion and green pepper very finely and fry in olive oil in a heavy saucepan for 10 minutes, then add the tomatoes (peeled and chopped if fresh ones are used), the peas, the fish and the thoroughly scrubbed mussels. After a minute or two stir in the rice. Then add hot water, allowing two cups to each cup of rice, which will work out to about 1 litre. Raise the heat a little and when it boils add a handful of chopped parsley, and the cloves of garlic, either put through a garlic press or crushed in a mortar. Season with salt if needed, pepper and saffron (one envelope or two pinches) and simmer gently for 20 minutes, partially covered.

Serve with crusty bread and red wine.

Arroz Gallego *Galicia*
Galician Rice

To serve 4

1 onion, 6 mushrooms, 1 clove garlic, olive oil, 2 large tomatoes, parsley, 400 g rice, pinch of saffron, teaspoon powdered cinnamon, salt, tomato sauce (no. 1 or 2, see page 224).

Heat some oil in a large pan or casserole, preferably one suitable for the table, and gently fry the peeled and sliced onion and mushrooms. Chop the clove of garlic and the parsley and scald and peel the tomatoes, cut them in quarters and remove the seeds. Put all this into the pan and cook for about 10 minutes. Then add the rice, stir well and pour in 1 litre of water; it should cover everything well. Season with plenty of salt, the cinnamon and saffron. Lower the heat, cover the pan and cook gently for 15–20 minutes, checking to make sure it does not become too dry and burn.

Serve the tomato sauce in a separate bowl.

Arroz Murciano   *Murcia*
Rice Murciano

To serve 4–6

Olive oil for frying, 1 kg of lean pork, 2 cloves garlic, 6 red peppers, ½ kg tomatoes, 1 envelope (about 2 pinches) saffron, handful chopped parsley, salt and pepper, water and 400 g rice.

Select a deep casserole with a lid, suitable for the oven. Pour into it about 1 coffee-cup of olive oil and set to heat gently on top of the stove. Meanwhile, trim and cut up the pork. When the oil is fairly hot put in the pork and brown it lightly all over, remove and set aside. Put in the whole peeled cloves of garlic and brown well – remove and also set aside. Add to the hot oil the chopped and peeled tomatoes and the red peppers cut into strips. While this is cooking gently, take the fried garlic cloves and crush them in a mortar, together with the saffron, and the well-chopped parsley. By this time the tomatoes and peppers should have begun to soften; give them a stir and return the pork to the pan together with the garlic and parsley mixture. Add about one cup of water to the pan, put on the lid and allow to cook for 20 minutes, when most of the liquid should have been absorbed. Now put in the rice, stirring well, and allow to cook for a minute or two before adding about 1 litre of hot water (twice the volume of rice). Season with salt and pepper, cover the casserole and put into a moderate oven, 350° F, gas 4, for 30 minutes.

This is rather a bland dish, with pleasantly subtle flavours, which goes well with a green salad tossed in vinaigrette dressing.

Arroz con Huevos   *Valencia*
Rice with Eggs

To serve 4

4 eggs, 4 large even-sized tomatoes, 50 g lean ham, butter, salt, 1 onion, ¾ litre beef or chicken stock, 250 g long-grain rice, 2 cups tomato sauce (no. 1 or 2, see page 000).

Hard-boil the eggs, remove shells and cut in half. Cut the tomatoes in half, remove the seeds, and put a tiny piece of butter in each. Sprinkle with salt and pepper and put into the oven for 10 minutes (or under a grill but do not allow them to brown). Sauté the chopped ham in butter and fill the tomato halves with it.

Chop the onion and fry it in butter in a saucepan, add the rice, cook a minute or two then add ¾ litre of stock. Cover and cook gently for 20 minutes. When the rice is ready strain off any liquid that has not been absorbed and pile it on to a large serving dish. Surround with stuffed tomato halves and hard-boiled eggs and pour hot tomato sauce over the rice.

Arroz con Judias Blancas   *Aragon*
Rice with White Beans

This is rather a fattening dish.

To serve 4

¼ kg large white beans, ham stock, 1 onion, 1 clove garlic, a small teaspoon paprika, hot dried red pepper, bay leaf, 100 g rice, 3 potatoes, oil, 50 g *jamón serrano* or smoked ham, salt.

Soak the beans overnight, then boil them in the ham stock with the cut-up onion and garlic, the washed and de-seeded hot pepper, the bay leaf and paprika. Cook for 1–2 hours until the beans are almost done (if they are old and very dry, they take longer). Then add the rice, the potatoes, which should be peeled and cut up, and more stock or water if necessary. Meanwhile cut the ham into cubes and fry it in a little oil, then mix it together with the oil into the rice and bean mixture. The dish should be thick with the beans almost disintegrating.

Arroz con Mahonesa   *Andalusia*
Cold Rice with Mayonnaise

To serve 4

½ kg hake or cod, 1 carrot, 1 bay leaf, sprig parsley, piece celery, salt, 400 g rice, 1 cup mayonnaise, ½ clove garlic.

Simmer the fish with the carrot, celery and herbs in salted water for 10 minutes. Strain off the liquid into another pan and boil the rice in it for 15–20 minutes. Butter a mould and put in half the drained rice. Flake the fish, removing any bones and put a layer on top of the rice. Cover it with mayonnaise into which you have crushed a ½ clove of garlic. Put in the rest of the rice and cover with a weighted plate. When completely cold turn out and pour over it the rest of the mayonnaise.

Serve with tomato salad (see page 56).

Arroz con Jerez   *Andalusia*
Rice with Sherry

To serve 4

1 onion, 2 tablespoons olive oil, 250 g rice, 2 glasses of sweet sherry, 2 cups chicken stock, salt, a little butter.

Chop the onion finely and fry it gently in olive oil, add the rice and stir for a minute or two, then pour in the sherry. When it has been absorbed add the stock. Lower the heat and cook covered for about 15–20 minutes. Add a few knobs of butter and salt to taste just before serving. This goes well with cold meat or fish dishes.

Pasta

As everybody knows pasta in all its various forms is an Italian invention. The Spanish, however, have firmly adopted one or two of these, notably the tiny pastas in the shape of stars or shells for soup, and perhaps the best loved of them all – cannelloni. Cannelloni were first introduced into Barcelona by the Italians more than a hundred years ago and are now an established favourite for certain feast days – especially St Stephen's Day, or our Boxing Day, 26 December. Much of the best ready-made cannelloni is still manufactured in Barcelona, one of the best being El Pavo which is sold in wafer-thin oblongs and packed in a yellow box. These should be boiled for 15 minutes in plenty of salted water before being filled. Some brands only need to be soaked, but follow the instructions on the packet.

In England excellent Italian cannelloni pasta is sold in many continental food shops, usually in the shape of a tube, cut into suitable lengths for stuffing.

Canalones   *Catalonia*
Cannelloni

This recipe is a favourite of mine as it is deliciously rich, but it may be varied to suit individual tastes. Other stuffings may be used, such as puréed spinach or tuna fish. Always cover the cannelloni with a rich béchamel sauce, with or without the addition of cheese.

To serve 4

2 to 4 pieces of cannelloni according to size, per person.

For the filling: 2 tablespoons olive oil, $\frac{1}{4}$ kg minced beef, 2 or 3 chicken livers, 1 onion, 1 can tomatoes, 2 tablespoons of tomato paste, 2 cloves garlic, 2 teaspoons oregano, 1 teaspoon sugar, 2 teaspoons wine vinegar, pepper and salt. Approximately $\frac{1}{2}$ litre béchamel sauce, a little finely grated Parmesan cheese or in Spain hard Manchego cheese.

The filling takes longest to cook so start this first. Mix the minced beef and chicken livers. Heat the oil in a saucepan and fry the finely chopped onion for a few minutes, then stir in the meat, turning it over with a wooden spoon until it is brown and smoothly blended. Add the can of tomatoes, including the juice, and the tomato paste, cook for a few minutes more and then add the crushed garlic, the oregano, vinegar, sugar and seasoning. If necessary add a little water, stir thoroughly and cook covered on a low flame for about an hour. Meanwhile prepare the pasta according to the directions on the packet. When the filling is ready pour a thin layer of it into a large shallow earthenware dish – a rectangular dish is nice for this, or alternatively individual dishes may be used. Use the rest of the mixture to fill the cannelloni. If flat pasta is used put a spoonful on to each piece and roll it up to form a tube – otherwise spoon the filling into the ready-made tubes. Arrange the filled pasta side by side in the dish, if necessary in two layers. Have ready the béchamel sauce and pour it evenly over the cannelloni. Cover with grated cheese and put it into a moderate oven, 350° F, gas 4, for about ½ hour. If you are using individual dishes allow them to cool for at least a quarter of an hour before serving. Serve with a lettuce salad, crusty bread and red wine.

Maccarones con Legumbres
Macaroni with Vegetables

This makes a pleasant change from the usual macaroni cheese.

To serve 4–6

A variety of any vegetables available such as peas, broad beans, green beans, carrots, aubergines or courgettes, making about ½ kg prepared weight, 400 g macaroni, 1 large onion, 1 red pepper, 2 cloves garlic, 1 can tomatoes or 8 fresh peeled and chopped tomatoes, a little butter or olive oil, salt and pepper, 2 tablespoons chopped parsley, grated cheese, a little freshly ground black pepper.

Prepare the mixed vegetables, excluding the onion, garlic, red pepper and tomatoes. Put them into enough boiling salted water to barely cover them and cook for 10–15 minutes, or until they are just tender, no more, then strain them. At the same time cook the macaroni in boiling salted water for 10–15 minutes or according to directions on the packet. Heat a little butter or olive oil in a large saucepan and fry the chopped onion, garlic and red pepper. After 5 minutes add the tomatoes, salt and pepper and the cooked mixed vegetables and cook slowly for 10 minutes or so to make a thick sauce. Stir in the cooked drained macaroni. Select a suitable ovenproof dish and rub the inside with butter or oil – pour the contents of the saucepan into it, flatten it down and cover with a mixture of grated cheese and chopped parsley. Grind a little black pepper over it and dot with butter. Put it into a hot oven or under the grill until the top turns brown. Serve with a green salad.

Fideos a la Catalana   *Catalonia*
Vermicelli a la Catalana

In Spain ribs of pork are sold quite cheaply; they do not have a great deal of meat on them but what there is is quite delicious, and combined with vermicelli they make a good family dish.

To serve 4
½ kg pork ribs cut into pieces, lard for frying, 2 onions, 1 clove garlic, 1 can tomatoes or 6 fresh tomatoes, 2 tablespoons chopped parsley, 4 *butifarrones*, 300–400 g vermicelli according to appetite, pepper and salt.

Heat the lard in large saucepan and brown the pieces of pork ribs. Chop the onions and garlic fairly small and add them to the pan. Allow to cook gently for about 5 minutes and then add the can of tomatoes, or the fresh tomatoes peeled and chopped. Stir in the parsley. Cut the *butifarrones* into about 1-inch lengths and stir them in, continue to cook for another 10 minutes or so, then add the vermicelli broken up into pieces. Blend thoroughly, cook for a few moments, and then add about 1 cup of hot salted water, perhaps a little more if it seems dry. Season with pepper and cook gently until the vermicelli is tender, about 15 minutes. Transfer to a hot serving dish.

Coca Mallorquina   *Mallorca*
Mallorcan Pizza

In Mallorcan bakers' shops one can buy a delicious version of the Italian pizza. It is usually made in one large piece, the baker cutting off as much as you want.

The base of these pizzas is made from left-over bread dough. The baker will probably save you some if you ask him the night before, but an equally good pizza may be made with ordinary shortcrust pastry.

To serve 4

¼ kg shortcrust pastry or bread dough, ½ kg of spinach or the large outside leaves of a cos lettuce, 2 onions, 3 cloves of garlic, 8 tomatoes or 1 can of tomatoes, olive oil, a tablespoonful of oregano, pepper and salt, about 12 black olives.

Oil a large rectangular baking tray and roll out the dough or pastry to fit it. Wash and shred the spinach or lettuce leaves and boil them with only a tablespoon or so of water and a little salt for about 10 minutes. Drain thoroughly. Fry the sliced onion and garlic in oil for about 10 minutes, then add the tomatoes (fresh ones should be peeled and chopped) oregano and pepper and salt and cook for a further 5 minutes, stirring all the time.

Spread the cooked spinach or lettuce evenly over the pastry base, followed by a layer of the onion, garlic and tomato mixture. Sprinkle with pieces of the chopped black olives and put into a pre-heated moderate oven, 375° F, gas 5, and bake for about 20 minutes. Serve hot or cold with a green salad. This makes a very good addition to a picnic.

Eggs

It has been said that no Spaniard can ever be bothered to time an egg for three minutes exactly, which is why soft-boiled eggs are never served in Spain. Whether this is true or not, eggs, boiled or otherwise, are certainly not a traditional breakfast food. Nevertheless they are an important part of Spanish cooking. They are served poached in soups, hard-boiled for hors-d'œuvre and used in many sauces. They are also featured in dishes such as eggs Flamenca, and of course the Spanish omelette which is a favourite standby for lunches and picnics.

At the time of writing eggs are even more expensive in Spain than they are in the U.K. but they are of consistently good quality and are still an economical buy for most households. They are still sometimes sold singly or in pairs, but these days it is more usual to see them in the familiar six-egg plastic carton.

Tortilla
Spanish Omelette

To serve 4

2 large potatoes, 2 large onions, olive oil, 4 eggs, salt.

Peel the potatoes and onions and chop them into ¼-inch cubes. Mix them together. Take a medium-sized frying-pan and put in a small cup of olive oil. It is essential to use olive oil for this dish. Heat the oil gently and add the diced vegetables, stirring well and sprinkle with plenty of salt. Put a lid on the pan – a saucepan lid will do, it does not have to fit exactly, and stew the onion and potato slowly in the oil, stirring from time to time. Meantime, beat the eggs well in a large bowl. When the vegetables are tender (it takes 15–20 minutes) carefully remove them from the pan leaving as much oil behind as possible and add them to the egg mixture. Beat together thoroughly with a fork. Drain most of the oil from the pan, leaving just enough to cover the bottom and reheat. When the oil is fairly hot pour in the egg mixture and lower the heat – shaking the pan to prevent sticking. Flatten the mixture down with a fork until it fills the whole pan evenly and cook gently until it comes away from the sides. Remove from heat and place a heatproof plate over the frying-pan. Quickly turn the contents of the pan upside down on to the plate, being careful not to burn your wrist in the process. Then slide the *tortilla* back into the pan to cook the other side. Alternatively, a simpler way of cooking both sides of the *tortilla* is to slide the frying-pan under a hot grill to do the top. It should look like a solid cake when both sides are cooked and may be eaten hot or cold. Serve with salad. .

There are many ways of varying this basic recipe. Cooked vegetables such as peas, asparagus, red or green peppers cut in strips, green beans or cooked spinach may be added to the beaten eggs at the same time as the cooked onion and potato mixture, or substituted for either the onion or the potato. A little chopped cooked chicken or ham may also be added with advantage.

Pastel de Tortillas
Omelette Cake

To serve 4

6 eggs, 1 onion minced, 100 g puréed spinach (frozen is ideal), 100 g canned tomatoes, olive oil, salt, ¼ litre thick well-seasoned béchamel sauce.

Fry the onion in a tablespoon of olive oil until it is soft, remove from the pan and reserve. Take three small bowls and beat 2 eggs with a pinch of salt in each, add the onion to one, the spinach to another and the tomatoes to the third, beating each one well. Heat a little more olive oil if necessary in the pan in which the onion was cooked and make three omelettes (see previous recipe), one after the other, keeping them hot as you do so. Have ready the hot béchamel sauce and sandwich the omelettes neatly together with a layer of sauce between each to make a cake. Pour the remainder of the sauce on top and serve hot. Tomato sauce may be used instead of béchamel if preferred.

Tortilla Madrileña con Riñones   *New Castile*
Omelette with Kidneys

To serve 4

2 onions, olive oil, butter, 3 lambs' kidneys, parsley, 1 glass dry sherry,
4 small tomatoes, 150 g smoked ham, 6 eggs, salt and pepper.

Chop 1 onion finely and sauté it in a mixture of oil and butter.
When it begins to soften add the chopped cleaned kidneys and
chopped parsley. Cook gently for 10–15 minutes, then add the
sherry and allow it to bubble. Remove from the pan and keep
warm. Cut each tomato in half and fry or grill, reserving on a
separate plate. In the same pan in which the kidneys were cooked
fry the other onion, also finely chopped, add the chopped ham,
then pour in 6 eggs, well-beaten and seasoned, to make a flat
round omelette. Turn over to cook on both sides. Serve with the
kidneys on top and surrounded with tomato halves. Sweetbreads
may be used instead of kidney.

Torta de Huevo
Tiny Omelettes

To serve 4

3 eggs, 2 teaspoons flour, pinch of mint, ½ teaspoon salt, ½ teaspoon baking
powder, pinch oregano, oil for frying.

Beat the egg whites until stiff, add yolks and beat again. Stir
flour, oregano, mint, baking powder and salt lightly into eggs.
Drop by teaspoonfuls into deep oil and fry. Drain and serve with
chilli sauce as an hors-d'œuvre.

Tortilla Coruñesa   *Galicia*
Bacon Omelettes from Coruña

To serve 2

4 eggs, paprika, 60 g lean bacon, olive oil, parsley.

Beat the eggs in a bowl and season with salt and 1 teaspoon of
paprika. Chop the bacon and fry it in hot oil, then add a handful

of finely chopped parsley and fry quickly. Remove from the pan
and drain on kitchen paper, then add it to the egg mixture. Pour
half the mixture at a time back into the hot oil to form two
omelettes. Smoked bacon gives the best flavour.

Tortilla Estilo Badajoz   *Extremadura*
A Piquant Omelette

To serve 4

200 g *chorizo*, paprika, 1 small thin hot pepper (red or green), 8 eggs, oil and
salt.

Cut the *chorizo* into slices and fry in a large pan. Wash and remove seeds from the pepper, slice and add to the pan together
with a teaspoon of paprika and cook for 10 minutes more. Beat up
the eggs with 2 tablespoons of water and salt to taste, and pour
them into the frying-pan. Stir round with a fork, and when
cooked fold over to form an omelette. Divide into 4. The pieces
of pepper are *very* hot.

Tortilla con Sardinas Frescas   *Balearic Islands*
Omelette with Fresh Sardines

To serve 4

8 fresh sardines, juice of ½ lemon, 2 teaspoons paprika, salt, 4 eggs, 1 clove
garlic, 1 tablespoon chopped chives or parsley, coffee-cup olive oil.

Remove the scales from the sardines under a running tap, cut off
the heads, clean them and open them out flat. Remove the backbone. This is easy if you run your thumbnail firmly down the
back first on the skin side. Sprinkle them with salt, lemon juice
and paprika. Beat the eggs with the crushed garlic and herbs and
a little salt. Heat the olive oil in a frying-pan and pour half the
egg mixture into it. Lower the heat and lay the sardines evenly
on top. Pour in the rest of the eggs. Cook gently for about 15
minutes, then carefully turn the omelette over (see *tortilla* recipe
on pages 89–90) and cook on the other side for a further 15 minutes.

Turn on to a hot dish and serve at once. A tomato and onion salad goes well with this.

Tortilla con Espárragos   *Mallorca*
Omelette with Wild Asparagus

To serve 1

A few spears of wild asparagus, 2 eggs, salt, pepper, a little water and butter.

Put the asparagus into boiling salted water for about 3 minutes. Drain and cut into fairly small pieces. Beat the eggs, seasoning and water together as for a French omelette. Heat a little butter in a small frying-pan and pour in the egg mixture. When it begins to set sprinkle on the pieces of asparagus and cook a little longer. Fold the omelette in half and serve at once.

Huevos a la Flamenca   *Andalusia*
Eggs Flamenca

This dish which is so typically Spanish can easily be made in England provided you can get some good *chorizo*. Smoked lean ham may be substituted for *jamón serrano*.

To serve 4

1 coffee-cup of olive oil, two potatoes, 1 onion, 1 sweet red pepper, 4 slices of *jamón serrano*, 200 g each of cooked peas and green beans (frozen ones are suitable), 1 small can of asparagus tips, 4 tomatoes, scalded, peeled and chopped, 2 tablespoons tomato paste, pepper and salt, 8 eggs, 8 thin slices of best-quality *chorizo*, 1 tablespoon chopped parsley.

Peel the potatoes and cut them into small dice. Heat the oil in a large pan and fry these until they are golden, remove and reserve. Chop the onion, the red pepper and two slices of ham and fry them in the same oil until the onions are transparent. Then add the peas, beans and the asparagus tips, the tomatoes and the tomato paste. Stir in the fried potatoes and about half a cup of water. Season with pepper and salt and blend everything well together. Cook gently for about 5 minutes stirring occasionally.

Select a large oval earthenware dish, or use 4 individual dishes if you prefer, and brush them with a little oil. Pour in the vegetable mixture and make some hollows on the surface for the eggs. Carefully break each egg into a cup and pour one into each hollow. Arrange slices of *chorizo* and the remaining ham cut into triangles over the top as a decoration and sprinkle with chopped parsley. Put into a moderate oven, 350° F, gas 4, for about 15 minutes, or until the whites of the eggs are just set. Serve at once.

Huevos a la Extremeña   *Extremadura*
Eggs Extremadura

This is a simpler version of eggs Flamenca.

To serve 4

1 coffee-cup olive oil, 1 large onion, 8 tomatoes or 1 large can, 8 medium potatoes, 150 g *chorizo*, 150 g ham, 1 cup cooked peas, 8 eggs, salt and pepper.

Peel the potatoes and put them to boil. Heat the oil in a large saucepan and fry the chopped onion and peeled and chopped tomatoes. When the potatoes are just cooked drain them, chop them small and add them to the tomato mixture. Cut up the ham and *chorizo* fairly finely and add it to the pan, stir thoroughly, season with salt and pepper and cook gently for 15 minutes. Take a large shallow earthenware dish or 4 small ones and pour the mixture into it. Make some hollows on the surface and break an egg into each. (If you break each egg into a cup first it is easier not to damage the yolks.) Sprinkle the top with peas and bake in a moderate oven, 375° F, gas 5, until the whites are set and the yolks still soft – about 15 minutes. Serve with a salad, red wine and crusty bread.

Huevos con Hierbas
Eggs with Herbs

To serve 4

1 cut clove of garlic, about 50 g butter, 1 tablespoon olive oil, a few spring onions, 2 tomatoes, salt, black pepper and paprika, 8 eggs, approximately

¼ litre béchamel sauce, grated Manchego or Parmesan cheese, 1 tablespoon finely chopped chervil or coriander leaves, 1 tablespoon finely chopped parsley, 1 tablespoon finely chopped basil.

Rub four small earthenware dishes with garlic and put a little butter and oil in each. Scatter some of the mixed chopped herbs, chopped spring onion and peeled diced tomato in each one and season with salt, pepper and paprika. Place in a moderate oven for about 5 minutes. Remove the dishes from the oven and break two eggs into each taking care not to damage the yolks. Put them back into the oven for about 10 minutes, or until the whites are just set, then spoon a little béchamel sauce over each one. Sprinkle with grated cheese and the rest of the herbs and put under a grill for 2 or 3 minutes to brown.

Huevos a la Castellana *Old Castile*
Eggs a la Castellana

To serve 4

1 onion, olive oil, 200 g good-quality minced beef, 4 eggs, 1 breakfast-cup béchamel sauce, ½ cup grated cheese, pepper and salt.

Heat the oil in a frying-pan and fry the finely chopped onion, add the meat and cook for 10 minutes. Season well. Take 4 individual earthenware dishes and put a layer of meat into each one, then carefully break an egg on top. Put them into a hot oven for 10 minutes or until the egg whites have set and then pour over them a coating of béchamel sauce and sprinkle with grated cheese. Replace in the oven until the cheese is slightly brown. Serve with small pieces of fried bread.

Huevos al Plato Gitanilla *Andalusia*
Gipsy Eggs

To serve 4

Olive oil, 2 or 3 cloves of garlic, a handful of almonds, 2 slices bread, 1 teaspoon saffron, 1 teaspoon cumin seed, 1 teaspoon ground cinnamon, salt, 8 eggs.

Heat the oil and fry the chopped garlic. Blanch and split the almonds and add to the pan. Fry them till golden and set aside. Fry the 2 slices of bread crisply. Crush all these in a large mortar with a little of the oil in which they were fried, together with the saffron and other spices. When it forms a thick paste add the rest of the oil and a little hot salted water and pour into a large shallow ovenproof dish. Break the eggs over the top and cook in a moderate oven until the whites are set, about 15 minutes.

Huevos Estilo Gallego   *Galicia*
Galician Eggs

To serve 2

3 tomatoes, 1 sprig parsley, bay leaf, salt, oil, 2 tablespoons butter, 100 g mushrooms, 4 eggs.

Cut up the tomatoes and fry in a little oil, add the parsley, bay leaf and salt and make into a sauce with a little water. Put through a sieve and reserve. Dot the butter over the bottom of an earthenware dish and cover with sliced mushrooms, pour the sauce over them and cook gently till the sauce has thickened. Carefully break the eggs one by one into the dish (it is easier to break each one into a cup first) not damaging the yolks, and put the dish into a hot oven for 15 minutes. Serve in the same dish, very hot.

Piparrada   *Basque Country*
Pipérade

To serve 4

1 cup thick tomato sauce (no. 1 or 2, see page 224), 2 onions, olive oil, 6 fresh green peppers, salt, 6 eggs.

Prepare the tomato sauce. Chop the onions very finely and fry them in hot oil, wash and remove the seeds from the peppers, cut them into strips and put them to fry gently with the onion. Add the tomato sauce and any salt necessary. When the peppers are tender, pour in the beaten eggs and mix well. Serve either as scrambled eggs or in the form of an omelette.

Pisto Castellano   *Old Castile*
Fried Vegetables and Eggs

To serve 4

4 small courgettes, 4 small onions, 2 tablespoons lard or oil, 50 g lean smoked bacon, 4 small potatoes, 1 medium can red peppers, 1 medium can tomatoes or 4 large ripe fresh ones, 1½ cups beef stock, salt, pepper and 4 eggs.

Thinly slice the courgettes 1 hour before they are needed. Sprinkle with salt and put between two plates with a weight on top to extract any surplus water. Rinse and drain thoroughly. Unless the skins are very tough it is better not to peel them. Chop the onions and bacon and fry in 2 tablespoons of oil or lard. Peel and chop the potatoes and add them to the mixture, then add the drained courgettes, stir and cover the pan, allowing the vegetables to stew gently. After 5 minutes add the can of tomatoes, or fresh ones (first scalded and peeled), and the cut-up red peppers. Pour in the stock and cook with the lid off until reduced by half. Beat the eggs with salt and pepper and pour them into the vegetable mixture, stirring until they thicken. Serve with triangles of fried bread.

Huevos a la Riojana   *Old Castile*
Scrambled Eggs Riojana

To serve 4

6 eggs, 6 tomatoes, 100 g *chorizo*, 100 g lard, 1 crusty loaf, salt and parsley.

Scald and peel tomatoes, squeeze and remove seeds, cut up finely and put them in a frying-pan with lard to make a thick sauce. When it has cooled, add the beaten eggs. Season with salt and a little chopped parsley and stir with a beater. When the scrambled eggs are cooked add the bread cut in triangles and fried in oil, together with the *chorizo* sliced and fried.

This is a fine dish for a light evening meal – use the best *chorizo* you can find – Rioja or Pamplona.

Huevos Rellenos   *Asturias*
Stuffed Eggs

To serve 4

8 eggs, 1 small can tuna in oil, 1 small can red peppers, 2 tablespoons butter, a little mustard ready mixed, 1 crisp lettuce, vinaigrette dressing.

Hard-boil the eggs and cut them in half lengthways. Mash the yolks together with the can of tuna and the canned peppers (drain them first). Soften the butter and blend in the mustard. Add this to the tuna fish mixture and mix together thoroughly until you have a smooth consistency. This may be either spooned into the empty egg whites or piped in with a fancy nozzle. Cut up the lettuce and arrange it on a flat dish with plenty of vinaigrette dressing and the eggs on top.

Serve as an hors-d'œuvre or a supper dish.

Fish

Whatever one might think about the smells involved, the fish markets of Spain are certainly visually exciting places. There is usually a good selection of exotic creatures ranging from the enormous blue-black tuna to the delicate red mullet and the minute fry of the anchovy. There is the grotesquely ugly angler-fish, which looks all mouth but which is a great favourite with the Spaniards, and the spotted moray eels, their evil little faces glaring ferociously even in death. There are great heaps of glistening prawns, beady-eyed and still tangled with threads of pale green seaweed, and glutinous white masses of tiny squid. There is a charming little fish called a *boga*, rather like a sardine but with delicately coloured vertical stripes, and the *chicharro*, a glamorous relation of the horse-mackerel. Many fish have rather endearing Spanish names such as *maceta* (sluggish), or *tiñoso* (clever), which are not much help if you want to know what kind of fish it is. A pocket guide such as *The Observer's Book of Fish*, or Alan Davidson's *Mediterranean Seafood* could be well worth taking to Spain if you really want to know exactly what you are buying.

There is a very efficient system for the transport of fish in Spain, and even the most central districts are supplied with fresh fish daily, particularly Madrid, which is famous for its seafood. Fish is far more popular than it is in England, and the Spanish housewife or her maid takes great care in selecting her choice for the day, going early to the market and diligently peering into gill-slits and prodding for firmness. A fresh fish should smell of the sea, and should have bright red gills and a clear rounded eye. Some of the fish offered for sale is alas not like this at all, and in spite of the fact that it is frequently sluiced down with water to freshen up its appearance it is obviously on the point of decay. Who buys this fish and for what purpose we have not yet discovered. There is another class of fish known as *con hielo*, literally 'with ice'. It is preserved on ice in the holds of fishing boats and usually sold surrounded by ice but not actually frozen. Care should be taken when buying this kind of fish as it may have been quite some time at sea.

Dried salt cod, or *bacalao*, features largely in Iberian cooking. It is probably eaten at least once a week in most households throughout Spain and is served in nearly all restaurants, usually as *bacalao a la vizcaína*. The cod is caught in the north Atlantic off the Newfoundland banks and is imported to Europe and the Iberian peninsular ready dried and salted, or brought back and cured in Spain. Every fish market and village shop has its salt cod, and sometimes other kinds of fish which have been locally dried. In the cities the supermarkets sell it cut into neat pieces in plastic bags or packets. It is harder to find in England, although many of the larger fish shops and delicatessen stock it. It is well worth buying a whole fish to hang by the tail in an airy place and cut off pieces as it is needed; it should keep for months. The tail-end is the tastiest, although the thicker part towards the head has less wastage of skin and bone. Half a kilo is generally sufficient for four people as there are usually other filling ingredients in the dish.

Pescado a la Sal
Fish Cooked in Salt

Murcia

This is an unusual and effective method of cooking a whole fairly large fish. Any of the bream family, grey mullet, or a flat fish such as turbot may be used. The fish must be absolutely fresh and classically should not be gutted although you may prefer to do this. Do not de-scale it or remove the head, just wash it.

To serve 4

1 large whole fish, a lot of rock or sea salt, melted butter or hollandaise sauce.

Choose a shallow ovenproof dish into which the fish fits neatly. Cover the bottom with a layer of coarse salt, damp it slightly and put in the fish. Pour in more salt, pressing it down and damping it as you go. When the dish is full and the fish completely covered, give a final sprinkling of water, press it down well and put it into a moderate oven, 350° F, gas 4, and cook for about an hour. When you remove it the salt will have become a solid block which has to be split with a hammer and a strong knife or even a chisel. Prise off the salt casing and the skin of the fish should come away with it, leaving the succulent tender flesh perfectly cooked. Remove any bits of salt left in the dish and serve as it is, with melted butter or hollandaise sauce.

Mero a la Vizcaína
Baked Grouper

Basque Country

This fish is considered a great delicacy in Spain. Halibut may be substituted.

To serve 4

4 thick steaks of grouper or halibut, salt, juice of 1 lemon, olive oil or butter, 1 wine glass of white wine or cider, 2 onions, 2 cloves of garlic, 2 tablespoons chopped parsley, ¼ kg fresh tomatoes or one medium can of tomatoes, 1 teaspoon sugar, 1 small hot red pepper or ½ teaspoon of chilli powder, a small can of red peppers, fresh breadcrumbs.

Put the pieces of fish into a shallow earthenware dish. Season well with salt and pour over the lemon juice, the wine and a little

olive oil or butter. Cover the dish with foil or buttered paper and
bake in a moderate oven, 350° F, gas 4, for 20 minutes. Meanwhile
chop the onions and garlic finely and soak the hot red pepper in
a little water. Fry the onions and garlic in olive oil, add the
parsley and tomatoes (chopped and peeled if fresh ones are used)
and simmer to make a thick sauce. Remove the seeds from the
pepper and pound it in a mortar. Add it to the sauce (or add the
chilli powder). Stir in the sugar and some salt. Take the fish from
the oven and spoon most of the liquid from it into the sauce, then
pour the sauce over the fish. Cover with breadcrumbs. Put strips
of canned red pepper over the top to form a lattice and sprinkle
with olive oil, put it back uncovered in the oven for 10 minutes.
Serve in the same dish.

Mero a la Valenciana *Valencia*
Grouper a la Valenciana

To serve 4

1 kg of fresh grouper (or halibut), 1 lemon, 1 tablespoon vinegar, 4 cloves
garlic, olive oil, 2 tablespoons flour, parsley, salt, white pepper, saffron.

Cut up the fish and sprinkle the pieces with lemon juice and
vinegar. Chop the garlic and fry it in plenty of oil till golden.
Remove and reserve. Dip the pieces of fish in seasoned flour and
fry them in the same oil, and when lightly browned on both sides
add a tablespoon of flour mixed with a little cold water and stir.
Cover the pan and cook slowly, shaking from time to time to
prevent sticking. Add a little more water if necessary. When the
fish is about half done add the pieces of fried garlic crushed with
the parsley and a pinch each of pepper and saffron. Serve the fish
in individual earthenware dishes with the sauce strained over it.

Mero al Jerez *Andalusia*
Grouper in Sherry Sauce

To serve 4

Four fresh grouper steaks (or substitute halibut), 2 tablespoons olive oil, salt, 2 tablespoons blanched almonds in slivers, 1 glass sherry (medium to dry), parsley.

Oil a shallow ovenproof dish and put in the pieces of fish whole, including the skin. Sprinkle with salt and the rest of the olive oil and scatter the almonds on top. Pour on the sherry and bake in a moderate oven, 350° F, gas 4, for about ½ hour, basting frequently. Add the finely chopped parsley before the fish is quite done and serve in the same dish.

Merluza Koskera
Hake with Mussels

To serve 4

4 slices of hake or cod (no need to thaw if frozen), 2 eggs, a dozen big mussels, 2 cloves garlic, olive oil, flour, salt, parsley, 1 glass dry white wine, 1 small cup cooked peas, 1 small can asparagus tips.

Boil the eggs until hard. Scrub the mussels and bring them to the boil. When they open, remove them and reserve the liquid. Reject any that do not open. Heat about 4 tablespoons of olive oil in a deep saucepan and fry the chopped garlic, then dip the pieces of fish in seasoned flour and fry them on both sides to a golden brown. Add the wine and enough water from the mussels to cover the fish and shake the pan gently over a low heat until the sauce thickens and the fish is cooked through. Check for seasoning. Finally add the peas, asparagus tips and mussels and put into a hot serving dish. Decorate with chopped parsley and slices of hard-boiled egg.

Merluza a la Gallega   *Galicia*
Hake a la Gallega

To serve 4

8 hake or cod fillets, salt, 2 sprigs thyme, bay leaf, parsley, olive oil, wine vinegar, 1 large onion, 6 medium potatoes, 4 or 5 cloves of garlic, 3 teaspoons cayenne pepper.

Poach the fish with a bay leaf, sprigs of thyme, parsley, 1 tea-spoon salt and a tablespoon of wine vinegar added to the water. Ten minutes should be enough. Strain and reserve the stock. Meanwhile cut the onion and peeled potatoes into thin rounds and sauté them in plenty of olive oil in a deep pan. Add the garlic, crushed, and a handful of chopped parsley, lower the heat and cover the pan. Cook gently for 3 or 4 minutes, then add about a cup of the fish stock and continue cooking with the lid on for about ½ hour, or until the vegetables are tender. Drain, and keep warm. Meanwhile make a sauce with 6 tablespoons of olive oil and 2 of vinegar and 3 teaspoons of cayenne pepper. Heat this mixture through in a little saucepan, stirring well. Reheat the fish steaks and serve on a bed of the potato and onion mixture with the hot sauce poured over them.

Merluza a la Mahonesa *Catalonia*
Cold Hake with Mayonnaise

To serve 4

4 thick slices of fresh or frozen hake (or substitute cod), 12 small mushrooms, lemon juice, 12 mussels, 12 small potatoes, salt, mayonnaise, slices of lemon for garnish.

Thaw the fish if frozen. Peel the mushrooms and simmer in a little water and lemon juice. Scrub the mussels and bring them to the boil, cook until they open. Throw away those that do not open. Use the water from the mussels to just cover the pieces of fish in the large pan, and season with salt. Put over a gentle heat and when it starts to simmer add the drained mushrooms and cook gently until the fish is done, about 10 minutes. Remove the pieces of fish and mushrooms and allow to cool completely.

Serve cold with mayonnaise and small boiled potatoes, and garnish with the mussels and slices of lemon.

Truchas de León
Leonese Trout

Leon

The rivers of Leon, as of Navarre and Aragon, are famous for their trout. The fishermen grill them on a wire grid over a wood fire on the river bank, using pork fat from their *bocadillos* (packed lunches usually consisting of bread and fat *serrano* ham) to baste them. At home trout may be cooked as follows.

To serve 4

4 or 8 trout according to size, pork dripping, salt, 2 lemons.

Clean the trout, leaving the heads on, and sprinkle well with salt. Put a knob of dripping on each and place under a hot grill. Turn the trout once and baste frequently till the skin is blistered and golden.

Serve at once with quarters of lemon and crusty bread.

Truchas Rellenas
Stuffed Trout

Asturias

The rivers of Asturias are also full of trout. They are usually served grilled or fried, but there is an unusual alternative combining fish and meat, as does the following recipe.

To serve 4

4 trout, salt, lemon juice, 2 slices of cooked chicken, 2 slices of ham, 1 small onion, 8 stoned olives, 100 g crushed toasted almonds, 1 canned red pepper (optional), butter, white pepper.

Wash the trout and split them open, remove the guts and backbone. Sprinkle them inside and out with lemon juice and salt. Mince the chicken, ham and onion together, finely chop the olives and red pepper, and mix into the minced meat. Add the almonds, season with salt and pepper, and stuff the trout with the mixture. Tie the fish up with thread, put a knob of butter on top and parcel each one in buttered foil, not too tightly, but be sure they are well sealed in. Put them on to a baking tray and bake in a moderate oven, 350° F, gas 4, for 40 minutes. Serve hot with the juices spooned over them.

Salmón con Ternera   *Galicia*
Salmon with Steak

A strange combination of fish and meat.

To serve 4

4 slices of salmon, 1 bay leaf, a few slices of onion, salt, 4 pieces of tender steak or veal, 8 cooked prawns, 1 thick slice of ham, 4 tablespoons fresh breadcrumbs, 1 tablespoon finely chopped parsley, 1 clove garlic, 50 g butter.

Poach the salmon for 10 minutes in a little salted water with the onion rings and the bay leaf. Butter a flat oval baking dish and put in the slices of steak or veal, well beaten and sprinkled with salt. Put the salmon on top and arrange the peeled prawns and the ham cut into strips around the meat and fish. Mix the breadcrumbs, parsley and finely chopped garlic together and sprinkle them on top. Melt the butter in a little saucepan and pour it over the ingredients in the dish. Bake in a hot oven, 400° F, gas 6, for about 10 minutes, or until the meat is cooked as you like it, and serve in the same dish.

Lenguados Tinerfeños   *Canary Islands*
A Canary Island Way of Cooking Sole

1 sole for each person, chopped fresh herbs including marjoram, parsley, fennel, tarragon or dill, ground white pepper, salt, plenty of butter, breadcrumbs.

Clean the fish and wash them under running water. Melt a little butter in a saucepan and put in all the chopped herbs. Coat the fish with this mixture, dip in breadcrumbs, season with salt and pepper, and put them into hot butter, dark side down. Fry quickly on both sides and eat straightaway.

Lubina Asturiana
Asturian Casserole of Bass

Asturias

To serve 2

1 bass, 1 onion, salt, pepper, olive oil, 1 teaspoon paprika, 1 glass white wine, 10 mussels, chopped parsley.

Clean the fish and cut it into slices. Chop the onion finely. Put the fish and onion into a casserole, season with plenty of salt, pepper and paprika, and pour in the wine. Cover and cook in a moderate oven, 350° F, gas 4, for 30 minutes. Meanwhile scrub the mussels and bring them to the boil. Drain when they have all opened. Arrange the slices of fish on an ovenproof plate and decorate it with the mussels and triangles of fried bread. Strain the juices from the casserole and pour them over the fish. Put back into the oven for 5 minutes and serve sprinkled with very finely chopped parsley.

Besugo a la Guipuzcoana
Barbecued Bream

Basque Country

To serve 2

1 bream, olive oil, sea salt, 1 lemon, 4 cloves garlic.

Clean the bream, removing the fins and scales. Hang it up by the head while you prepare a wood fire. When the fire is red and the flames have died down, put a metal grill over the hottest part. (You could just grill the fish at home in the ordinary way, but it would not taste quite the same.) Thoroughly brush the fish with olive oil, using a feather if you have no brush, rub it with coarse salt and place it over the fire, turning it until it is thoroughly cooked. Chop up the garlic and fry it quickly in a small pan, then add the juice of the lemon. Split the fish in half and pour this mixture over it. Eat at once.

Almost any other fish may be cooked in this way.

Besugo al Horno   *Asturias*
Casserole of Bream

To serve 2

1 bream weighing about 1 kg, 2 lemons, 1 clove garlic, 1 onion, 12 tablespoons
olive oil, flour, 1 tablespoon pine-nuts, 1 glass white wine, chopped parsley,
pepper and salt.

Clean the bream and pour over it the juice of one lemon and 4
tablespoons of oil. Allow to stand in a cool place for 2 hours.
Select an earthenware casserole to fit the fish, heat the rest of the
oil and fry the garlic, roughly chopped. When browned remove
and set aside. Flour the bream and brown it well on both sides.
Pound the fried garlic and pine-nuts with the finely chopped
onion in a mortar and add this to the bream, then pour in the
wine, the juice of the other lemon and a little water. Sprinkle
with chopped parsley, season well, cover and allow to cook gently
in a moderate oven, 350° F, gas 4, for 30 minutes. If you have
no lid to fit the dish use foil. Serve in the same dish.

Variations of this dish are traditional fare for Christmas Eve
all over Spain.

Besugo Asado a la Madrileña   *New Castile*
Baked Bream

To serve 2-3

1 large bream (1-1½ kg in weight), 2 lemons, olive oil, a glass of dry white
wine or sherry, 1 dried bay leaf, 2 cloves garlic, parsley, salt and pepper.

Clean the fish but leave the head on. Make some diagonal cuts
on one side of the fish and place a slice of lemon in each cut. Take
a large shallow ovenproof dish, preferably earthenware, pour in
a little oil and put in the fish, well seasoned with salt and freshly
ground black pepper, with the cut side uppermost. Pour over it
the rest of the oil, the juice of one lemon and the glass of wine.
Sprinkle it with crushed garlic and parsley and the crumbled bay
leaf and put into a moderate oven to bake. Baste it frequently and
allow ¾-1 hour cooking time or until the fish is cooked through
to the bone.

Serve in the dish in which it was cooked.

Marmitako
Basque Country

Fresh Tuna Fish

This dish is served in Basque restaurants in late summer, when the tuna come, following the shoals of anchovy.

To serve 4

1 coffee-cup olive oil, 1 onion, 2 cloves garlic, 1 kg potatoes, salt, 1 teaspoon cayenne pepper, 1 large tin red peppers or two fresh red peppers, 1 kg fresh or frozen tuna or *bonito*.

Heat the oil in an earthenware casserole and fry the chopped onion and garlic, then add the cut-up raw potatoes, salt and cayenne pepper, the red peppers cut into strips and the tuna fish cut into thick steaks. Cover with water and cook gently for $\frac{1}{2}$–$\frac{3}{4}$ hour, or until the fish is cooked through and the potatoes tender. Serve in the same casserole.

Note. Fresh tuna which is common in Spain and Portugal is not usually sold in English fish shops, but it may be ordered from the larger ones. Frozen tuna is excellent.

Bonito con Aceitunas
Andalusia

Fresh Tuna with Olives

To serve 4

4 steaks of fresh or frozen tuna, 1 cup olive oil, 1 glass white wine, a little wine vinegar, 2 cloves garlic, 1 bay leaf, sprig thyme, ground black pepper, salt, flour, 100 g stoned green olives.

Wash the fish and place it in a large shallow dish. Make a marinade with the oil, wine, vinegar, herbs, chopped garlic and salt. Pour this over the fish and leave to stand in a cool place for 2 hours. If frozen fish is used allow it to thaw thoroughly first. Remove the fish from the marinade and dip it into flour, then fry the pieces in hot oil until golden on both sides, remove and keep hot. Using the same pan, make a sauce with the marinade. Boil until it has reduced a little, strain it, add the chopped olives and serve with the fish.

Tenca Murciana
Tench Murciana

Murcia

To serve 2

1 tench, 1 tablespoon lard, 2 tablespoons flour, 1 large glass dry white wine
(or dry cider), a bunch of herbs tied together (thyme, basil, fennel, parsley,
bay leaf), 2 cloves garlic, ground black pepper, salt, 1 tablespoon butter,
3 egg yolks, chopped parsley.

Clean the fish and remove the head. Scald and remove the skin.
Cut it into pieces (roughly 1-inch cubes), removing any bones.
Flour the fish and fry it in hot lard for 5 minutes, then add the
wine and let it bubble. Lower the heat and add the bunch of
herbs, salt, pepper and 2 whole cloves of garlic. Cover the pan
and cook gently for 15 minutes, adding water if it becomes dry.
When the fish is cooked, take out the herbs and garlic and remove
from heat. Add the egg yolks, stirring in carefully some small
pieces of butter and the chopped parsley. Reheat and serve with
small boiled potatoes and white wine.

Anguila al Horno
Eel Cooked in the Oven

*Catalonia and the
Balearic Islands*

Either conger or moray eel is used in this dish, and though the
common river eel may also be cooked in this way, it tends to be
rather oily. It is best to use only the centre section of a large eel,
avoiding the bony tail end.

To serve 4

1 medium-sized eel, flour, salt, olive oil, 4 tomatoes, 2 onions, 4 potatoes,
1 large glass white wine, 2 cloves garlic, 1 tablespoon chopped parsley,
2 tablespoons crushed, blanched almonds, several lettuce leaves, preferably of
the Cos variety.

Skin and chop up the eel, discarding the head. Dip the pieces in
seasoned flour and fry them in olive oil until golden. Transfer to
an ovenproof dish and keep warm. In the same oil fry the peeled
tomatoes, chopped onion and sliced raw potato for about 10
minutes. Mix this with the eel in the ovenproof dish and pour in

a large glass of white wine. Sprinkle with a mixture of chopped garlic, parsley and almonds and completely cover with a layer of washed shredded lettuce leaves. Sprinkle with oil and bake in a moderate oven, 350° F, gas 4, for about an hour or until the eel is cooked.

Rape con Patatas   *Andalusia*
Angler-fish with Potatoes

Angler-fish is often combined with shellfish such as mussels or prawns, possibly because the texture of the flesh is similar to lobster. Here is a simple recipe which savours the fish in its own right.

To serve 4

¾ kg angler-fish, flour, salt, olive oil, 2 onions, ½ kg tomatoes or 1 large can tomatoes, ¾ kg potatoes peeled and cut into thick rounds, 1 small can red peppers.

Clean and slice the fish and dip into seasoned flour. Heat the oil in a saucepan and brown the pieces of fish. Take them out and put in the onion and tomatoes, peeled and roughly chopped. Cook for about 5 minutes. Add the pieces of raw potato and cover with water. When the potato is about half cooked put back the fish and continue to cook very gently for about ½ hour.

Serve decorated with thin strips of red pepper.

Salmonetes a la Parrilla   *Catalonia*
Grilled Red Mullet

To serve 4

1 or 2 red mullet per person, depending on the size of the fish, sea salt, olive oil, juice of 2 lemons, plenty of chopped parsley, *romesco* sauce (see pages 215–16.)

Slit the mullet and remove the guts leaving behind the liver. (It is probably better to get your fishmonger to do this.) Leave the heads on, but scrape off all the scales. Wash the fish and sprinkle them with coarse sea salt, olive oil and lemon juice. Leave them in a cool place for 1–2 hours if possible before grilling. Put them under a hot grill. When they are nicely crisp serve them with the juices from the grill-pan poured over them and sprinkled with chopped parsley. Serve the *romesco* sauce in a separate bowl.

Caballas a la Parrilla   *Canary Islands*
Grilled Mackerel

To serve 4

8 small or 4 medium-sized mackerel, olive oil, 2 cloves garlic,
sprig parsley, paprika, vinegar, salt, ½ lemon.

Clean and wash the mackerel and make 2 diagonal slits in each side. Fill with a mixture of finely chopped parsley and a little crushed garlic. Sprinkle the fish with olive oil, paprika and salt, and grill for a few minutes on each side until the skin is crisp and the fish cooked through.

Serve the fish straight away, with the juices from the grill-pan, diluted with a little wine vinegar and lemon juice, poured over them. If you line the grill-pan with foil and place the fish on it you will not waste any juice.

Pescados Fritos   *Andalusia*
A Variety of Fried Fish

This dish is usually served as a *tapa* or appetizer in Cadiz and Malaga but is substantial enough for a supper dish served with white wine and good bread. The Andalusian housewife uses whatever fish she has to hand, but they should be small and perfectly fresh.

To serve 4

2 young hake, cut up, 2 small sole cut in pieces, 2 squid cut into rings (if available), ¼ kg small sardines (sprats could be used), 200 g *chanquetes* or *boquerones* (tiny fish like whitebait, eaten whole), 2 small red mullet, cut up, flour, sea salt and plenty of olive oil.

Clean and wash the fish and coat them with well-salted flour. Heat about ¼ litre of olive oil in a large shallow pan and when smoking hot put in sufficient fish for one person, using some of each kind. Fry quickly, turning them over and over until they are crisp and moving them around the pan so that they are done as evenly as possible.

Serve immediately.

Filetes de Espada   *Andalusia*
Fried Swordfish Fillets

To serve 4

4 large or 8 small fillets of swordfish, or substitute cod or halibut, 2 eggs, 1 whole head of garlic, peeled and finely chopped, 1 teaspoon cinnamon, a good pinch of powdered saffron, salt and freshly ground black pepper, olive oil for frying.

Beat the eggs and add the garlic and spices, pepper and salt. Lay the fillets flat in a dish and pour the mixture over them. Allow to stand in a cool place for about an hour. When ready to eat, fry the fillets quickly in hot olive oil.

Zarzuela de Pescado *Catalonia*
A Mixture of Fish in a Piquant Sauce

Zarzuela means a light opera or musical comedy, and this celebrated Catalan dish is certainly very colourful and delightful to look at. It has become widely popular with tourists and Spaniards alike and is served in Spanish restaurants everywhere. The ingredients vary according to what fish are available, but usually include at least two kinds of white fish, some prawns, a lobster and sometimes mussels or squid.

To serve 4

The fish: ¼ kg halibut, ¼ kg hake (angler-fish, grouper, monk-fish or turbot may be used), 1 freshly boiled lobster, about 12 freshly boiled prawns, 12 mussels (optional).

For the sauce: 4 tablespoons olive oil, half an onion, herbs as available, 2 cloves of garlic, 2–3 tomatoes or 1 small can of tomatoes, 1 tablespoon chopped parsley, 1 glass white wine, 1 small glass brandy, 1 teaspoon paprika, pinch saffron, a few peeled crushed almonds, pepper and salt.

Clean the fish and cut them into neat pieces. Flour them. Boil any trimmings with half an onion, salt and herbs in a little water to make a fish stock. Divide the lobster in pieces, remove the dark line of gut that runs down inside the body and crack the claws. Scrub the mussels if used and boil them until they open. Remove the top half of the shell. Heat the oil in a heavy pan and lightly brown the pieces of floured fish. Remove them and put into a large round earthenware serving dish to keep warm. In the same oil gently fry the chopped garlic, the peeled chopped tomatoes (or canned tomatoes) and the parsley. Cook for a few minutes, then add the wine, brandy, paprika, saffron and crushed almonds with plenty of pepper and salt. Add about a cupful of strained fish stock and stir over a low flame until the sauce is well blended. Now put in the pieces of fried fish and cook gently in the sauce for about 10 minutes, making sure they do not disintegrate. Lastly add the legs of lobster and the prawns still in their shells. Transfer the contents of the pan to the warmed earthenware dish and put the mussels, the lobster pieces and the claws on top as a decoration. Put into a hot oven for 5 minutes and serve immediately.

Caldereta Asturiana   *Asturias*
Asturian Fish Stew

All the fish in this recipe live along the rocky Asturian coast, and have firm flesh which is suitable for this kind of dish. They are what might be found in a typical day's catch by an Asturian fisherman, but most may be obtained in this country too.

To serve 4–6

Approximately 2 kg of assorted whole fish such as *dorada* (or any other sea bream), red or grey mullet, hake, weever* or bass, assorted shellfish such as a few each of limpets, mussels, clams or *abalones*, about 6 prawns, 4 tablespoons olive oil, 1 chopped onion, 1 tablespoon paprika, salt, 4 whole peppercorns, chopped parsley, 2 pinches grated nutmeg, a glass of sherry, 1 sweet red pepper (fresh or canned), 1 small hot red pepper.

Wash and clean the fish and cut them up. Scrub the shellfish and bring any bivalves (mussels, clams and *abalones*) to the boil in a little water till they open. Heat the oil in a deep pan and fry the chopped onion for a few minutes, then add the pieces of fish. Brown lightly and add about 1 litre of water, including the

* Weever fish are quite common in the English Channel and are good to eat. However they have venomous spines along their backs, and great care must be taken to remove these.

strained stock from the shellfish. Bring to the boil and add the spices, parsley and sherry. If you are using canned red pepper, simply chop it up and put it in. If a fresh pepper is used both it and the small hot pepper should be de-seeded, washed and finely chopped before adding to the pan. Season with plenty of salt and put in the limpets. Lower the heat and allow to simmer for $\frac{1}{2}$–$\frac{3}{4}$ hour. Put in the remaining shellfish, still in their shells and the whole prawns. Cook for 15 minutes. The resulting stew should be fairly thick and very tasty. Serve in small earthenware bowls with bread and Ribiera wine, or dry cider.

Suquet de Pescado
Fish Stew Using Three Kinds of Fish

Catalonia

To serve 4

2 tablespoons olive oil, 2 tablespoons butter, 4 large cloves garlic, 1 tablespoon flour, 4 fresh tomatoes or 1 small can of tomatoes, 1 tablespoon finely chopped parsley, about $\frac{1}{2}$ litre of water, salt and pepper, $\frac{1}{4}$ kg each of 3 different kinds of white fish, such as cod, turbot, halibut or angler-fish. A *picada* (see page 221) may be added to this dish.

Heat the butter and oil in a large saucepan and brown the finely chopped garlic, stir in the flour and cook until it starts to colour, then add the tomatoes, peeled and chopped, if fresh, and the parsley. Stir in the water and seasoning. Add the *picada* if used. Cut the fish into neat pieces, removing as many bones as possible and put it into the pot. Cook gently for about 20 minutes, shaking the pot to prevent sticking, and adding a little more water if necessary. Serve with crusty bread and white wine.

Sardinas en Cazuela de Barra
Casserole of Fresh Sardines

Murcia

To serve 4

About 24 fresh sardines, 1 cup tomato sauce (no. 2 or 3, see pages 224–5), 3 green peppers, 1 large onion, white pepper, 1 envelope saffron (about 2 pinches), salt, oil, parsley, 3 cloves garlic.

Cut off the heads of the sardines, remove the guts and the scales and wash thoroughly under a running tap. Take a deep earthenware casserole and put in a layer of tomato sauce to cover the bottom. Arrange half the sardines over this, then a layer of half the onion, peppers, garlic and parsley, all chopped very finely and well seasoned with salt (coarse sea salt is best), pepper and saffron. Repeat with the rest of the sardines and vegetables. Pour a generous amount of olive oil over everything and cover the pot. Cook very gently for about 1 hour, shaking carefully from side to side occasionally so that it does not burn.

Serve hot in the casserole in which it was cooked with plenty of crusty bread and red wine.

Empanadillas de Pescado   *Basque Country*
Fish Pasties

To serve 4

For the pastry: 2 cups plain flour, 50 g butter or margarine, 2 cups water, salt.

For the filling: ½ kg white fish (angler-fish, hake, cod, or de-salted salt cod), about 12 mussels if available, one onion, 1 bay leaf, lemon juice, olive oil for frying, 1 egg, breadcrumbs.

To make the pastry: put 2 cups of water in a saucepan and bring it to the boil. Add the butter or margarine and when it melts remove it from the heat. Stir in 2 cups of sieved flour and ½ teaspoon of salt. Work it into a dough and turn it out on to a pastry board. Allow to cool slightly before rolling out as thinly as possible without breaking the pastry. Cut into rounds of about 4 inches diameter.

For the filling: cook the fish and scrubbed mussels together in a little salted water with a bay leaf for 15 minutes. Chop the onion very finely and fry it in a little butter until soft, then stir in a tablespoon of flour and cook until it thickens. Take the fish and mussels from the water in which they were cooked, remove skin and bones, and cut up the fish. Take the mussels out of their shells, which will have opened, and chop them. Put the fish and mussels into the onion mixture and blend everything together thoroughly, using a little of the fish stock to make a thick porridge-like consistency. Add the juice of half a lemon and test for seasoning. Allow to cool slightly, then put a spoonful of the filling on to each round of pastry and fold over, dampening the edges and pressing them together. Brush the pasties with beaten egg and coat with breadcrumbs. Fry them in plenty of hot olive oil till crisp and golden and serve with tender young broad beans (frozen ones may be used).

In my opinion dried salt cod make the tastiest filling for *empanadillas*, but you must remember to put it to soak in cold water the night before.

Pastel de Pescado *Galicia*
Fish Pie

To serve 4–6

24 blanched almonds, 3 tablespoons olive oil, 2 cloves garlic, 4 onions, 1 bay leaf, 6 potatoes, 6 tomatoes, ½ kg of fresh cod or hake in thin fillets, salt and pepper.

Fry the almonds in oil, then remove them and put in the chopped garlic, onions and bay leaf and allow to cook slowly. Meanwhile peel and boil the potatoes and mash them into a purée with plenty of seasoning. When the onion is tender, add the tomatoes, peeled and chopped, season with salt and cook for 10 minutes. Reserve one-third of this mixture for use as sauce. Add the fried and crushed almonds to the remainder and cook a little longer. Take out the bay leaf. Grease an ovenproof dish and line the bottom and sides with puréed potatoes, then fill it with alternating layers of the fried mixture and thin fillets of fish, starting with the mixture. Cover with a layer of puréed potatoes and bake in a hot oven for 40 minutes.

It may be served in the same dish or turned out carefully and covered with the reserved sauce.

Croquetas de Caballas
Mackerel Croquettes

To serve 4

4 large potatoes, 1 large can of mackerel in oil, 1 teaspoon cumin seed, 1 tablespoon wine vinegar, flour, salt, pepper, egg and breadcrumbs, oil for frying.

Peel, cut up and boil the potatoes till tender. Mash them and blend with the canned mackerel, including all the oil. Add the crushed cumin seed, vinegar, pepper and salt. If the mixture seems too moist, thicken with a little flour. Form into croquettes and coat each with beaten egg and breadcrumbs. Fry in oil till crisp on the outside.

Serve with green sauce (see page 222) or with baked vegetables (page 191).

Pulpo con Papas
Octopus with Potatoes

You will probably only find octopus in specialist fish shops in Britain; for example, those catering for a Greek or Italian community. In Spain octopus is very popular and is usually eaten as a *tapa*, or an hors-d'œuvre. From the culinary point of view one of the chief characteristics of this creature is its toughness. The larger the animal the tougher it is, so that any way of preparing octopus involves long slow cooking. Beating it with a stick or against a stone before cutting up will help to make it more tender. Some shops sell them ready beaten.

Another good way of tenderizing a fair-sized octopus is to cut it up roughly and pressure cook it for 20 minutes before using it in any recipe.

To serve 4

1 octopus of about 1 kg, 4 tablespoons olive oil, 2 onions, a handful of chopped parsley, 1 bay leaf, ½ kg potatoes, 2 cloves of garlic, a pinch of saffron, salt.

Wash the octopus and remove the eyes, beak and stomach. Cut it into pieces, using the body and the tentacles. Chop the onions.

Heat the oil in a suitable saucepan and gently sauté the onions for about 5 minutes. Add the pieces of octopus and the chopped parsley and cook gently until the juices start to run. Add a little water if necessary, the bay leaf and some salt. Cover and continue to cook for at least an hour, keeping an eye on the pan to make sure it does not get dry. By this time the octopus should start to become tender. Put in the potatoes peeled and sliced, the garlic and saffron pounded together in a mortar. Add a little more water if required and cook for a further 30 minutes, when the octopus should be reasonably tender and the potatoes soft.

Pulpo Catalan   *Catalonia*
Octopus Catalan

1 octopus of about 1 kg, olive oil, 1 or 2 onions, about 2 glasses dry white wine, 1 clove garlic, chopped parsley, salt, paprika, pepper.

Prepare and cut up the octopus as before and lightly stew the pieces in oil with the chopped onions. Add the wine and an equal amount of water, the crushed garlic and parsley. Season with salt, paprika and pepper and simmer for 1–2 hours or until the octopus is tender.

Pulpos Guisados   *Catalonia and the*
Stewed Octopus   *Balearic Islands*

This recipe is especially successful using the young octopus of up to 8 inches in length (including the stretched-out tentacles) which are sold in fish markets all round the Mediterranean in spring and summer. Cuttlefish are also very good cooked in this way, and these are common in British waters. Seaside fish shops sometimes sell them fresh for bait or they may be bought frozen elsewhere.

To serve 4

8 small fresh octopus, 1 tablespoon olive oil, 1 large clove of garlic, 4 large Mediterranean spring onions (or substitute shallots), 1 sweet red pepper,

1 tablespoon tomato paste, 2 teaspoons paprika, a pinch of cayenne, a small
sprig of fennel (optional), 2 tablespoons of finely chopped parsley, some dry
white wine, 2 tablespoons wine vinegar, salt.

Wash the octopus under a running tap, turning the bodies inside
out. Carefully remove the ink bags and stomach. The horny beaks
and the eyes will have to be taken out with a knife. A little of the
ink may be reserved to add later to the sauce if liked, but this
sometimes has a very strong flavour. Cut the tentacles and bodies
into roughly 1-inch pieces – this is most easily done by holding
the fish up by the tip of the body and snipping off appropriate
lengths with sharp scissors. Put all the cut pieces into a colander
and thoroughly wash again. If cuttlefish are being used prepare
them in exactly the same way but remove the central bone,
which octopus lack.

Heat some olive oil in a suitable saucepan and put in the octopus with the crushed garlic. Cook very gently while preparing
the onions or shallots, which should be cut into rings, and the red
pepper which should be de-seeded, washed and cut into thin
rings or strips. Add these to the pan. Cook for about 5 minutes
and then add the tomato paste and the herbs and spices. Stir
thoroughly and pour in enough white wine to almost cover
everything (the fish will give off a certain amount of its own
liquid). Add 2 tablespoons of vinegar and salt to taste and leave
to simmer very gently for about an hour. Cuttlefish may take
longer.

It is a widely held view among Spanish cooks that a few corks
added to the pot will make the octopus tender – this does appear
to work although I do not know why.

This dish is best served hot in small individual earthenware
dishes to start a meal, but it is also good as a lunch or supper dish
with plenty of bread and dry red or white wine.

Calamares en su Tinta   *Basque Country*
Squid in their own Ink

To serve 4
1 kg tiny squid, 2 onions, 2 tomatoes, olive oil, 2 cloves garlic, chopped
parsley, breadcrumbs, 1 small glass brandy, salt.

Wash the squid well, removing the stomach and the back bone, cut off the tentacles, and reserve the bags of ink in a cup. Push the tentacles into the bodies of the squid. Put the chopped onions and peeled chopped tomatoes into hot oil and fry gently, using a large frying-pan. When the onions begin to soften add the squid and cook until they become opaque, about 15 minutes. Remove the squid and put them into a large shallow earthenware dish. Make a sauce in the frying-pan by adding the finely chopped garlic and parsley, the breadcrumbs, a glass of brandy, a little water and salt. Cook for a few minutes and add the ink from the bags. Pour this sauce over the squid. Cover and cook gently either on top of the stove or in the oven for 1 hour or until the squid are tender. Serve in the same dish with triangles of fried bread and white rice.

Fishmongers can usually get squid if you order them; frozen ones are quite good. If you live by the sea you may be able to get them from local fishermen, who sometimes catch squid and cuttlefish in their nets.

Centolla a la Vasca   *Basque Country*
Basque Spider Crab

Spider crabs are not fished commercially in this country because although they are extremely common in the English Channel, they are inferior to those found in more southerly waters. In Spain, however, they are served as a speciality in restaurants all along the Cantabrian coast from San Sebastian to La Coruña. As they contain less white meat than the common crab and have a stronger, sweetish flavour, it is necessary to blend other strong-tasting ingredients with the flesh. Allow one for each person and serve the crab in its own well-cleaned shell.

For each person
1 spider crab, 2 tablespoons olive oil, 1 clove garlic, 1 small onion,
1 tablespoon tomato paste, 1 tablespoon sherry, 1 tablespoon brandy, salt,
pepper and a very little cayenne pepper, 1 tablespoon finely chopped parsley,
1 tablespoon breadcrumbs, a little butter.

Spider crabs are prepared in exactly the same way as ordinary crabs, so bring a large pan of water to the boil and add 1 tablespoon of salt. The Universities Federation for Animal Welfare recommends that crabs should be anaesthetized before boiling by destroying the two nerve centres with a special awl. As this requires practice and is a delicate operation to carry out, especially on a lively crab, the alternative is to plunge the crab into a gallon of rapidly boiling water. This should kill the crab in 15 seconds. Exactly the same applies to lobsters. The flame should be high enough to keep the water boiling when the crab goes in and the crab should be held under the boiling water for at least 2 minutes with tongs or two wooden spoons. Since both crabs and lobsters have well-developed nervous systems and are therefore capable of feeling pain it is obviously kindest to follow these instructions to the letter. Having done so proceed to boil the crab for 10–20 minutes according to size. When the crab has cooled a little remove it from the water with two spoons and lay it on its back. Twist off the legs. Press with both thumbs on the mouth which will give under pressure and should be removed in one piece with the stomach bag which is directly behind it. Prise the body out of the shell. Remove the feathery white lungs (dead mens' fingers). Scoop the meat from the shell and crack the larger sections of the legs and scrape out the meat. This method of preparation applies to all crabs.

Heat the olive oil in a small frying-pan and put in the garlic clove. When it starts to colour remove it. In the same oil gently fry the very finely chopped onion, stirring until it starts to soften, then add the mashed crab meat, the tomato paste, the sherry and the brandy. Season with salt, pepper and a tiny pinch of cayenne and add sufficient water to make a thick mixture. Cook gently for a few minutes, stirring all the time. Thoroughly clean the outside of the shell and fill it with this mixture. Sprinkle the bread-crumbs and finely chopped parsley on top, dot with butter and put into a hot oven for 5 minutes. Serve immediately.

Llagosta a la Catalana   *Catalonia*
Lobster a la Catalana

Llagosta in Catalan, or *langosta* in Castilian Spanish, refers to the spiny lobster or salt-water crayfish. This creature is found more often in warmer seas but it does occur off the south and west coasts of England. It lacks the large claws of the common lobster and some say that it has a superior flavour. For culinary purposes it may be treated in the same way. The common lobster is called in Spanish *lubrigante* or *bogavante*.

Lobster tastes best if it is freshly killed – if boiled lobster is required follow the instructions for killing crabs and lobsters on page 123. This recipe, however, requires that the lobster be killed with a knife. This is not as formidable as it sounds if the following instructions are carried out.

First, if your lobster is of the clawed variety make sure these are firmly held shut by strong elastic bands; the fishmonger will usually do this. Now, using a thick cloth or towel to get a good grip, grasp the lobster firmly by the body from above with your left hand and hold it down hard. The flicks of the tail which propel the lobster when it is free in the water are quite powerful and can easily jerk it out of your grasp. Next, take a heavy sharp-pointed knife in your right hand and pierce the shell just behind the head; this will sever the spinal cord and kill the lobster instantly. (Alternatively plunge the lobster into fast boiling water for about 2 minutes, or until dead.) The head may then be cut off and the lobster divided.

Cut the head and body in half longitudinally and twist off the legs and claws. The intestinal tract, which is a dark line running the length of the abdomen, should be removed; it is not poisonous, but it may taste bitter. The only other inedible part is a small jelly-like sac in the head which should be discarded. The coral, if any, is also in the head and looks black when in its raw state, and this is a delicacy. If the lobster has claws these should be cracked with a smart blow from a hammer before cooking.

To serve 4

1 large lobster, a coffee-cup of olive oil, 1 finely chopped onion, 1 bay leaf,
a sprig of thyme, 2 cloves garlic, 75 g bitter chocolate, 10 toasted hazelnuts,
a tablespoon chopped parsley, a pinch of saffron, a small piece of dry toast or
rusk, pepper and salt, a tablespoon of brandy, a little dry white wine,
triangles of fried bread for garnish.

Kill and cut up the lobster as above. Heat the oil in a large shallow casserole or earthenware dish and gently fry the chopped onion with the bay leaf and thyme. Add the pieces of lobster and turn them over and over in the hot oil until the shell turns red. Remove from the heat. Peel the garlic cloves and crush them in a large mortar with the chocolate, hazelnuts, finely chopped parsley, saffron and the piece of dry toast or rusk. Pound all this to a paste, adding the brandy little by little. Season with salt and freshly ground black pepper and dilute with a little white wine to make a thick sauce. Pour this sauce over the lobster in the earthenware dish and put it into a moderate oven, 350° F, gas 4, for 20 minutes. Decorate with small triangles of fried bread and serve in the same dish.

Llagosta a la Costa Brava   *Catalonia*
Lobster a la Costa Brava

To serve 4

2 medium lobsters, 6 tablespoons olive oil, 2 tablespoons wine vinegar, salt,
white pepper, *all-i-oli* (optional), mayonnaise.

Follow the instructions for killing and dividing lobsters given on pages 124–5. Make a vinaigrette dressing with the oil, wine vinegar, salt and pepper. Line a grill-pan with foil and put the pieces of lobster and the cracked claws into it shell side down and soak them well with the dressing. Put under a hot grill for about 20 minutes, or until the flesh is tender, basting frequently with the dressing.

Serve coated with *all-i-oli* (see page 216) if liked, though I prefer to omit it. Serve a bowl of mayonnaise separately.

Dried Fish

Bacalao a la Graciosa   *Canary Islands*
Salt Cod Graciosa

This dish was my first experience of dried salt fish and always reminds me of the tiny remote island of Graciosa in the Canaries.

The island is covered almost entirely with white sand and sulphur-coloured volcanic rocks. The only two villages are clusters of low dazzlingly white flat-roofed houses, with no roads, no cars and no electricity. An occasional camel led by a woman in a long sun-bleached skirt would be met wandering across the sand carrying a load of alfalfa. All the men of the villages were away fishing most of the time. The combined shop and bar opened at 4 a.m. to serve black coffee and cognac to those about to set off to the fishing grounds, from whence they would return the next day laden with fish, some of which would be split open, salted and sun-dried on the rocks.

To serve 4
½ kg salt cod or any other kind of dried salt fish, 2 large onions, 4 potatoes, 2 green peppers, 6 tomatoes, large handful parsley, a little oil.

Wash the fish well under the tap and soak overnight, changing the water once if the fish seems very salty. The next day remove all the skin and bones and break the fish into small pieces. Peel

the onions and potatoes, de-seed the peppers and slice all the vegetables into thin rounds, keeping them in separate heaps. There is no need to skin the tomatoes for this dish. Chop the parsley roughly. Cover the bottom of a deep saucepan with oil (not too much) and put in all the ingredients in layers until the pot is full. Start with a layer of tomato and finish with a layer of potato. This is because the juice starts to run from the tomatoes first – and the potatoes take longest to cook. Put the lid on the pan and cook very gently for ¾ hour, or until the potatoes are tender. Shake the pan gently from time to time to prevent sticking, and use an asbestos mat on a gas cooker.

In the Canary Islands the other kinds of dried fish used are *vieja* (old woman), *rubio* (flying fish) and *cherne* (stone bass), but salt cod (*bacalao*) is probably the best, and is the only one available in England.

Bacalao a la Vizcaína   *Basque Country*
Biscay Salt Cod

To serve 4

½ kg dried salt cod from the thickest part of the fish, olive oil for frying, flour, 4 onions, ¾ kg tomatoes or 2 cans of tomatoes, 2 cloves of garlic, 4 small dried hot red peppers (in the Basque country these are called *ñoras*), 1 slice of bread, 2 sweet red peppers or one small can of peppers, 2 tablespoons of chopped parsley, 2 tablespoons of fresh breadcrumbs.

Soak the cod overnight. Next day put it into fresh water and bring to the boil. Drain, remove the skin and bones and cut it into neat pieces approximately 1½ inches square. Dip the pieces into flour and fry them in deep oil until golden. Drain well and set aside. Meanwhile soak the hot red peppers in a little hot water.

There are two ways of making the sauce which is an integral part of this dish. The first is the correct one, but to some may be a counsel of perfection. It is as follows: heat some oil in a frying-pan and make a *sofrito*: gently stew in the oil three of the onions finely chopped, adding ½ kg of the peeled and chopped tomatoes when the onions are half done. In another pan heat a little oil and quickly fry the slice of bread until crisp, remove and drain thoroughly. In the same oil fry the garlic, the remaining onion and tomatoes and the de-seeded hot red peppers, all very finely chopped. Crumble the fried bread into this mixture, and when the onions are sufficiently tender put it through a sieve or blender to reduce it to a purée. Add it to the first pan containing the *sofrito*.

An easier way, which to my mind produces a dish of comparable quality, is simply to make a single *sofrito* including all the onions, the garlic, the tomatoes, the soaked and de-seeded hot peppers (or a teaspoon of chilli powder) all of which must be very finely chopped. The fried bread may be omitted. This makes a sauce of a good consistency though it lacks the interesting combination of textures produced by the first method.

Spread a thick even layer of whichever sauce you have chosen to use in the bottom of a shallow ovenproof dish, preferably earthenware, and cover it with the pieces of fried cod. Pour the rest of the sauce over the cod and smooth it down. Cut the sweet red peppers into strips (fresh ones should first be grilled until black, the skin rubbed off, and the seeds removed) and arrange them on top of the dish. Scatter a mixture of breadcrumbs and parsley over the dish, sprinkle with olive oil and put it into a hot oven, 375° F, gas 5, for 20 minutes. Serve in the same dish.

Bacalao al Pil-Pil $\qquad$ *Basque Country*
Salt Cod al Pil-Pil

This dish takes its name from the onomatopoeic Basque word *pil-pil* – meaning very slow boiling. It really only works well if the cod used is not too hard and dry in the first place; you will find it varies considerably in this respect.

To serve 4

½ kg *bacalao* from the thickest part of the fish, ½ litre olive oil, 4 cloves of garlic, 2 red or green fresh hot peppers for garnish.

Soak the cod for 24 hours, changing the water at least three times to make sure it is absolutely de-salted and plumped up to a soft consistency. Cut it into neat pieces and remove any bones and scales.

Heat some of the oil in a frying-pan and throw in the chopped garlic cloves, brown them lightly then remove them and set aside. Now add the thoroughly drained bacalao, skin side down, and fry it to a light golden brown, turn it once and fry the other side leaving the skin side uppermost. Drain off any surplus oil, and keeping the pan on a very low heat gradually pour back the oil, gently shaking the pan in a circular motion as you do so. Move the fish carefully round in the oil until the juices from the fish start to combine with the oil to form a thick sauce. Add the rest of the oil gradually until the fish is almost covered – this takes a little time and practice. Basque chefs make this dish in the flat round earthenware bowl in which it is traditionally served, but a frying-pan with a handle is far easier to manage. When the sauce is thick and white the fish is ready and may be transferred to four individual serving dishes. Cut the hot peppers into rings (discarding any seeds) and sprinkle them over the top as a garnish – to be eaten with discretion as they are very hot. The fried garlic may also be added if liked.

Purrusalda   *Basque Country*
Salt Cod Casserole

This is also the name of a local dance.

To serve 4

8 potatoes, ½ kg salt cod from the tail end, 1 bay leaf, 12 leeks, water, salt and oil.

Soak the cod overnight. Peel and cut up the potatoes, peel and wash the leeks, cut lengthwise, leaving some of the green part; skin and bone the fish and cut into pieces. Put all these ingredients into an earthenware pot, add 1 tablespoon of olive oil, cover with water and add the bay leaf and a very little salt. Heat slowly and simmer very gently for 1 hour.

Serve very hot in the same casserole.

Bacalao a la Llauna   *Catalonia*
Salt Cod Casserole

To serve 4

¾ kg dried salt cod, 4 cloves garlic, 1 sprig parsley, chopped, 6 tomatoes, toasted breadcrumbs, oil for frying.

Llauna is the Catalan word for casserole. Soak the fish overnight, remove the skin and bones and cut it into cubes. Fry them in oil. Put the fish in the *llauna*, pour over the oil from frying and cover it with chopped tomatoes, parsley and garlic. Put it into a moderate oven, 350° F, gas 4, and cook for 30 minutes. Add more oil if needed and finally sprinkle with toasted breadcrumbs. Cook for a further 15 minutes, when it should be ready.

Bacalao Zaragozano
Salt Cod Zaragozano

Aragon

To serve 4–6

¾ kg dried salt cod, previously soaked overnight and cut into eight pieces,
2 tablespoons olive oil, 3 cloves garlic, ½ bay leaf, 3 onions, 4 potatoes,
3 tomatoes, parsley.

Warm the oil in a deep pan and add the chopped onions and
peeled and sliced potatoes and ½ bay leaf. Stew them in the oil
gently till they begin to turn golden, then add the sliced tomatoes. Place the pieces of cod skin side down over the vegetables
and put in the peeled cloves of garlic whole. Cover the pot; if
using gas it is a good idea to use an asbestos mat as the fish must
be cooked gently to prevent sticking and burning. Chop a good
handful of parsley, add to the pot and continue cooking for ½–¾
hour, or until the fish is done.

Serve with rough red wine and crusty bread.

Bacalao a la Gallega
Salt Cod from Galicia

Galicia

To serve 4

½ kg salt cod cut into eight pieces, flour, olive oil, parsley, 2 cloves garlic,
2 green peppers, 2 red peppers, 16 tiny onions or shallots, water, ground
white pepper.

Soak the cod overnight, scald it and remove the skin and bones.
Flour the pieces and fry them in olive oil. When they are light
brown on each side transfer them to a large earthenware dish and
cover them with roughly chopped parsley, chopped garlic, the
peppers cut into strips, and the tiny peeled onions. Season with
white pepper and add a breakfast cup of water (enough to cover
the fish). Put the lid on the dish, or cover tightly with foil, and
cook in a moderate oven, 350° F, gas 4, for 1½ hours or until the
onions are tender.

Serve with good crusty bread and Ribiera – or dry cider.

Giraboix   *Valencia*
Salt Cod a la Jijona

To serve 4–6

½ kg dried salt cod, 6 onions, 6 potatoes, 2 cups green beans, ½ cabbage, 1 hot red pepper, *all-i-oli* sauce (see page 216), 2 slices brown bread.

The cod should be soaked in cold water overnight. Cut up the fish and remove the bones. Put it into a large saucepan with the chopped onions, peeled and cut-up potatoes, cut-up green beans, shredded cabbage and whole hot red pepper. Cover with water and boil gently for about an hour.

When it is nearly ready, toast slices of brown bread and crumble it into a soup tureen. Strain the liquid from the fish and vegetables into the tureen, sprinkle with tiny pieces of the hot red pepper and serve as soup. The fish and vegetables are then arranged on a large dish, covered with *all-i-oli* and served as a second course.

Croquetas de Bacalao
Salt Cod Croquettes

To serve 4–6

½ kg salt cod, ½ kg potatoes, 2 shallots, 2 egg yolks, 1 tablespoon butter, ground black pepper, oil.

Soak the cod overnight, then simmer in fresh water for 20 minutes. Remove the skin and bones and shred the cod as finely as possible. Peel and boil the potatoes and sauté the finely chopped shallots. When the potatoes are cooked, mash them thoroughly and add the butter, fish and the shallots and the two egg yolks. Season with pepper and form the mixture into small croquettes. Roll them in flour and fry in hot oil. (Use the oil in which the shallots were fried.) Serve with a salad.

The water in which the cod was simmered makes a good basis for fish soup for the following day.

Meat

Shopping for meat in Spain can be confusing as the carcass is divided in a different way and the pieces may be unrecognizable. However, there is usually a chart hanging up in the shop showing the cuts, and a blackboard with the day's prices clearly marked.

The quality of Spanish meat has improved tremendously in the past decade, due partly to better breeding and management of stock and partly to the higher standard of living in general, and since the animals are not yet reared as intensively as in this country the meat still retains its old-fashioned flavour which, sadly, some of us in England have almost forgotten.

Pork and lamb are especially good, whereas beef varies considerably, for in a country where for centuries cattle have been reared either for the plough or the bullring, a great deal of it is bound to be tough and stringy. This is well-suited for the traditional stews which need long slow cooking. However, beef of superb quality is produced in some regions, particularly in the north where the pastures are rich. You will find a kind of beef known as *ternera* on many menus and mentioned in recipes. It is neither beef nor veal as we know it, but a one-year-old animal which is both tasty and tender. As far as I know beef cattle are never killed at this age in England.

That economical and versatile animal, the pig, is, above all other animals, important in Spanish cooking, and although roast pork is still something of a luxury in many homes, parts of the pig are used in almost every meat dish. *Tocino*, or salted pork fat (the fat is stored in crystalline salt), has a distinctive flavour which is an integral part of many dishes. All the various kinds of sausage (collectively known as *embutidos*), used both in cooking and eaten as they are, such as *chorizo*, *morcilla*, *sobresada* (see pages 29–30), are derived from the pig. Many villagers and farmers still make their own sausages using the fat, blood and intestines of the animal and blending them with spices and nuts. The sausages are boiled in huge cauldrons and hung up to last the family for the year. The traditional yearly pig-killing, called a *matanza*, is a big family occasion – almost a festival. It takes place some time between November and January, usually just before Christmas, and is a time of great feasting and enjoyment for everybody. The old-fashioned Large White pig is a favourite as it yields a great deal of fat, but there is also a rather long-legged lean blackish pig which does well in the more arid regions, particularly in Extremadura. Here, in the autumn, each household in the village turns out its pig in the morning to fatten on the acorns in the scrubby oak forests. Droves of pigs may be met in the evening hurrying home, each pig to its own sty. Baby pigs of three to eight weeks old are a special Spanish delicacy, and in the region of Old Castile, and particularly in the old romanesque city of Segovia, sixty miles from Madrid, any restaurant worthy of its name will serve a delicious dish of suckling pig.

Young lambs not yet weaned and generally known as *lechazos* are an Easter speciality and they are always roasted, either in the oven or on a spit. In country districts the village baker will often roast suckling lambs or pigs for the local inhabitants on special occasions. These ovens are frequently fired with aromatic woods such as olive, pine and eucalyptus: meat cooked in this way tastes wonderful. Kid is often eaten as an everyday dish instead of lamb as it costs less, and a great many country people with a small patch of land keep a goat or two as a valuable source of milk and meat. Most recipes for lamb may be used for kid as well, though a little extra seasoning may be necessary as the meat tends to have less flavour than lamb.

With regard to offal, Spaniards do not believe in wasting anything. No part of the animal is despised and in fact I came across an old recipe from Aragon which included the tails of ewes cut off to facilitate lambing. The dish was rather quaintly called *espárragos montaneses*, 'mountain asparagus'. Apart from the usual range of offal – such as tripe and pigs' trotters – cows' noses, lights and even blood are on sale and put to good use by the Spanish housewife. In old Spanish cookery books there are always a few recipes for using blood, but these I have not included as they are impractical for this country.

Most of the cuts of meat mentioned in the following recipes should be easily obtainable in Britain, but where they are not I have suggested possible alternatives.

Escalopes Zingara   *Andalusia*
Escalopes of Veal in Sherry Sauce

To serve 6

12 small veal escalopes, 2 tablespoons flour, 2 tablespoons chopped onion, ½ green pepper, 6 mushrooms, 100 g minced ham, small glass sherry, 2 tablespoons butter, 2 tablespoons oil, 1 teaspoon cornflour, salt.

Pound the flour and ¾ teaspoon salt well into the veal with a mallet. Heat the butter and oil in a pan and lightly brown the escalopes on each side. Remove to a shallow casserole or baking dish into which they will fit side by side. Add the chopped onion, minced green pepper, minced peeled mushrooms and minced ham to the oil and butter in the pan, cook until tender and lightly browned. Place a mound of this mixture on each escalope. Add the sherry to the pan, bring to the boil and add one cup of water, stirring in all the browned bits from the bottom. Thicken with the cornflour, add salt to taste and pour over the escalopes. Finish cooking in a moderate oven for 30 minutes.

Ternera a la Asturiana   *Asturias*
Veal Asturiana

To serve 4

1 kg stewing veal or chuck steak, flour, salt and pepper, 100 g lard, stock or water, 1 onion, 1 cup tomato sauce (no. 3, page 225).

Heat the lard in a frying-pan, and put in the seasoned and floured meat in one piece, browning well on both sides. Add a little stock or water and cover the pan, keeping it on a low heat. Meanwhile fry the finely chopped onion in a separate pan, and when it is soft add the tomato sauce and continue to cook for a few minutes longer, stirring constantly. Finally put the whole mixture through a sieve and pour it over the meat in the other pan. Put the lid on again and cook slowly till the meat is tender, approximately 1½ hours. Serve the meat sliced and covered with the sauce.

Carne Machada a la Andaluza   *Andalusia*
Beef with Almonds and Olives

To serve 4–6

1 kg good-quality lean beef in one piece, 100 g blanched almonds, 100 g green olives, 1 teaspoon cinnamon, olive oil, 1 onion, 1 tomato, 1 clove garlic, stock, salt and a glass of red wine.

Make some deep cuts in the meat and fill them with a mixture of blanched almonds cut into strips, chopped stoned olives, salt and cinnamon. Tie up the meat and brown it in hot oil in a casserole. When it looks golden brown all over put in the onion cut into four, the tomato peeled and also cut into four, and the whole clove of garlic. Add the glass of wine and about an equal amount

of stock, or more if necessary. Season well, cover the casserole
and cook on a very low flame till the meat is tender, about 2–3
hours.

To serve, slice the meat and strain the sauce over it.

Carbonade de Carne   *Aragon*
Pot-Roasted Beef

To serve 4

1 kg beef, such as silverside, salt and flour, 2 tablespoons olive oil, 2 onions,
1 tablespoon chopped parsley, 1 tablespoon wine vinegar, 1 tablespoon
tomato paste, ground black pepper, 2 cups stock or water, 2 small segments of
bitter chocolate.

Lightly flour the piece of beef and sprinkle it with salt. Heat the
olive oil in an ovenproof pot with a lid and sear the meat on all
sides. Remove it and put the sliced onions into the oil, lower the
heat and stir in the tomato paste, vinegar, parsley, black pepper
and the stock or water. Put the meat back into the pot and cook
in a low oven, 275° F, gas 1, for 2½–3 hours, or until it is tender.
When ready remove the meat and keep it hot. Make a sauce in
the casserole by adding the grated chocolate.

Serve the meat sliced on a dish and covered with sauce. The
addition of dark chocolate is of Mexican origin, but it is now
typically Spanish and makes a beautifully smooth, rich sauce.

Asada de Vaca   *Aragon*
Pot-Roasted Beef

To serve 4

1 kg braising steak cut into slices 2 inches thick, 50 g seasoned flour, 50 g lard,
4 ripe tomatoes, 1 onion, 1 green chilli or ½ teaspoon chilli powder.

Pound the seasoned flour well into the meat. Heat the lard in a
large casserole and brown the pieces of meat on both sides. Remove and keep warm. Peel and chop the tomatoes and slice the
onion, remove the seeds from the chilli pepper and chop it. Put

all these ingredients into the fat in the casserole and cook gently for about 5 minutes. Add about ½ litre of water, stir well and put back the slices of beef. Cover the casserole and transfer it to a moderate oven, 350° F, gas 4. Cook for about 1½ hours, or until the meat is tender.

To serve arrange the slices on a hot dish and pour the sauce over them.

Estofado de Buey   *Asturias*
Stewed Beef

To serve 6

1½ kg shank of beef or other stewing cut, 1 tablespoon lard, 8 onions,
4 carrots, 4 turnips, 200 g *tocino* or fat bacon, ¼ litre red wine, 1 breakfast-cup
wine vinegar, a bunch of aromatic herbs including thyme, parsley, mint and a
bay leaf, a knuckle of veal, salt and pepper.

Use a large saucepan or casserole with a tightly fitting lid. Heat the lard and well brown the piece of beef – (it should be in one piece) on both sides. Peel and slice the vegetables and add them to the pot. Put in the bacon, chopped. Lower the heat and when the onions are softening add the red wine and vinegar, the bunch of herbs tied with thread and the knuckle of veal, pepper and salt. Cook uncovered for 1 hour on a low heat until the sauce has reduced. Then lower the heat still more and cover the pot tightly; use foil under the lid if necessary. Cook for 2 hours. Remove the bunch of herbs.

Serve the meat in a large dish surrounded by vegetables and covered with its own sauce.

Rabo de Toro   *Leon*
Bull's Tail

To serve 4

1 bull's tail (in England, oxtail), 2 tablespoons lard or dripping, flour, salt,
2 tablespoons olive oil, 3 onions, 1 clove garlic, ½ kg carrots, ¼ kg mushrooms,
2 celery stalks, about ¼ litre water.

Choose a tail with plenty of gristle between the joints as this is what gives the dish its flavour. Wash it, cut it into joints and roll them in salted flour. Heat some dripping, preferably good beef dripping, in an ovenproof pot and gently brown the joints on all sides. In a separate frying-pan fry the onions cut into rings in hot olive oil. Scrape the carrots and cut them into rounds, peel the mushrooms and leave them whole unless they are very large. Wash and cut up the celery. When the onions are starting to turn brown pour them into the pot containing the bull's tail and add the rest of the vegetables, including the whole garlic. Stir everything together and add a little salt if necessary (no pepper). Add as little water as possible, about $\frac{1}{4}$ litre, because the sauce should be very thick. Cover the pot tightly and put it into a moderate oven, 350° F, gas 4, for 2 hours. Check to make sure it does not dry up completely; if necessary a little more water or stock may be added. Serve the meat in the same pot or on a large heated plate surrounded by the vegetables and sauce.

Porcella Asada   *Mallorca*
Roast Suckling Pig from Mallorca

As I said in the introduction to this chapter roast suckling pig is one of Spain's gastronomic triumphs. The method of preparation varies from region to region but it is always roasted, either plain or stuffed. The baby pig itself is generally referred to as a *cochinillo*, while when cooked in the Balearic Islands it is a *porcella*, in Old Castile a *lechal* and in Navarre and the Basque country a *lechona*. It is interesting to note that in this simple old recipe from Mallorca (adapted from Luis Ripoll's *Cocina de las Baleares*), the killing of the pig is referred to as a 'sacrifice'. A very small pig is best for this recipe.

To serve 6

One suckling pig of about 2 kg, 3 lemons, $\frac{1}{4}$ litre olive oil, salt.

Having sacrificed your pig, or bought it at the butcher's shop, remove the intestines and rub the skin hard with pumice stone (if bought at the butcher's this will not be necessary). Wash the piglet thoroughly and rub it inside and out with plenty of lemon juice. Make a mixture of the rest of the lemon juice, the olive oil and about 2 teaspoons salt. Put the pig in an oiled earthenware dish, pour the mixture over it, and put it into a hot oven, 400° F, gas 6, and roast until crisp, basting frequently (approximately 2 hours). A little foil may be put over the ears and nose to stop them blackening. Serve it in the dish in which it was cooked, with roast potatoes and broad beans.

Lechona Asada Vasca   *Basque Country*
Roast Suckling Pig from the Basque Country

This recipe makes an impressive festival dish for a large party.

To serve 8–10

One suckling pig of about 4 kg, plus the liver, olive oil, salt, 6 hard-boiled eggs, a red apple for garnish.

For the stuffing: 100 g fresh breadcrumbs, a little milk, 1 wineglass dry sherry, a small glass of brandy, 2 tablespoons chopped parsley, two eggs, 4 finely chopped onions, ¼ kg each of minced pork and veal, a sprig each of thyme and rosemary, salt and pepper.

The pig should be ready opened and cleaned by the butcher. Wash it thoroughly and rub it inside and out with sea salt.

Soak the breadcrumbs in a little milk, then thoroughly mix together all the ingredients for the stuffing, including the finely chopped liver. Shell and slice the hard-boiled eggs and line the inside of the pig with them. Push in the stuffing and sew the piglet up with a strong needle and thread. Brush the outside with olive oil and wrap it loosely in foil. Stand the parcel on a rack in a roasting-pan and roast in a pre-heated moderate oven, 350° F, gas 4, for about 2½ hours; then remove the foil and cook for a further ½ hour or so at a higher temperature, 400° F, gas 6, to crisp the outside. Make gravy in the usual way, using the juices in the roasting tin, and serve separately.

Serve the pig on a large grand dish surrounded by roast whole red and green peppers and watercress, with a red apple in its mouth.

Cochinillo Asado de Segovia   *Old Castile*
Roast Suckling Pig from Segovia

Segovia specializes in roast suckling pig, where it is cooked and
stuffed in many ways. Here is a simple one.

To serve 6–8

1 suckling pig of about 3½ kg. To prepare the pig for roasting rub the inside
with a mixture of salt and coarsely ground black pepper.

For the stuffing: 1 large stale loaf, 1 chopped onion, 1 clove chopped garlic,
200 g seedless raisins, a few leaves of mint or pinch of dried mint sprigs, sage,
½ teaspoon pepper, ¼ teaspoon celery salt.

Remove crust from bread and slice it, moisten in hot chicken
stock (a cube may be used) and squeeze out excess liquid. Fry in
a little hot fat. When the mass leaves the pan easily, add the other
ingredients and mix well. Stuff the pig and sew it up. Roast in a
hot oven till well done, about 2½–3 hours. Do not baste, but
occasionally prick the skin. When the pig is done, pour a glass of
red wine over it and put a red apple in its mouth.

This stuffing may also be used for turkey.

Lomo de Cerdo Trufada
Fillet of Pork with Truffles

Pork fillet is very popular with Spaniards. The quality of the
meat is usually superb, and there are many ways of preparing it.
As a general rule it is at its best cooked slowly in a sauce as there
is little or no fat on the meat and it can be dry. Various kinds of
stuffing add a subtle flavour and texture. The following recipe is
one of the simplest and most luxurious.

To serve 4

2 medium-sized pieces of pork fillet, about 1 kg in all, 4 thick rashers of
bacon, salt and pepper, one small can of truffles, 1 coffee-cup olive oil, a glass
of dry sherry, 2 tablespoons finely chopped summer savory.

Cut the bacon and truffles into strips and push them into the
pork fillets with a knitting or larding needle. Sprinkle liberally
with salt and a little ground black pepper. Heat the olive oil in a

heavy saucepan and carefully brown the fillets on all sides. Pour in the sherry and let it bubble for a few seconds then lower the heat and stir in the chopped savory. Cover the pan and cook over a very low flame for about an hour or until the pork is tender.

To serve, arrange the meat slices in the centre of an oval serving dish, and pour the juices from the pan over it. Fried potatoes are usually served with this dish in Spain.

Lomo de Cerdo Relleno
Stuffed Pork Fillet

This recipe is one of my own favourites.

To serve 4-6

2 long pieces of pork fillet, about 1 kg in all, flour, salt, pepper, 50 g butter or lard, 1 large glass of dry sherry.

For the stuffing: 1 cup fresh breadcrumbs, 100 g finely chopped chicken livers, 4 rashers finely chopped fat, salt bacon or 50 g *tocino*, 1 tablespoon chopped chives, 1 tablespoon chopped chervil, 1 tablespoon chopped fennel, a very little rosemary, 1 tablespoon of chopped capers, 1 beaten egg.

Trim the fillets and slit them lengthways without cutting them right through. Flatten them out and sprinkle with salt. Prepare the stuffing – thoroughly mix all the dry ingredients, bind with the beaten egg and a tablespoon of sherry. Press half the stuffing into each fillet and tie up with string into a neat sausage shape. Roll in the seasoned flour. Heat the butter or lard in a heavy saucepan or casserole and carefully brown the fillets on all sides. Lower the heat a little, pour in the rest of the sherry and let it bubble. Add enough water to come about halfway up the fillets. Cover tightly and cook either on a very low flame or in a slow oven, 300° F, gas 2, for about an hour, turning once halfway through. (It may be necessary to add a little more liquid.) When the fillets are cooked through, remove them from the pan and arrange in slices on a heated oval serving dish. Serve the liquid separately as a sauce. New potatoes in season go well with this dish, or if you have cooked the pork in the oven, jacket potatoes can go in at the same time. Broad beans make a good additional vegetable.

Lomo de Cerdo a la Baturra   *Aragon*
Pork Fillet a la Baturra

To serve 4

8 strips of pork fillet of one finger's thickness, 4 thick slices ham, salt, flour,
olive oil, 1 onion, a handful of stoned olives, 1 tablespoon tomato paste,
pepper, 1 glass red wine, 1 tablespoon butter, 2 hard-boiled eggs.

Baturra is a local nickname for an Aragonese peasant.

Dip the fillets in seasoned flour and fry them in a deep casserole in hot oil. When brown remove from heat. In a frying-pan
brown the slices of ham and place them on top of the pork, then
in the same oil in which the ham was fried make a sauce with the
finely chopped onion, the olives cut into rings, the tomato paste
and the glass of red wine. Make the butter into a ball in your
hands and roll it in flour, put this into the sauce and cook gently
till the sauce thickens. Check seasoning. Pour the sauce over the
meat and cook for $\frac{1}{2}$ hour on a low heat with the lid on. When the
fillets are done serve very hot in the same dish, sprinkled with
finely chopped hard-boiled egg.

Lomo de Cerdo Almendrado   *Catalonia and*
Fillet of Pork with Almonds   *the Balearic Islands*

Almonds are one of Mallorca's major products and they are
probably the finest grown anywhere. They are carefully har-
vested and stripped of their green covering by hand and so are
expensive even on their native island. They are used in many
dishes and this one is especially nice.

To serve 4–6

Approximately 1 kg pork fillet in two long pieces, 100 g crushed toasted
almonds, salt and pepper, flour, 50 g lard, 1 small glass dry sherry, $\frac{1}{4}$ litre
stock, 2 tablespoons chopped spring onions or shallots, a little cream.

Make two longitudinal incisions in each fillet without cutting
right through. Sprinkle with salt and press a layer of crushed
almonds into each incision. Tie the fillets up again neatly and
roll them in seasoned flour. Heat the lard in a large heavy pan

and brown the meat carefully all over. Lower the heat, add the sherry and allow to bubble, then add the onions or shallots and cook gently for a few minutes. Pour in the stock and cover the pan. Cook gently for an hour, turning the meat once and make sure it does not stick. Stir in the cream. Serve the meat in slices with the juices poured over it. Garnish with triangles of fried bread. Creamed potatoes are a good foil for the crunchy texture of the almonds.

There is a similar recipe from Aragon, using red wine and water and no cream – this is equally good, and is usually served with potatoes and a salad of lettuce and raw onions.

Lomo de Cerdo con Judias Blancas *Catalonia*
Fillet of Pork with Haricot Beans

To serve 4
½ kg haricot beans, ½ kg pork fillet, 2 cloves garlic, lard, parsley.

Soak the beans overnight and simmer in salted water for about 1½ hours, or until tender. Drain them and allow to get cold. Cut the pork into neat slices and sprinkle with plenty of salt. Heat about 2 tablespoons of lard in a large frying-pan and fry the chopped garlic, turning it round in the fat until it browns, then remove it. Put in the slices of pork and fry them gently until cooked through and golden, remove and keep hot. Now put the beans into the fat and turn carefully without breaking them up until slightly coloured. Put the beans on a heated dish with the slices of pork on top. Sprinkle with chopped parsley.

Chuletas de Cerdo *Balearic Islands*
Con Salsa de Granada
Pork Cutlets with Pomegranate Sauce

This recipe comes from Mallorca where pomegranates are often used to add their special flavour to meat dishes.

To serve 4

Lard, 4 large pork cutlets or 8 small ones, 2 onions, seeds and pulp of 2 pomegranates, a glass of dry white wine, an equal amount of milk, salt and pepper.

Heat the lard in an earthenware dish or casserole of suitable size and brown the cutlets. Add the finely chopped onions and lower the heat. When the onions start to become transparent stir in the pomegranate seeds and pulp. Cover the dish and cook for about 10 minutes, then add a glass of dry white wine and a glass of milk and perhaps a little water if it seems necessary. Season with pepper and salt and cook very gently with the lid off until the pork is tender. Take the dish straight to the table and serve either with plainly boiled potatoes or, in the Mallorquin way, with potatoes cut into thick slices and slowly fried in oil or lard.

Lechazo Asado   *Old Castile*
Roast Baby Lamb

To serve 6–8

1 baby lamb of about 2 kg (you will probably not find this in England, but as an alternative choose the most tender cut of lamb you can find), salt and pepper, lard, 1 bay leaf, one glass of white wine (in Spain, use Valdepeñas), 1 clove garlic, 2 tablespoons chopped parsley, 1 tablespoon of vinegar.

Rub the lamb with salt and pepper and smear it with a little lard. Put it in a roasting tin with the bay leaf and place it in a hot oven, 425° F, gas 7, for about $\frac{1}{2}$ hour. When it begins to colour remove it from the oven and carefully pour over most of the wine. Put it back into the oven and continue to cook until done, basting occasionally. It should take about 2 hours. When the lamb is ready transfer it to a hot serving dish and keep hot. Crush the garlic clove and add this with the chopped parsley and the rest of the wine to the juices in the pan. Bring it to the boil, scraping up all the brown bits from the pan to make a sauce. Serve this in a separate sauceboat. Roast aubergines, red or green peppers and roast potatoes may be served with this dish, or a green salad if you prefer it.

Ternasco
Young Lamb, Roasted

Aragon

To serve 4

1 kg of very young lamb, 1 glass of white wine, juice of 2 lemons,
4 tablespoons lard, salt.

The lamb should be in one piece. Choose the joint you prefer.
Sprinkle it with salt and place it in an ovenware dish with the
lard. Put it into a hot oven, 375° F, gas 5, until it browns, then
turn it over and add the lemon juice and the white wine. Lower
the oven to 350° F, gas 4, and roast for 1½ hours. Serve with the
vegetables of your choice.

Chuletas de Cordero con Salsa de Jerez
Lamb Cutlets with Sherry Sauce

Aragon and Navarre

To serve 4

8 lamb cutlets, salt, 100 g butter, 1 cup fresh breadcrumbs, 1 glass dry sherry,
1 tablespoon finely chopped chervil, 1 tablespoon finely chopped parsley,
1 teaspoon finely chopped capers, watercress for garnish.

Flatten the cutlets out with a wooden spoon and sprinkle them
with salt. Melt the butter in a small saucepan and brush the cutlets with a little of it. Dip them in breadcrumbs, put them under
a hot grill or on a *plancha* (see page 28) and cook for about 7
minutes on each side. When cooked arrange them on a serving
dish and keep hot. Gently reheat the rest of the butter and pour
in the sherry, allow to bubble, lower the heat and add the
chopped herbs and capers. Cook for a minute more and pour the
resulting sauce over the cutlets. Garnish with watercress and
serve at once.

Chuletas de Cordero a la Navarra   *Navarre*
Lamb Cutlets a la Navarra

To serve 4

8 lamb cutlets, 50 g lard, a little oil, 1 small clove garlic, 1 onion, 100 g lean ham, 6 ripe tomatoes or 1 can of tomatoes, salt and pepper, 200 g of good-quality *chorizo*, preferably Pamplona.

Lightly fry the cutlets in a mixture of lard and oil, transfer them to an ovenproof dish and keep warm. In the same fat fry the garlic and onion, chopped fairly finely, and when transparent add the ham cut in little dice. If you are using fresh tomatoes, peel them, cut them up and add them to the pan. Canned tomatoes may be put straight in and broken up with a wooden spoon. Season with salt and pepper and stir over a low flame until a thick sauce is formed; it will take about $\frac{1}{2}$ hour. Add a little stock or water if it starts to get too thick. Pour the sauce over the cutlets and cover the entire dish with thin slices of *chorizo* (remove the skin first). Put into a hot oven for 5 minutes and serve. Pork chops or cutlets may be cooked in the same way.

Caldereta Extremeña   *Extremadura*
Stewed Kid

To serve 4

1 kg kid, plus 200 g of the liver (if you cannot get kid lamb may be used), olive oil, cayenne pepper, salt, 1 glass white wine, bay leaf, 1 fresh sweet red pepper, 4 cloves garlic, ground black pepper.

Heat some oil in a heavy saucepan and fry the chopped garlic. Remove and reserve. Cut the kid or lamb into small pieces, dust them with cayenne pepper and salt and brown them in the oil. Pour in the wine, let it bubble, then add about a cup of water and the bay leaf. Cover the pan and cook gently for 15 minutes. Meanwhile mince the liver, or chop it finely, cut the red pepper into very thin strips and crush the fried garlic. Add all this to the kid, and a little more water if needed. Add a little black pepper, cover the pan and cook on a low flame until the meat is tender. The sauce should be very thick. Serve with crusty bread.

Cordero a la Pastora   *New Castile*
Shepherdess Lamb

To serve 4

1 lean shoulder of lamb, 2 tablespoons olive oil, 1 tablespoon flour,
1 tablespoon of cayenne pepper, 1 onion, 100 g lamb's liver, ½ lamb's brain,
2 big cloves of garlic, 1 sprig of fresh thyme, 2 cups stock, 2 tablespoons wine
vinegar, salt and black pepper.

Cut the lamb into chunks and dust them with flour, salt and
cayenne pepper. Chop the liver finely. Heat the oil in a large
saucepan and put in the chopped onion. Cook for a few minutes
and then add the pieces of lamb including the bone and the liver.
Brown the meat, then lower the heat and cover the pot. Crush
the garlic and mash it together with the thoroughly washed and
cleaned brain and the thyme leaves. Add this to the lamb with
2 cups of stock or water, and the vinegar. Season with a little salt
and ground black pepper. Cover the pot and cook gently for
1 hour, or until the meat is very tender. This dish is best left for
a few hours before serving, or better still made the day before
to allow the flavours to blend. It should then be reheated.

Serve in an earthenware casserole accompanied by red wine
and baked potatoes, or crusty bread.

Carnero con Ajo   *Catalonia*
Mutton with Garlic

To serve 4

Take half a leg of mutton or lamb and get the butcher to cut it into rounds
1 inch thick leaving the bone in the middle; 40 small or 20 large cloves garlic,
olive oil, meat stock, a small tin of tomato paste, 6 peppercorns, a bay leaf,
1 teaspoon paprika, salt.

Peel the garlic but do not chop it. Heat plenty of olive oil in a
deep pan and brown the slices of meat on each side, two at a
time. Lower the heat and when all the slices of meat are browned
put them in the pan and add the whole cloves of garlic. Allow
them to stew a little but not to brown. Carefully add enough
stock to just cover the meat, together with the tomato paste,

peppercorns, bay leaf and paprika. Add salt to taste and simmer very gently for $1\frac{1}{2}$–2 hours, or until the meat begins to come away from the bone.

This is best served with plenty of boiled potatoes. The garlic flavour is not as strong as one might expect as the garlic is stewed whole and slowly. The sauce may be thickened with a little cornflour if desired.

Estofado de Carnero *Extremadura*
Pot-Roasted Mutton

To serve 4–6

1 leg mutton, 4 thick rashers of bacon, 4 onions, 2 carrots, 1 sprig thyme, 1 bay leaf, 1 sprig mint, salt, pepper, 1 cup stock.

Remove the bone from the meat (or get your butcher to do this) and substitute the bacon, cut into long strips, pushing it in with a knitting or larding needle. Tie up the meat and put it into a large deep casserole, together with the cut-up onions and carrots, seasoning, and the herbs tied in a bunch. Pour in the stock and cover the casserole tightly, using foil under the lid if necessary. Cook slowly in the oven for 3–4 hours at 300° F, gas 2, turning the meat occasionally, and adding a little more stock if needed. When the meat is tender (the time will vary according to the age of the animal) remove the bunch of herbs and serve the meat in slices with the juices from the pan poured over it.

Riñones al Jerez
Kidneys in Sherry Sauce

To serve 4

$\frac{1}{2}$ kg beef kidneys, 1 tablespoon lard, 4 tablespoons dry sherry, 2 tablespoons tomato paste, salt, nutmeg and pepper, parsley, bread.

Choose very tender kidneys and, after removing the white tissue, cut them into small thin slices. Heat half of the lard in a frying-pan and when it is hot enough sauté the kidneys, seasoned with salt, for 5 minutes. Heat the sherry in an earthenware casserole and when it is reduced to half the quantity, add the tomato paste and a little salt, pepper and grated nutmeg. Put in the kidneys and cook for 10 minutes.

Serve in a dish, decorated with triangles of bread fried in the rest of the lard and sprinkled with chopped parsley, or serve in individual earthenware dishes.

Higado Frito   *Leon*
Fried Liver

The Spaniards have a way of making plain foods more interesting – here is a simple way to cook liver.

To serve 4

½ kg pigs' liver cut into thin slices, 2 tablespoons olive oil, 1 large clove garlic, flour, salt, 2 tablespoons sherry.

Dip the pieces of liver into slightly salted flour. Heat the olive oil gently in a frying-pan and throw in the garlic cut into largish pieces. Put in the liver before the oil gets too hot and allow it to cook on a medium heat, turning often to brown evenly. When it is about half cooked sprinkle with sherry and continue to cook until the juices which run from the liver are brownish instead of red (about 20 minutes). Serve immediately, pouring all the oil and juices from the pan over the liver; the pieces of garlic may be removed if preferred. This is good eaten either with fried potatoes or fresh bread and red wine.

Higado de Ternera
Calves' Liver

To serve 4

½ kg calves' liver, white bread, 4 tablespoons olive oil, 1 tablespoon flour, ½ cup stock, 1 tablespoon chopped parsley, salt and pepper, 1 tablespoon butter, 1 egg yolk, juice of ½ a lemon, watercress.

Cut the liver into very thin slices or ask your butcher to do so, and cut a slice of bread for each piece, roughly the same size.

Heat the olive oil in a frying-pan and carefully fry the pieces of liver until they are just cooked through; if you cook them for too long they will harden. Remove the liver and keep it warm. Raise the heat and fry the pieces of bread until they are crisp, remove and keep hot. Stir the flour into the hot oil, add the stock and lower the heat. Cook for 3–4 minutes, stirring to make a thick sauce, then add the chopped parsley, salt and pepper. Remove it from the heat and stir in the egg yolk, butter and lemon juice.

Arrange the pieces of fried bread on a large hot dish with a piece of liver on each and some of the sauce spooned over the top. Wash the watercress and serve separately.

Sesos de Cordero   *Leon*
Lambs' Brains

To serve 2

2 lambs' brains, 1 onion, 2 sprigs parsley, wine vinegar, 1 carrot, flour, salt, oil, 1 egg.

Wash the brains and remove any skin and bits of membrane. Put them in a pan of cold water with some chopped onion, one sprig of parsley, and a teaspoon of salt and simmer for 15 minutes. Remove the brains and reserve the stock. Cut the brains into strips and marinate for 2 hours in a little diluted vinegar, with some thin rounds of onion and carrot, salt and pepper. Dip the slices of brain into flour and beaten egg and fry them in hot oil. Remove and keep hot. In the same oil make a sauce with a little flour and stock from the brains, adding some finely chopped parsley and a teaspoon of the vinegar marinade. Pour this over the brains and serve hot with fried bread.

Lengua Estofada   *Navarre*
Stewed Tongue

To serve 4

1 small ox tongue, 2 carrots, 1 large onion, 2 tomatoes, 2 cloves garlic, oil, salt and pepper, parsley, thyme, 1 clove, a small piece of dark chocolate, 2 cups stock or water, 2 green peppers, boiled carrots, boiled potatoes.

Boil the tongue for 30 minutes, remove from the water and when cool enough remove the skin and small bones with a sharp knife. Heat the oil in a deep casserole and brown the tongue lightly, then put in the chopped carrots, onion, the peeled tomatoes and garlic, the herbs, the clove, the piece of chocolate, the pepper and salt. Add the liquid and tightly cover the casserole. Cook in a slow oven for 3 hours, turning the tongue over from time to time. About ½ hour before it is ready put in the green peppers cut into strips. When the tongue is completely tender cut it into slices and arrange it on a dish with the sieved sauce poured over it, surrounded by boiled carrots and small boiled potatoes.

Manos de Cerdo   *Asturias*
Pigs' Trotters

To serve 4

6 pigs' trotters, a bunch of herbs (parsley, thyme, bay leaf), 2 carrots, 2 turnips, flour, oil, salt and pepper, 8 red peppers, 1 clove garlic, 1 onion, 2 tomatoes, 1 glass dry sherry.

First wash the trotters and cut them in half. Cover with cold water, bring to the boil and skim. Then add the bunch of herbs and the chopped carrots and turnips. Simmer for 30 minutes. When the trotters are cooked take the flesh off the bones and cut it into small pieces. Flour them and fry lightly in oil. Cut the tops off the peppers. Remove the seeds. Stuff them with pieces of fried trotter and put back the tops. Take an ovenproof earthenware casserole with a lid and heat a little oil in it. Fry the finely chopped onion and garlic, a little fresh parsley and the tomatoes, add the sherry and some of the stock in which the trotters were cooked to make a sauce. Put in the stuffed peppers, cover the dish and cook in a moderate oven, 350° F, gas 4, for 45 minutes or until the peppers are cooked.

Serve with pieces of fried bread.

Albondigas en Salsa   *New Castile*
Meat Balls in Sauce

To serve 4

¼ kg minced beef, ¼ kg minced pork, 2 tablespoons fresh breadcrumbs, a little milk , 1 egg, flour, oil, ½ kg potatoes, 1 onion, 1 clove garlic, small glass of sherry, saffron.

Mix the minced meats with the breadcrumbs soaked in milk and the beaten egg. Season with salt and form into small balls. Flour them and brown them all over in hot oil. Put them into another saucepan. Peel the potatoes and cut them to roughly the same size as the meat balls and put them into the saucepan with the meat balls. In the pan in which the meat balls were browned fry the finely chopped onion and garlic, add a tablespoon of flour and stir until it thickens, then add the sherry and about 2 cups of water. Season with salt and saffron. Pour this sauce over the meat balls and potatoes and cook gently for ¾ hour.

Croquetas a la Española   *New Castile*
Spanish Croquettes

To serve 2

50 g ham, 250 g cooked pork or chicken, ½ onion, tablespoon lard, 1 tablespoon flour, ½ litre stock, salt, pepper and grated nutmeg, pinch cinnamon, 2 eggs, dried breadcrumbs, oil for frying.

Mince the meats and onion together, season with salt and pepper and fry in hot lard, stirring all the time. Add the flour and cook a little more, then add the stock and bring to the boil, still stirring. Put in the cinnamon and nutmeg and allow to simmer for 15 minutes. Remove from the heat and stir in one beaten egg. Cool a little and with floured hands make the mixture into small croquettes, about the size of half a sausage. Dip them in beaten egg and breadcrumbs and fry in hot oil until light brown and crisp on the outside and soft inside.

Empanadas
Pasties

Galicia

Empanada in general means pie and may apply to the huge round flat pies of Galicia, cut and sold in wedges, or to the small pies the size and shape of a Cornish pasty usually made at home. In Spain the pastry for these small pasties may be bought ready-made in wafer-thin discs. Many fillings are used, either sweet or savoury or a mixture of both – the following fillings are some of the more unusual ones. (The raisins used are improved if plumped out first in a little sherry.)

To serve 4

¼ kg shortcrust pastry rolled out thinly and cut into circles approximately 4 inches in diameter.

Minced Beef and Pumpkin Filling

100 g cooked minced beef, 200 g of pumpkin, 50 g pine-nuts or crushed blanched almonds, 50 g seedless raisins, 1 tablespoon sugar, ½ teaspoon each of ground cloves and cinnamon, a little salt.

Peel and cut the pumpkin into small squares and simmer in a little salted water until tender, then mash or reduce to a purée in an electric blender. Add the rest of the ingredients and mix together thoroughly.

Pork and Apricot Filling

150 g finely diced cooked pork, 100 g finely chopped cooked apricots (dried are best but fresh or canned ones may be used), ½ tablespoon sugar, 100 g mixed seedless raisins and currants, 50 g crushed toasted almonds, pinch of salt, a little meat stock to moisten if necessary.

Mix all ingredients well.

Tongue and Cider Filling

200 g cooked minced tongue, 50 g pine-nuts or crushed blanched almonds, 50 g seedless raisins, a little sugar, salt, a pinch of nutmeg and ground cloves, cider to moisten.

Thoroughly blend all these ingredients together.

Put about a tablespoon of whatever filling you choose to use in the centre of each circle of pastry, dampen the edges, fold over and press down. Make two tiny cuts in each and brush with milk or beaten egg. Put them on a greased baking sheet and bake in a moderate oven, 375° F, gas 5, for 15–20 minutes or until the pastry is crisp and golden.

Empanadas de Pascua   *Balearic Islands*
Easter Pies

It is traditional in many parts of Spain to kill a very young lamb at Easter and this recipe from Mallorca makes use of any small pieces of meat trimmed off before the roasting. In this country use the most tender cut of lamb you can find.

To serve 4

For the pastry: ½ kg plain flour, 1 teaspoon salt, 100 g lard, 1 coffee-cup olive oil, 1 coffee-cup water, 1 egg yolk.

For the filling: about ½ kg of lamb cut into small neat pieces, a little olive oil, 100 g *tocino* or fat bacon cut into dice, 100 g *sobresada* (optional), skins of 2 oranges and 1 lemon, a little salt and pepper, a little wild thyme.

Sieve the flour and salt into a bowl and rub the lard into it with your fingers. Make a well in the centre and put in the egg yolk, the oil and water. Mix with a fork until a stiff dough is formed and knead it gently into a ball with floured hands. Allow it to stand in a cool place while you prepare the filling.

Gently heat the oil in a saucepan, or better a *greixonera*, and put in the lamb, *tocino*, *sobresada* (cut up), the fruit skins, salt, pepper and thyme. Garden thyme will do if you have not got any wild thyme, but use less. Cover closely and cook over as low a flame as possible (use an asbestos mat) for about ½ hour, checking now and then to make sure it does not dry up. When the pieces of lamb are cooked remove the fruit skins and any surplus oil.

Keep aside enough dough to make lids for the pies and divide the remainder into four; mould each piece into a hollowed out ball. The walls of the ball should be reasonably thin and the base flattened to make a little dumpy pie-shape. Fill each pie with the prepared meat; a little of the orange and lemon peel may be cut into fine strips and put in as well. Dampen the rim and cut rounds to make lids. Pinch up the rims as neatly as possible. Put into a fairly hot oven, 375° F, gas 5, for 40 minutes or until the pastry is cooked.

Eat hot or cold.

Poultry and Game

In general the poultry reared in Spain is much the same as in this country, and includes all the familiar domestic birds bred specially for the table – chicken, duck, goose and turkey.

Of all these chicken is by far the most popular. Although rather yellowish and scraggy in appearance when plucked, the Spanish chicken is unexpectedly good. *Pollos* or young male birds are the best choice for roasting, while the *gallina*, usually a hen past her laying prime, is excellent for stewing or boiling. In spite of the fact that there are now plenty of fat white broiler chickens in the freezer cabinets of the supermarkets and even in some village stores, many Spanish housewives of the older generation still prefer to buy their chickens live from the market. A good healthy looking bird has a recognizable value and in fact is still often used as a payment in kind. A doctor friend of ours frequently receives payment of this sort from his country patients, and a large and lively cockerel once spent two days perched, crowing loudly, on a high shelf in his kitchen before being eventually caught by his Scottish wife.

Although also very good, ducks and geese are less commonly seen, probably because they do not thrive particularly well in the dry climate in many parts of Spain. Where in other countries villagers with a small piece of land might keep one or two geese, in Spain you are more likely to see a few turkeys strutting about round their owner's back door. These are nearly always the old-fashioned Bronze turkey, which in this country has almost disappeared in favour of the larger and fatter Broad Breasted White, which is easier to rear under the intensive systems now used in Britain. Although an excellent table bird, in my opinion the White turkey has not as good a flavour as the Bronze.

As well as poultry Spaniards eat a lot of game. This includes wild birds and animals such as partridge, pheasant, quail, woodcock, snipe, pigeon, wild duck, venison, wild pig, wild rabbit and hare. As in many other Mediterranean countries small birds such as thrushes and larks are also counted as game, but it seems rather pointless to include any recipes for these. On the whole, the Spaniards like to eat their game well-hung in spite of the generally higher temperatures. The exceptions are rabbit, quail and pigeons which should be eaten on the day after they are killed.

The partridge is far and away the most popular of all the game birds. Partridges used to be extremely common throughout Spain, so much so that they were an everyday dish in their season for many rural families. They are still relatively common today, especially the Red-Legged or French partridge, with its black bib and delicate blue markings. In the villages you often see a plump French partridge in a tiny cage hung outside on a sunny wall. This is for no sentimental reason – it is either being fattened to eat, or used (illegally now) as a decoy.

Quail are a rather rarer delicacy, and these tiny succulent birds are delicious cooked in the Spanish way – wrapped in a vine leaf, roasted for 20 minutes only and served on a slice of toast or fried bread. In Britain quails may be obtained by post from The Claxby Quail Farm, Alford, Lincolnshire.

Both wild and domestic rabbits, and hares too, are widely eaten throughout Spain. One of the most delicious methods of cooking them comes from Mallorca and includes a lot of tiny onions and a rich sauce. In Spain you can usually buy rabbits at the butcher's shop; or you can buy live rabbits at the local market. Many villagers breed rabbits for the table and will sell you one ready skinned and cleaned to order.

When young and tender most game and poultry is delicious simply roasted in the usual way. But if you have any doubts about the age of the bird or animal the slower methods of cooking such as braising or pot-roasting are more suitable, and some of the Spanish methods of cooking in this way are both simple and unusual.

Pollo al Jerez   *Andalusia*
Chicken in Sherry Sauce

To serve 4

1 chicken, 2 onions chopped, 3 cloves garlic mashed, 2 bay leaves, 1 teaspoon oregano, ½ teaspoon chilli powder, about 24 green olives, 2 wine glasses sherry, a little cornflour.

Cut the chicken into joints. Just cover the pieces with boiling water and simmer for 15 minutes. Add the onion, mashed garlic, bay leaves, oregano and salt and cook gently for 30 minutes. Just before the chicken is fully cooked add the chilli powder, olives and sherry and simmer for 5 minutes or until the chicken is tender. If necessary, thicken the sauce with a little cornflour blended with cold water, and cook for a further 2–3 minutes. Serve with plain boiled rice.

Pollo Extremeño
Extremadura

Chicken in Wine

To serve 4

1 medium-sized tender chicken, 1 large glass red wine, 1 cup stock, a
bouillon cube, 2 tablespoons lard, 2 tablespoons butter, salt, fried bread
cubes.

Cut the chicken into eight pieces, season with salt and brown in
hot lard. Add the stock together with the dissolved bouillon cube
and the wine. Allow to bubble for a few seconds then lower the
heat and add the butter. Cover tightly and cook until the chicken
is done, about 1–1½ hours. Serve with fried bread cubes.

Pollo en Chilindrón
Aragon

Chicken in Chilindrón Sauce

Pork, rabbit or lamb may also be cooked *en chilindrón*.

To serve 4–6

1 chicken, 1 clove garlic, 6 tablespoons olive oil, salt and pepper, 1 onion,
2 green or red peppers, pinch toasted saffron, 2 teaspoons paprika, 200 g
smoked ham (*serrano* should be used if possible), ¼ kg tomatoes, 1 small hot
red pepper.

Cut the chicken into joints and season with salt and pepper. Heat
the oil in a large saucepan and fry the chopped garlic. Remove the
garlic, and brown the chicken joints in the hot oil. Take them
out and set aside. Put the chopped onion and peppers into the
oil, lower the heat and cook until they are soft, then add the
paprika, saffron, cubed ham and the peeled and chopped tomatoes. Put the pieces of browned chicken and the tiny hot red
pepper (cut up and with the seeds removed) into the sauce, cover
the pot and cook very gently until the chicken is tender, about 1
hour.

To serve, arrange the chicken pieces on a dish and cover with
the sauce.

Pollo en Chanfaina   *Catalonia*
Chicken in Samfaina Sauce

To serve 4

1 medium chicken, 1 tablespoon lard, 1 tablespoon oil, 1 onion, 2 aubergines, 2 courgettes, 100 g ham, 1 green pepper, 1 red pepper, 1 can tomatoes or 6 fresh ones, bay leaf, thyme, pinch ground nutmeg, salt and pepper, 1 cup chicken stock.

Cut up the chicken and brown the pieces in a mixture of hot oil and lard. Chop the onion, aubergines, courgettes (it is best not to peel these last two) and ham and put them in the pot. Cut the peppers into strips and add them. Sauté the mixture for 10 minutes, then add the canned or fresh (peeled) tomatoes and the herbs and seasoning. Pour in the stock and cover the pan. Lower the heat and cook gently for ¾ hour. Serve with triangles of fried bread.

The sauce in which the chicken is cooked is called *samfaina* and may be used equally well with pork fillet.

Pollo Tomatero   *Basque Country*
Chicken with Tomatoes

To serve 4

1 medium-sized tender chicken, 1 onion, 100 g ham in a thick slice, 4 or 5 tablespoons olive oil, ½ kg tomatoes or 1 large can of tomatoes, 6 peppercorns, 2 cloves garlic, 1 teaspoon sugar, salt.

Wash the chicken and cut it into joints. Rub the pieces thoroughly with salt. Heat 4 tablespoonfuls of olive oil in a heavy saucepan and brown the chicken joints all over, then remove them and keep them warm. Chop the onion and ham into small cubes and fry them gently in the same oil. When the onion starts to soften remove it and the ham from the pan and set aside with the chicken joints. Scald and peel the tomatoes if fresh ones are used, chop them up and put them into the hot oil (add a little more oil if necessary). Crush the garlic, in a press or a mortar, and bruise the peppercorns, then add them together with the sugar, and salt to taste, to the tomato, and cook, stirring all the time, until a thick sauce is obtained. Stir in the pieces of onion and ham. Put the chicken pieces into an ovenproof dish of suitable size and pour the sauce over them. Add a little water if it seems too thick, cover the dish and cook in a moderate oven, 350° F, gas 4, for 1 hour. Serve with baked potatoes and a green salad, or with plain boiled rice.

Pepitoria de Gallina   *New Castile*
Chicken Casserole

To serve 4

1 tender chicken of just over 1 kg in weight, a bunch of herbs (parsley, thyme and a bay leaf), 1 carrot, 1 small onion, 100 g ham, 2 tablespoons lard, chopped parsley, salt and pepper, 4 or 5 cloves garlic, 10 toasted hazelnuts, 1 clove, yolks of 2 hard-boiled eggs, 2 raw egg yolks.

First poach the chicken in water with the bunch of herbs, salt, pepper, carrot and onion until it is almost cooked. Remove it and reserve the stock. Heat the lard in a big saucepan or casserole and fry the ham cut into cubes and a little chopped parsley, then put in the chicken and carefully brown it on all sides. In a large mortar make a paste with the garlic and hazelnuts, 1 clove, 2 hard-boiled egg yolks and the rest of the chopped parsley. Dilute it with 2 or more ladles of the chicken stock and pour this sauce over the chicken in the casserole. Cover and cook gently for 20 minutes. Remove from the heat and stir in 2 raw egg yolks. Serve straight away.

Pechuga de Gallina a la Española   *New Castile*
Chicken Breasts a la Española

To serve 4

4 chicken breasts, 4 thick slices of ham, 2 tablespoons lard, 1 small onion, 1 carrot, 2 tablespoons flour, 2 breakfast-cups chicken or meat stock, 1 glass white wine or dry cider, salt, pepper, a little grated nutmeg, a handful of pine-nuts.

Slit the breasts and insert a slice of ham into each, tie up with thread. Heat the lard in deep pan or casserole and fry the onion and carrot, both finely chopped. When they are soft add the flour and stir for a minute then gradually add the stock, stirring well to make a thickish sauce. Add the wine and boil for 2–3 minutes. Lower the heat and put in the chicken breasts. Season with salt, pepper and nutmeg, cover and cook until the breasts are done, about 30–45 minutes, then add the pine-nuts and cook a few minutes more. If preferred the sauce may be put through a sieve before adding the nuts.

Salpicón de Pollo   *Canary Islands*
Cold Chicken and Salad

To serve 4–6

1 boiling fowl, bunch of herbs, salt, 4 carrots, vinaigrette dressing, parsley, 4 hard-boiled eggs, 1 crisp lettuce, 100 g green stoned olives.

Cut up the chicken and simmer with the herbs and whole peeled carrots until it is tender. Allow it to cool and remove the meat from the bones. Discard the skin. Arrange the pieces of cold chicken and sliced carrots on a large serving dish. Make a sauce by combining the vinaigrette, chopped parsley and 2 hard-boiled eggs mashed up with a pinch of salt. Pour this over the chicken and carrots and serve surrounded by lettuce and whole olives and the remaining hard-boiled eggs in slices.

Pato con Aceitunas   *Andalusia*
Duck with Olives

To serve 4

1 young duck weighing about 1½ kg, 2 tablespoons olive oil, 2 tablespoons butter, 4 small onions or shallots, 2 carrots, 1 tablespoon flour, 2 glasses of dry sherry or Madeira, about ½ litre of stock, 3 tablespoons tomato paste, 1 tablespoon finely chopped parsley, pepper and salt, 4 dozen green olives.

Wash and dry the prepared duck and heat the oil and butter in a large heavy pan with a lid. Slice the onions and carrots into rings.

When the oil and butter mixture is fairly hot but not actually sizzling put in the duck and the sliced vegetables. Carefully turn the duck over and over in the fat without damaging the skin until it is golden brown all over – about 20 minutes. When the duck is ready take it and the vegetables out and keep them warm. Lower the heat and stir the flour into the fat in the pan, gradually adding stock to make a sauce. Add seasoning. Pour in the sherry or Madeira, stir in the tomato paste and parsley and cook for a few minutes stirring all the time. Put the duck and the vegetables back into the pan and cover it tightly. Cook gently for about an hour turning the duck occasionally. Meanwhile remove the stones from the olives if they have them and rinse them well under the hot tap to remove any excess brine. When the duck is ready put it onto a heated serving dish, strain the sauce into a small saucepan and add the olives; cook just enough to heat them through. Pour over the duck and serve.

Pato en Salsa de Almendras *Catalonia*
Duck in Almond Sauce

To serve 4

1 medium-sized duck plus the liver, a little well-seasoned flour, 100 g lard, 1 onion cut into rings, 2 cloves garlic chopped, 4 fresh tomatoes or one small can of tomatoes, about 15 blanched and toasted almonds, a small glass of dry sherry, 1 tablespoon chopped parsley.

Joint the duck and remove any surplus fat. Wash and dry the pieces and dip them into well-seasoned flour. Heat the lard in a large shallow earthenware dish, or failing this a heavy-based saucepan, and gently fry the roughly chopped liver. Remove with a draining spoon and set aside. Put the onion and garlic into the pan and fry them gently until the onion begins to soften, then remove them and put them aside with the liver, draining off as much fat as possible. Put the pieces of duck into the remaining fat in the pan, adding a little more if necessary and brown them carefully on all sides. Add the peeled and chopped tomatoes. Lower the heat and leave to cook gently with a lid on the pan.

Meanwhile pound the liver, onion, garlic and toasted almonds together in a large mortar (or use an electric blender) to make a smooth paste. Dilute this with the sherry and add it to the duck. Stir in the chopped parsley and adjust the seasoning. Cover the pan and simmer gently for about an hour or until the duck is tender. It may be necessary to add a little more liquid (stock or water) during the cooking. If you have used an earthenware dish it may be taken straight to the table. Otherwise transfer it to a hot serving dish. Creamed potatoes go well with this.

Pavo Asado   *Old Castile*
Roast Turkey

In Spain there are still many free-range turkeys, almost always dark bronze or black, and possessing a delightful flavour when cooked. Here is a simple way to roast a good turkey.

1 fresh turkey, stuffing (see page 000), lard and salt, 2 glasses sherry, several sprigs of winter savory, flour, stock or water.

Stuff the turkey with the prepared mixture and sew it up. Rub the outside with salt and spread it generously with lard. Sprinkle it with the savory leaves and pour over the sherry. Roast in a moderate to hot oven, 375° F, gas 5, allowing 20 minutes to the pound and 20 minutes over. Serve with the juices from the pan made into a sauce with a little flour and stock or water, and a dish of puréed potatoes.

Game

Perdices con Leche   *Catalonia and the*
Pot-Roasted Partridges in Milk   *Balearic Islands*

This recipe from Mallorca is typical of the old country way of cooking game and other small birds in a pot, using milk. Old Mallorcan cookery books include many recipes for thrushes and other song birds cooked in this way. It is sad that there are so

few partridges and virtually no thrushes left on the island today although the pine forests and scrub-covered hillsides provide a perfect habitat for them. Pigeons could equally well be used for this recipe.

To serve 4

4 partridges or young pigeons, 2 large onions, 8 small sweet tomatoes, olive oil, a glass of sherry, ½ litre water and ¼ litre milk, 2 tablespoons Mallorcan capers (these are the best, but others may be substituted), 2 tablespoons parsley, 2 tablespoons stoned olives, salt and pepper.

Prepare the birds, reserving the livers. Heat a little olive oil in a large, deep earthenware casserole or a heavy saucepan and carefully brown the birds on all sides. Cut the onions into quarters and put them in. Put in the whole unpeeled tomatoes. Cook a little longer on a lowered flame, turning gently with a wooden spatula, then pour in the sherry, water and milk and season with pepper and salt. Cover the pot either with an earthenware plate or its own lid if you are using a saucepan, and simmer very gently on as low a flame as possible. Pound the livers, capers, parsley and olives together in a mortar and add them to the pot. Cover again and allow to cook undisturbed for at least 2 hours. In country districts the *olla* or earthenware pot would sit in the embers of a wood fire, with perhaps a few ashes heaped on top, and be left to cook until needed. The slow oven of an Aga is ideal for this dish provided the pot is tightly sealed. Greaseproof paper or foil put over the top, with the lid pressed firmly over it, makes a good tight fit.

Serve the birds straight from the pot, accompanied by plain boiled potatoes and brussels sprouts.

Perdices Asturiana   *Asturias*
Asturian Partridges

To serve 4

4 partridges cut in half, salt, 100 g salt pork or bacon, 12 small onions or shallots, 1 carrot, 50 g lard, 1 tablespoon flour, a bunch of aromatic herbs including thyme, parsley, marjoram and a bay leaf, grated nutmeg, salt, pepper, a glass of cider, and a little stock.

Rub the cleaned birds thoroughly with plenty of salt, then brown them in hot lard, and add the bacon or pork in small cubes, the whole peeled onions and the chopped carrot. Stir in the flour, cook a little longer, then add the cider. Put in the herbs and nutmeg and season with salt and pepper. Lower the heat, add a little stock, cover the pan and cook gently for 1½–2 hours. When the partridges are done arrange them on a plate surrounded by the onions and covered with sauce.

Perdices con Col   *Andalusia*
Partridges with Cabbage

To serve 4

4 partridges, 8 rashers of bacon, 1 cabbage, 100 g salt pork, 200 g *salchichón* or salami, 2 carrots, 8 tiny onions, a bunch of herbs including thyme, mint and a bay leaf, 1 cup stock, salt and a little butter or lard.

Rub the outside of the cleaned partridges with salt, and sprinkle some liberally inside. Tie two rashers of bacon securely round each bird. Cut up the cabbage finely and boil it in a little salted water

for 10 minutes, then drain it and mix into it the salt pork cut into tiny cubes, the *salchichón* in slices, the cut-up carrots, the peeled whole onions and the bunch of herbs tied with cotton. Put all this into a large ovenproof dish with a lid and place the partridges on top, pressing them down a little into the cabbage. Pour over about a cup of good stock and put a knob of butter on top of each bird. Cover tightly (using foil under the lid) and cook in a very moderate oven, about 300° F, gas 2, for 2 hours or until the partridges are done. Check occasionally to make sure it does not become too dry. Remove the bunch of herbs and cut each bird in half. Serve in the same dish, with plenty of crusty bread and accompanied by a good Rioja wine. Pigeons could be cooked in the same way.

Codornices en Salsa   *Balearic Islands*
Quails in Sauce

This recipe comes from Menorca where quails used to be abundant. For where to get quails in England, see page 159.

Allow one large or two small quails per person.

To serve 4

4 or 8 quails according to size, about 100 g butter, 1 tablespoon of chopped
parsley, 1 tablespoon of chopped summer savory, several leaves of mint
chopped, a pinch of thyme, 4 or 8 rashers of bacon, salt, pepper,
a medium-size glass of white wine, an equal amount of chicken stock,
1 tablespoon of flour.

Put a knob of butter into each bird and fit them into a greased
shallow earthenware dish or roasting tin. Smear a little butter
over each one, sprinkle with a mixture of the chopped herbs, salt
and pepper and cover each bird with a rasher of bacon. Mix most
of the wine with the stock and pour it over the birds. Put them
into a pre-heated moderate oven, 350° F, gas 4, and roast for
about ¾ hour, basting occasionally. Remove the bacon rashers,
raise the oven temperature to 400° F, gas 6, and continue to cook
until the quails are browned.

Transfer them to a serving dish and keep warm. Meanwhile
make a sauce with the juices in the pan: strain off any surplus fat
and stir in a level tablespoonful of flour. Cook on the top of the
stove for a minute or two, stirring all the time, and then add the
rest of the wine and a little stock or water and allow to boil for
about a minute. Pour the sauce over the quails and serve with
triangles of fried bread and the vegetables of your choice.

Codornices   *Galicia*

A Galician way of cooking quails.

To serve 4

400 g large white beans, 8 quails or 4 pigeons, 1 ham bone, 1 onion, 6 cloves
garlic, 2 tomatoes, oil, salt.

Another recipe which is good for pigeons too. Soak the beans
overnight, then put them to boil in about 1½ litres of salted water.
Clean the birds and, leaving them whole, sear them in a very
little hot oil, turning them over and over, and taking care not to
damage the skin. When the beans are half cooked, which will
take ½–1 hour according to their age, put in the birds, the
chopped onion, tomato and garlic and the ham bone, together

with the oil and any juices from the birds. Cook gently for another $1\frac{1}{2}$ hours, or until the beans are tender and the sauce has reduced considerably. Remove the ham bone and serve the quails on a large plate surrounded by beans and sauce.

Chocha a la Vizcaína
Woodcock Vizcaína

Basque Country

A *chocha* is a woodcock (also known as a *becada*).

For 2 people

2 woodcock, 50 g lard, 50 g bacon, 4 small onions, 2 cups of beef stock, a small glass of sherry, 4 turnips, 1 tablespoon of flour, salt.

Clean and salt the well-hung birds, leaving on the heads. Reserve the giblets. Heat the lard in a deep heavy pan or casserole and put in the woodcock, 3 onions and the bacon cut into 2 pieces. When browned pour in the stock and sherry and add the whole peeled turnips. Cover the pan and allow to cook gently for about 1 hour. In another pan fry the remaining onion chopped up finely with the chopped giblets, and when the onion is soft stir in the flour and all the liquid in which the birds were cooked, to make a thick sauce. Put the birds with beaks pointing upwards on a dish with the turnips and pour the strained sauce over.

Pichones
Young Pigeons

Balearic Islands

To serve 4

4 young tender pigeons, a little vinegar, 50 g of lard, 2 onions finely chopped, 2 tablespoons of tomato paste, a small glass of red wine, chicken stock, flour, pepper and salt.

Pluck and clean the pigeons, reserving some of the blood, to which you add 2 teaspoons of vinegar to prevent it from clotting. Heat the lard in an earthenware dish or heavy saucepan and brown the pigeons well all over, then lower the heat slightly and add the onions and tomato paste. Continue to fry gently for about

5 minutes, then add the wine and sufficient well-seasoned chicken stock to come about halfway up the birds. Cover the pan and allow to simmer gently for about an hour, or until the pigeons are tender. Take a small ladleful of the stock, allow it to cool a little, add the blood and vinegar to it and return it to the pan, stir it in thoroughly and remove the pan from the heat without allowing it to boil. If you have used an earthenware dish it may be taken straight to the table, otherwise transfer the pigeons, in their sauce, to a hot tureen.

Liebre Guisada   *Extremadura*
Stewed Hare

To serve 4

1 hare, ½ bottle of white wine (preferably Ribiera) or dry cider, 2 cloves garlic, a few cloves, ½ teaspoon grated nutmeg, 6 black peppercorns, 3 tablespoons good dripping or lard, 2 large onions.

Wash the hare and cut it up. Put it into a shallow dish and cover it with wine or cider; add the spices and crushed garlic cloves and marinate it for several hours.

When you are ready to cook the hare heat the dripping in a frying-pan and brown the well-drained pieces. Remove them and put them into an ovenproof casserole. Sprinkle with salt. Cut the onions into fine slices and fry them in the same fat. When they are half cooked pour them over the hare, and add the wine and spices from the marinade. Cover the casserole and put it into a pre-heated oven, 350° F, gas 4, and cook for 2–3 hours, or until the flesh of the hare is coming away from the bone. Serve with baked potatoes.

Conejo en Sarmorejo   *Canary Islands*
Rabbit en Sarmorejo

This is a delicious way of cooking rabbit practised in Tenerife. Any small unassuming-looking restaurant in, for example, Tacaronte or Oratava, both charming Spanish colonial towns with names of Quanche origin, will serve it for a comparatively modest sum. Sometimes it is served with fried potatoes, but more usually simply with fresh country bread and the purplish red Tacaronte wine, which leaves a bitter effervescent taste on the tongue.

To serve 4

1 medium-sized rabbit, salt, half a bottle of dry white wine, a small glass of vinegar, 2 sprigs of wild thyme, 2 teaspoons of oregano, 1 bay leaf, a coffee-cup of olive oil, 2 large cloves of garlic, 2 teaspoons of paprika, either a small piece of hot red chilli pepper or ½ teaspoon or less of cayenne pepper according to taste.

Cut the rabbit into joints, sprinkle with salt and put it into a shallow dish. Make a marinade to cover the rabbit with some of the wine, the vinegar, the thyme, oregano and bay leaf. Allow to stand for several hours, or better still overnight.

When ready to start cooking remove the pieces of rabbit and dry them, reserving the marinade. Gently heat the olive oil in a saucepan and thoroughly brown the pieces of meat, turning them frequently to colour as evenly as possible, then lower the heat and pour in the marinade, adding more wine to cover the rabbit pieces. Partially cover the pan and simmer gently. Meanwhile peel the garlic cloves and crush them in a mortar with the paprika, the finely chopped chilli pepper (or the cayenne) and a little salt. Add this to the pan and taste for seasoning. The sauce should be slightly hot, but not too much. Continue to simmer for up to an hour, or until the meat leaves the bone easily. Add more wine if necessary.

This is a dish which improves with standing and is even better if cooked the day before it is needed and reheated when required.

Conejo con Cebollitas *Mallorca*
Rabbit with Little Onions

Choose small evenly sized onions (pickling onions are ideal), or use shallots.

To serve 4

1 medium-sized rabbit or young hare, salt, 1 coffee-cup of olive oil, about

150 g *tocino* cut into small dice, a small glass of dry sherry, a sprig of thyme, parsley and a bay leaf tied together, about 15 small onions, seasoned flour.

Joint the rabbit and sprinkle with salt. Heat the olive oil in a large heavy saucepan and fry the *tocino* for a few minutes, then add the pieces of rabbit, turning them over until they are evenly browned. Lower the heat slightly and pour in the sherry, add the bunch of herbs and allow to cook gently for about 15 minutes. Meanwhile peel the onions but keep them whole. Roll them in flour. In a separate frying-pan heat a little oil and fry the onions, rolling them round until they are evenly golden. Remove them with a draining spoon and put them into the saucepan with the rabbit. Add a little water or stock, cover the pan and simmer gently for about ¾ hour, or until the rabbit is tender. Remove the bunch of herbs. Check the seasoning. Take out the pieces of rabbit and put them in the centre of a hot serving dish. Arrange the onions round them and pour the liquid from the pan over the meat. Serve at once. New potatoes are a good accompaniment to this dish.

Conejo Guisado   *Canary Islands*
Roast Stuffed Rabbit

To serve 4

1 domestic rabbit weighing about 1 kg, 100 g *tocino* or bacon fat, 1 cup fresh breadcrumbs, 100 g beef marrow or suet, ½ litre milk, chopped parsley, salt, pepper, 6 rashers bacon, 1 glass white wine, 6 onions, 2 cloves.

Clean the rabbit. Soak the breadcrumbs in the milk, stir in the marrow or suet, and the *tocino* cut into tiny dice. Add chopped parsley, pepper and salt and mix well to form a firm paste. Stuff the rabbit with this and sew it up. Put the rashers of bacon in a layer on the bottom of a baking dish, put the rabbit on top and pour over it the glass of white wine. Put it into a pre-heated oven, at 375° F, gas 5, to roast. It will take about 1½ hours. Turn the rabbit from time to time and baste it with the wine and juices. Make a purée with the onions cooked in a little water with the cloves and serve this with the rabbit.

Conejo al Ram *Catalonia*
Rabbit al Ram

To serve 4

1 rabbit, 2 tablespoons olive oil, 1 glass red wine, paprika, salt, a few lavender leaves, a sprig of rosemary, 200 g pork ribs, flour and water.

Make a marinade with the wine, oil, seasoning and herbs. Cut up the rabbit and leave to marinate for at least 2 hours. Fry the pork ribs in a little fat in a saucepan, and when they are browned add the pieces of rabbit and brown them. Mix a little flour with the marinade and strain it into the pan with the rabbit and pork ribs. Add a cup or more of water to cover the meat and allow to cook gently until tender, about 1½–2 hours according to the age of the rabbit.

Conejo a la Vinagreta *Catalonia and the*
Rabbit Vinaigrette *Balearic Islands*

Partridge, young hare or chicken may be cooked in the same way (allow one partridge per person). Traditionally a deep earthenware pot is used, covered with an earthenware plate full of water, but any suitable casserole will do provided it is well sealed.

To serve 4

1 medium-sized rabbit, 1 coffee-cup of wine vinegar, 1 coffee-cup of olive oil 2 coffee-cups of water, sliced onions, 2 cloves of garlic, a bay leaf, salt and 6 peppercorns, a handful of stoned green olives and a tablespoon of capers.

Prepare the rabbit, cutting it into joints. Put it into a suitably large pot with the vinegar, oil and water, sliced onions, garlic, bay leaf, salt and peppercorns. Cover tightly and bring it to simmering point on the top of the stove. Meanwhile pound the olives and capers in a mortar and add them to the pot. Transfer to a moderate oven, 350° F, gas 4. Cook for about 1½ hours, or until the meat is tender. Serve in the same pot with croûtons of fried bread.

Estofado de Conejo y Legumbres *Leon*
Rabbit and Vegetable Stew

A country dish designed to use whatever vegetables are available.

To serve 4–6

1 medium-sized rabbit, a little well-seasoned flour, 1 coffee-cup of olive oil, 1 glass of white wine, 1 bay leaf, a sprig of thyme, a tablespoon of chopped parsley, 1 onion chopped, 2 carrots chopped (black carrots are good for this), 250 g green beans or shelled peas, 250 g shelled broad beans, 4 potatoes roughly cut up.

Thoroughly wash and dry the rabbit. Cut it into fairly small pieces and roll them in the seasoned flour. Heat the olive oil in a large deep pan and carefully brown the pieces of rabbit. Lower the heat, add the wine and herbs and cook covered for about ½ hour, and then add the prepared vegetables. Pour in just enough water to cover and season with more pepper and salt if necessary. Simmer for about ¾ hour, by which time everything should be thoroughly cooked without being mushy. Serve with plenty of fresh crusty bread and white wine.

Capirotada *Balearic Islands*
Meat with Almond Sauce

This is a method of serving meat with almond sauce which originated in Mallorca where almonds are plentiful. Almost any kind of tender game or poultry may be used, young rabbit, chicken, or partridge being the most usual.

To serve 4

1 small rabbit or chicken or 2 partridges, a bunch of fresh herbs, ½ sliced onion, 50 g lard, 2 slices of white bread, 200 g blanched almonds, a stick of cinnamon or 1 teaspoon of ground cinnamon, salt and pepper.

Poach the prepared animal of your choice in well-seasoned water with the herbs and onion for about 30–40 minutes. While it is cooking pound or grind the almonds as finely as possible. When the meat is ready remove it and reserve the stock. Cut the meat into small neat pieces (discarding any skin and bones) and fry them lightly in lard until golden. Transfer to a hot serving dish and keep warm. Fry the bread in the same fat, drain thoroughly and crush in a mortar. Blend this with the almonds and about $\frac{1}{4}$ litre of the reserved stock. Pour this mixture into a saucepan with the cinnamon, a little pepper and salt if necessary and simmer gently for about 10 minutes, adding more liquid if needed and stirring to prevent it sticking. The resulting sauce should be smooth and thick.

Pour this over the pieces of meat and garnish with triangles of fried bread. Serve very hot.

Jabalí Estofado   *Asturias*
Stewed Wild Boar

There are plenty of wild pigs left in Spain even today, especially in the mountainous northern regions. Young animals are best roasted as for pork, and as a Spanish friend put it, using 'many spices and wild grasses' (herbs). These may include mountain herbs such as rosemary, thyme, fennel or oregano which should be strewn liberally over the joint when roasting. This recipe from Asturias is a typical way of preparing a tougher animal. Obviously wild pig or boar will not be available in English butchers' shops, but venison could be treated in the same way, using red wine instead of white, or alternatively ordinary fresh pork could be used, still using white wine, but cutting the cooking time down to about 1 hour, or until the pork is tender.

To serve 4

1 kg wild pig cut into slices, a coffee-cup of strong olive oil, a large glass of dry white wine and 2 tablespoonsful of wine vinegar, 2 bay leaves, 6 black peppercorns, a bunch of mountain herbs tied together, 2 large onions cut very finely, 4 cloves of garlic, 2 tablespoons chopped parsley, a little stock or water, salt and pepper.

The day before you are going to cook the meat, rub it well with olive oil and marinate it overnight in the wine and vinegar with the bay leaves, peppercorns and bunch of herbs. The next day remove the pieces of meat and dry them with a piece of kitchen paper, reserving the marinade. Heat the olive oil in a heavy saucepan and lightly brown the meat. Add the finely chopped onion, garlic and parsley and cook for a few minutes stirring gently. Pour in the wine and vinegar marinade including the herbs and peppercorns. Add enough stock to just cover the meat and season with salt. Cover the pan and cook very gently until the meat is tender. This will vary according to the toughness of the animal, but will take about 2–2½ hours. A good way to cook this would be to transfer it to a tightly covered casserole and put it into a slow oven.

To serve, arrange the slices of meat on a hot dish with the strained liquid poured over them.

Stews

There are many words in the Spanish language for stew besides *cocido*; most of them derive from the name of the cooking vessel. *Puchero*, *pote*, *cazuela* and *greixonera* are some examples. Originally a peasant dish designed for long slow cooking over a low fire, in a well-sealed vessel and perhaps with embers strewn over the top, Spanish stews are elastic in their ingredients though certain rules are generally adhered to. The basic ingredients tend to fall into three categories: dried pulses such as chickpeas, beans or lentils, fresh vegetables as available, and various kinds of meat, fresh or salted; and a spicy sausage – almost without exception the *chorizo*. It is this which gives Spanish stews their unique flavour and red-brown colour.

Nearly every region of Spain has its classic stew, the ingredients originally depending on the climate and what food was locally available. *Fabada asturiana* is perhaps the best known and appears on menus all over Spain. The black blood sausage, *morcilla*, which is an essential ingredient, is made in Asturias, and the special white beans called *alubias* are grown there too. These are rather like butter beans but are smaller and rounder, with a fat glossy appearance, and it is generally agreed that they have a superior flavour. In Catalonia a *pilota* or *picada* is often added to a stew to give extra flavour. This is either in the form of a ball of minced meat, almonds, garlic and spices rolled in flour, or it may simply be a thick paste of nuts, garlic, spices and seasoning. It is generally added halfway through the cooking.

The presentation of certain stews such as *olla podrida* and *pote gallego* is interesting. They are divided to provide three separate courses, as is the French pot-au-feu. First the liquid is strained off and served as a soup with tiny pasta or pieces of fried bread. The meats are cut up and served as a second course and the vegetables are separated and often served with a tomato sauce. In this way a substantial meal for a large family or gathering of people can be prepared under somewhat primitive cooking conditions.

Most of the ingredients for the following recipes may be obtained in Britain. A good Spanish stew can be a useful dish for those occasions when the exact number of guests and the time of their arrival is uncertain, as it is expandable, difficult to spoil, and improves with reheating.

Olla Podrida, o Cocido Madrileño   *Old Castile*
Rotten Pot, or Madrid Stew

Possibly one of the oldest national dishes of Spain, the *olla* was once unkindly said by the French to consist of two cigars boiled in three gallons of water. Richard Ford in his book *Gatherings from Spain* written in 1846 assures us that this is far from true, and gives the following recipe. He is most emphatic that only earthenware pots should be used, putting two on the stove to boil separately:

Place into No. 1 garbanzos, which have been placed to soak overnight, add a good piece of beef, a chicken, a large piece of bacon, let it boil once quickly, then let it simmer; it requires four or five hours to be well done. Meanwhile place into No. 2, with water, whatever vegetables are to be had, lettuces, cabbage, a slice of gourd, of beef, carrots, beans, celery, endive, onions and garlic, long peppers. These must be previously well washed and cut, as if they were destined to make a salad; then add red sausages, or chorizos, half a salted pig's face, which should have been soaked overnight. When all is sufficiently boiled, strain off the water and throw it away. Remember constantly to skim the scum off both saucepans. When all this is sufficiently dressed, take a large dish, lay in the bottom the vegetables, the beef in the centre, flanked by the bacon, chicken and pig's face. The sausages should be arranged around, en couronne; pour over some of the soup of No. 1 and serve hot . . . no violets come up to the perfume which a cooking olla casts before it; the mouth watering bystanders sigh, as they see and smell the rich freight steaming away from them.

This is the essence of a Spanish stew – it has changed little in a hundred years or so. *Cocido madrileño* is its more modern name. The recipe that follows is a version slightly simplified for the English cook.

To serve 4–6

½ kg chickpeas soaked overnight, half a boiling fowl, ¼ kg salted stewing beef with bone, a pig's trotter, 100 g smoked bacon in one piece, 100 g *tocino* cut up, 1 *morcilla*, 100 g *chorizo*, 1 large onion, ½ small cabbage, 2 carrots, ½ head of garlic, 2 leeks, turnips or other vegetables as available, pepper and salt.

Obviously you will need a very large pot for all this, and it should ideally be of earthenware. Having found a suitable vessel half fill it with cold water and put in the chickpeas, half boiling fowl, in one piece, pig's trotter, piece of beef, the bacon, *tocino* and the sausages. Bring it to the boil and skim, lower the heat and simmer for about 2 hours, adding more hot water if necessary.

Meanwhile prepare the vegetables. Peel and roughly chop the onion, shred the cabbage (not too finely), scrape and cut up the carrots, wash and cut up the leeks or other vegetables you are using. The half garlic head should remain in one unpeeled piece. Put all these vegetables into the pot and bring it back to the boil, add the pepper, and salt if necessary. Continue to simmer for an hour. When you are ready to serve this meal (it is a whole meal) remove the head of garlic and throw it away. Remove the meats and sausages with a draining spoon and cut them into fairly large pieces. Put the chickpeas and vegetables into the middle of a large heated serving dish, arrange the meat and sausage around them and pour over a little of the broth. The rest of the broth should be served first as soup with cubes of fried bread.

Ropa Vieja   *Old Castile*
Old Clothes

For this traditional dish you need either left-over cooked meat (chicken, pork or beef, or a mixture of all) or a piece of tough stewing beef which you have cooked very slowly for a long time. If there are any cooked chickpeas or beans available these may be added to the pot with great advantage.

To serve 4

2 large onions, 2 fresh peppers (red or green), 2 aubergines (optional), $\frac{1}{2}$ kg tomatoes, stock or water, salt and pepper, approximately $\frac{3}{4}$ kg cooked meats, olive oil.

Make a *sofrito* as follows – chop the onions fairly finely and stew them gently in hot oil, cut the peppers and aubergines into small pieces and add them to the pan when the onions are half cooked. Scald and peel the tomatoes and stir them into the mixture. Lower the heat and continue to cook for a few minutes, then add about a cup of stock and the chopped cooked meats. Season with salt and pepper. Cover the pan and cook gently for $\frac{1}{2}$ hour. Any beans or chickpeas should be added about 10 minutes before serving, just long enough to thoroughly heat through.

Olla Gitana   *Andalusia*
Gipsy Stew

To serve 4–6

200 g dried white beans, 200 g dried peas, 200 g green beans, 200 g squash or

pumpkin, 2 pears, 1 slice white bread, olive oil, 1 onion, 2 tomatoes, 1 clove garlic, salt, ground black pepper, 1 teaspoon paprika, 1 envelope (2 pinches) saffron, 1 teaspoon wine vinegar.

The dried beans and peas should be soaked overnight. Put 1¼ litres of cold water into a pot and boil the white beans for an hour, then add the dried peas and boil for another hour. This operation could be done in a pressure-cooker to save time. Then add the green beans and pumpkin cut up, and the pears cored and peeled and halved. Cook until everything is tender. Meanwhile fry the slice of bread in olive oil till crisp, remove and reserve. Chop the onion, tomatoes and garlic and fry in the same oil until soft, then season with salt, black pepper, paprika and saffron. Add this to the pot of stew. Crush the fried bread in a mortar, mix with vinegar and also put into the pot. Cook for a few more minutes and serve.

Cocido Extremeño   *Extremadura*

To serve 4–6

¼ kg chickpeas soaked overnight, 100 g stewing beef, 50 g bacon or a bacon bone, some pieces of boiling fowl, 1 large onion stuck with cloves, 4 potatoes, 200 g rice, ½ cabbage, 2 tablespoons tomato purée, 200 g each of *chorizo* and *morcon* (black sausage of the region) or black pudding, 1 teaspoon cayenne pepper, salt, mint.

Put the pre-soaked chickpeas in a large pot of cold water with the chicken, beef and bacon or bacon bone. Bring to the boil and simmer for 2 hours, skimming when necessary. Add more boiling water if it evaporates too much, then put in the whole onion, the potatoes peeled and cut into chunks, the rice, shredded cabbage, tomato purée, sausages and seasonings. Continue to cook for 30–40 minutes, or until the meat is tender. Serve the liquid separately as a soup, and the meats and vegetables arranged on a big serving-plate as a second course.

Lacón con Grelos   *Galicia*
Hand of Pork with Turnip Tops

To serve 4

250 g white beans, ½ kg of fresh hand of pork plus the bone, ½ kg turnip tops,
½ cabbage, salt and pepper.

This is one of Galicia's best-known dishes. It uses some of the
best products of the region, and is highly suitable for the cold
wet winter climate.

The beans should be soaked overnight. Put them into a large
pot with plenty of water and cook gently for an hour. Cut the
pork into small pieces and add to the pot, with the bone. Wash
and shred the turnip tops and the cabbage, put them in the pot
and season well with salt and pepper. Cook slowly for about an
hour, adding more hot water if necessary, until the meat is tender
and the stew very thick. Remove the bone before serving.

Fabada Asturiana   *Asturias*

To serve 6–8

400 g large white beans, 400 g salt pork, 1 salted pig's ear, 1 pig's foot, 400 g
salt beef (if not available fresh stewing beef may be used), 150 g *chorizo*, 200 g
morcilla, 100 g smoked ham, or 1 ham bone or knuckle, 100 g *tocino*, 1 onion,
1 small hot red pepper, 1 whole head of garlic, bay leaf, salt.

Soak the beans overnight in cold water. Soak the salt pork and
beef for a few hours (unless using fresh beef). Put the beans to
boil in fresh water in a very large pot with the bay leaf. Before it
comes to the boil put in the salt pork, the pig's ear and foot and
the beef, the onion and hot red pepper, all whole. Finally add the
head of garlic, whole and without peeling it. Cover the pot and
cook as slowly as possible for 1–1¼ hours, skimming and checking
occasionally to see if more liquid is needed; if so, add hot water.
Now add the smoked ham or knuckle, whole, the *chorizo* and the
morcilla, also whole, and the *tocino*, diced. Add salt if necessary
and simmer very gently for 2 hours or more. When everything is
thoroughly cooked remove the head of garlic and the bay leaf and
throw them away; transfer the beans and liquid to a large serving

dish. Cut the meats and sausage into large pieces and arrange them on top. Serve very hot. If there is any left over it is even better the next day. You will need plenty to drink with this dish, as it is extremely rich. In Spain this would be a *vino verde* (green wine) or dry cider.

Pote Gallego — *Galicia*

To serve 4–6

¼ kg white beans, ¼ cabbage, 3 turnips, 3 potatoes, ¼ kg chicken in one piece, ¼ kg stewing meat, 300 g cured ham (*serrano* should be used – otherwise smoked ham), 100 g salt pork, a head of garlic, 1 onion, oil, vinegar, salt.

Put the beans (soaked overnight) in the pot with water to cover and as soon as they start to boil add the chicken, meat and ham, together with the onion and the head of garlic, all whole. Then add the salt pork, also in one piece. After 2 hours add the potatoes and turnips cut into pieces and the finely chopped cabbage. When the vegetables are well cooked, add a tablespoon of oil, a little vinegar and salt. Let it boil a little more to reduce the liquid to a thick consistency. Serve the broth first, then the meat, chicken and ham cut into pieces, and the vegetables separately, with tomato sauce (nos. 1 or 3, pages 224–5).

Cachelada — *Leon*
Chorizo and Potato Stew

This dish is supposed to require special *chorizo* made in the Bierzo from locally reared pigs, as it is said that no other *chorizo* gives the same flavour from the fat, but it is very good made with ordinary *chorizo*.

To serve 4

1 kg large potatoes, 2 *chorizos*, salt.

Peel and cut the potatoes into big chunks, boil them with salt and pieces of cut-up *chorizo*. Do not use more water than necessary. When the potatoes are done drain them and serve with the pieces of *chorizo*. The liquid makes an excellent basis for vegetable soup for the following day.

Puchera Canario   *Canary Islands*

To serve 6

¼ kg chickpeas, ½ kg stewing beef, a small piece of salt pork, 1 bacon bone, 6-inch piece of cooking *chorizo*, 1 *morcilla*, 2 whole cobs of corn, a piece of pumpkin or squash weighing about 200 g, ½ cabbage, 4 potatoes, 2 pears, 1 sweet potato, 200 g green beans, salt, water, 2 cloves garlic, 1 envelope of saffron (2 pinches), 2 cloves.

Having soaked the chickpeas since the day before, put them in a large pot with plenty of water. Put in the beef cut into rough pieces, the salt pork, *chorizo* and black sausage also cut up, and the bacon bone. Boil gently for 1–2 hours skimming when necessary. The cobs of corn may be put in at the beginning if they seem to be tough, otherwise put them in after 1 hour's cooking. (All this may be done in a pressure-cooker to save time.) When the chickpeas are half done add the cabbage, cut up, the pears, peeled and cut in half (removing the cores), the pumpkin in cubes, the green beans in slices, the potatoes and sweet potato peeled and cut up. Cook for another hour. If the stew starts to get dry add some more boiling water. Just before the *puchero* is ready crush the garlic, saffron and cloves together in a mortar and add them to the pot.

This *puchero* has a characteristic sweetish taste and is usually served all together as one dish, with the sausage, meats and the cobs of corn cut up. It is quite delicious and very filling.

Carn d'Olla a la Catalana   *Catalonia*
This is an old Catalan dish.

To serve 4–6

250 g mutton or stewing beef, half a pig's ear, a thick slice of streaky salt pork or bacon, a neck of chicken, 250 g *cigrons* – beans from Catalonia (substitute butter beans), salt, 4 potatoes, a few celery leaves, a raw ham bone, a few inches of black pudding per person (should ideally be *butifarra negra*), pasta if liked.

This dish requires what is called in Catalonia a *pilota*, or ball, which is made as follows: 100 g minced beef, 100 g minced pork, 2 cloves garlic finely chopped, chopped parsley, cinnamon, black pepper, 200 g crushed pine-nuts, 2 tablespoons breadcrumbs, salt and egg to bind. Mix all together to make an elongated ball and roll it in flour.

Soak the beans overnight. Boil the stewing meat, pig's ear, neck of chicken, salt pork and the beans slowly for 2–3 hours. Then put in the prepared *pilota*, the potatoes, peeled and cut up, celery leaves, black pudding in one piece, and the raw ham bone. Boil for $\frac{1}{2}$–$\frac{3}{4}$ hour. When the dish is ready, strain off the liquid for soup (small Italian pasta may be added) and serve the meats and beans as a second course.

Guisado de Cerdo   *New Castile*
Stewed Pork

To serve 4–6

1 kg lean pork, 2 tablespoons oil, 2 tablespoons lard, 1 onion, 2 carrots, 1 tablespoon flour, approximately $\frac{1}{2}$ litre, beef stock, salt and 4 potatoes.

Put the oil and lard to heat in a saucepan with a large bottom and cut the meat into small cubes. Brown the meat gently on all sides then add the finely chopped onion and carrots. When the onion becomes transparent add the flour, and cook for a few minutes stirring all the time – then add the well-seasoned stock. Cover the saucepan, lower the heat and allow to cook slowly. Meanwhile peel and chop the potatoes into quarters and put them into the stew. If it becomes dry add a little more stock. It is ready when the meat is tender and the potatoes cooked.

Callos a la Madrileña   *New Castile*
Tripe a la Madrileña

To serve 4–6

1 kg blanched tripe, 1 pig's foot, 1 bay leaf, salt, 1 lemon, 1 *morcilla* and a 6-inch piece of *chorizo*, 150 g lean ham, 2 red peppers, 2 glasses of white wine, 1 small glass of brandy (optional), 2 tablespoons lard or pork dripping,

2 onions, 2 cloves of garlic, 1 tablespoon paprika, 1 tablespoon finely chopped parsley, a pinch of thyme, freshly ground black pepper, $\frac{1}{2}$ teaspoon cayenne pepper.

First wash the tripe and pig's foot and simmer them for 1 hour with salt and a bay leaf. Cool a little, cut the tripe into neat 2-inch squares and remove the flesh from the pig's foot. Sprinkle with salt and lemon juice. Cut the *morcilla* and *chorizo* into slices, dice the ham and de-seed and chop the red peppers. Put all these ingredients into a large heavy saucepan and pour in the white wine and brandy if used, add sufficient stock from the tripe to cover everything well and simmer gently. In a frying-pan heat the lard and put in the onions very finely chopped and the crushed cloves of garlic, stir in the paprika, parsley, thyme, black pepper and cayenne pepper. Cook gently for 10 minutes, then add to the pot of tripe, stir everything well together and season with more salt if necessary. Cover the pot and cook very gently for 2 hours or more until the tripe is tender and well flavoured and the sauce is thick. (A little cornflour blended with cold stock may be added to thicken the sauce.) Serve in a very hot tureen. Small boiled potatoes in their skins go well with this dish.

Callos a la Asturiana   *Asturias*
Asturian Tripe

To serve 4–6

1 kg tripe, 1 lemon, vinegar, 1 pig's foot, 2 marrow bones, 2 large onions, $\frac{1}{2}$ head garlic, 1 leek, 1 bay leaf, 1 teaspoon oregano, 1 tablespoon chopped parsley, coffee-cup olive oil, 100 g smoked ham, 100 g *chorizo*, 1 small tin tomato paste, pinch of pepper, $\frac{1}{2}$ small hot red pepper, 1 green pepper, salt, a glass of white wine.

On the day before this dish is needed prepare the tripe as follows: wash it well and rub it with cut lemon, pour over some vinegar and leave it to soak for 15 minutes. Then cover it with cold water and bring to the boil. Simmer for 15 minutes. Change the water and add the pig's foot, marrow bones, 1 onion, the whole garlic, the leek, bay leaf, oregano, parsley and salt. Add plenty of tepid water and cook gently for $2\frac{1}{2}$ hours. Leave to cool.

Next day cut the ham into slices and fry in olive oil, remove it and fry the sliced *chorizo* – remove this also and in the same oil fry the other onion, finely chopped. When the onion is soft add the tomato paste, a pinch of pepper, the hot red pepper (cut up and de-seeded), and the green pepper cut into thin strips. Add sufficient strained stock from the tripe to make a thick sauce and cook for a few minutes more. Cut the prepared tripe and the flesh from the pig's foot into pieces and put into a deep pan, with the fried ham and *chorizo*, and pour in the sauce. Add the wine and salt to taste and cook very gently for 2 hours or more. This dish improves with long slow cooking. Serve hot with a bottle of rough red wine and crusty bread.

Callos a la Catalana   *Catalonia*
Catalan Tripe

To serve 4–6

1 kg blanched tripe, olive oil, 2 onions, 3 tomatoes or 1 small can tomatoes, 1 glass white wine, 2 cups stock (from the tripe), salt, pepper, 3 tablespoons chopped parsley, 2 cloves garlic, ½ kg potatoes.

To prepare the tripe wash it thoroughly and simmer for 2 hours, or until it is fairly tender. When it is ready cut it in pieces and reserve some of the stock. Heat the olive oil in a large heavy saucepan and fry the finely chopped onions and peeled and chopped tomatoes for 5 minutes, then add the pieces of tripe, the wine and 2 cups of the tripe water. Season, and continue to simmer for ½ hour, then put in the potatoes, peeled and cut up as you wish, but not too small. Peel and crush the garlic, and add it to the stew, together with the chopped parsley. Check the seasoning. Cover and cook slowly for another ¾ hour by which time the potatoes will be cooked and the stew thick and delicious.

Vegetables

Spain and her islands produce an enormously wide variety of vegetables ranging from the ordinary to the exotic. In fact it is hard to think of any vegetable that is not grown somewhere between the cold mountainous regions of the north and the sub-tropical islands of the Canaries off the African coast.

In Asturias and Galicia the cabbages and turnips – and the apples – are as good as ours in England, hard and firm and crisp from the cold and rain. Further south on the dry dusty central plains of Castile and La Mancha, maize, lentils, chickpeas and beans are grown, also spices and the small hot red peppers sometimes called *chorizeros*. In the fertile valleys of the far south aubergines, small sweet artichokes, broad beans, huge water melons and gourds, red and green peppers, cucumbers and all the salad vegetables are grown in profusion.

The Canary Islands produce most of the subtropical vegetables such as sweet potatoes, mangoes, papayas, avocado pears, and of course early potatoes, and the exquisite tiny sweet tomatoes from the islands of Lanzarote and Fuerteventura.

The Spaniards prefer to eat their vegetables as a separate course, and since they are in such abundance they form a major part of the Spanish diet. There are many dishes that are made up entirely of one or more vegetables. Broad beans are one of the most popular, and these are also dried for use in the winter months. The protein value of dried pulses has always been relied upon by those who could not afford meat very often, and the great variety of dishes made from beans, lentils and chickpeas is one of the features of Spanish cooking.

Les Escalibades   *Catalonia*
Grilled Vegetables

This is a method of cooking aubergines, green or red peppers, and tomatoes over a charcoal or wood fire, but it could be done under the grill if there is sufficient space.

To serve 4–6
4 aubergines, 4 green or red peppers, 4 large tomatoes, ¼ litre olive oil,
1 tablespoon finely chopped parsley, salt, 1 clove garlic.

Put the whole unpeeled vegetables over a fire or under a hot grill. Turn them until they are well-blackened all over. Allow to cool slightly. Meanwhile prepare a dressing of olive oil seasoned with salt, crushed garlic and finely chopped parsley. Peel the vegetables, cut them into strips and sprinkle liberally with the olive oil dressing. Serve with meat either grilled or cooked over a fire, and accompanied by *all-i-oli* if liked.

Legumbres Asados
Baked Vegetables

To serve 4–6

2 green peppers, 2 red peppers, 8 onions, 8 carrots, 4 potatoes, oil and salt.

Choose vegetables of an even size. Cut the peppers in half, wash and remove seeds, remove outer skin from the onions, scrub the potatoes and carrots. Arrange the vegetables in rows on a large baking tray and sprinkle with salt and olive oil. Bake in a moderate oven, 350° F, gas 4, for 1 hour or until the potatoes are done. Serve with cold meat or fish croquettes.

Menestra a la Palentina   *Old Castile*
Vegetable Stew a la Palentina

This is a stew to be made in the spring when plenty of young vegetables are available.

To serve 4–6

2 tablespoons olive oil, a knob of lard, 200 g smoked fat bacon, 1 onion, 2 cloves garlic, 1 tablespoon chopped parsley, ¼ kg green beans, 1 lettuce, 2 globe artichokes, 2 courgettes, ½ kg small new potatoes, ¼ kg shelled peas, ¼ kg broad beans, ¼ litre white wine, a little stock or water, salt, pepper, grated nutmeg, 100 g chopped cooked chicken, ¼ litre tomato sauce (no. 2 or 3, see pages 224–5).

Heat the oil and lard in a large saucepan and fry the bacon cut into smallish cubes, add the finely chopped onion and the chopped garlic and parsley. Wash and chop the lettuce, green beans and artichokes, scrape the potatoes and slice the courgettes. Put all these into the pan with the shelled peas and shelled broad beans. Mix with the oil and add the wine and about ½ litre of mild chicken or ham stock or water. Season with salt, pepper and nutmeg and cover the pan tightly. Simmer very gently for ½ hour and then stir in the chopped cooked chicken and tomato sauce. Heat through and serve.

Pisto Manchego
Vegetable Hash
New Castile

To serve 4

2 onions, 2 tablespoons oil or lard, 50 g bacon, 4 courgettes, 4 ripe tomatoes or a can of tomatoes, 4 green peppers, 3 tablespoons ham or chicken stock, seasoning.

Chop the onions and fry them in the oil or lard in a deep sauce-pan. Put in the bacon cut into pieces. Cook for 5 minutes or so and then add the courgettes, peeled and cubed (if they are small there is no need to peel them). Cook gently with the lid on until the courgettes are beginning to soften, then add the peeled, de-seeded and cut up tomatoes, and the peppers with their skins removed (you do this by grilling them until they are black, then rubbing off the skins) and cut into strips. Season with salt, add a little stock and simmer gently until the volume is reduced. Skim off any surplus oil and serve with bread.

Tumbet
Baked Vegetables and Egg
Balearic Islands

To serve 4

Olive oil, 2 green or red peppers, 4 potatoes, 2 courgettes, 3 large onions, butter, fresh breadcrumbs, 4 eggs, salt, pepper, and prepared tomato sauce (no. 2 or 3, see pages 224–5) or tomato paste.

Fry the peppers cut into strips, the onions in rings, the potatoes peeled and cubed and the unpeeled courgettes in slices. Beat the eggs together with salt and pepper. Grease a pie-dish or casserole with butter and coat the inside with breadcrumbs. Put a layer of fried vegetables in the bottom and pour over a little beaten egg and some tomato sauce, then some more vegetables. Repeat till the dish is full, finishing with egg and a sprinkling of breadcrumbs. Bake in a moderate oven, 350° F, gas 4, for ½ hour. It should be crusty and golden.

Calabacines y Tomatos   *Catalonia*
Courgettes and Tomatoes

To serve 4–6

1 kg courgettes, ½ kg small ripe tomatoes, 2 cloves garlic, ¼ litre olive oil.

Wash the courgettes and slice them thinly. It is better not to peel them unless they are large and coarse. Sprinkle with salt and leave in a colander to drain for ½ hour. Blanch and peel the tomatoes and chop them. Heat the olive oil in a saucepan and gently fry the chopped garlic for 10 minutes without browning. Dry the courgettes with a cloth and put them into the oil, stirring thoroughly. Cover the pan and allow them to stew very gently for 15 minutes – they will sweat enough liquid to prevent them from browning. Add the chopped tomatoes and continue to cook for 10–15 minutes, stirring occasionally. Serve very hot as a separate course.

Judias Verdes a la Española   *New Castile*
Green Beans a la Española

To serve 4

1 kg green beans (runner or French), ½ litre tomato sauce (no. 2 or 3, see pages 224–5), 2 tablespoons olive oil, 1 small onion, 100 g ham, 2 cloves garlic, parsley, ground white pepper, ½ teaspoon cumin seeds, salt.

Slice the beans (string them first if you are using runner beans) and cook for 10 minutes in salted water. Prepare the tomato sauce. Heat the oil in a saucepan and fry the chopped onion and garlic, and the ham cut into cubes. Add the tomato sauce and plenty of finely chopped parsley. Bring to the boil and add the drained beans, crushed cumin seeds, and pepper and salt if necessary. Simmer for 15 minutes.

Pimientos Rellenos
Stuffed Peppers

Basque Country

To serve 4

4 large green or red peppers, 100 g minced beef, 100 g minced pork, 1 onion, 1 egg, salt and pepper, tomato sauce (no. 3, page 225), a little stock.

Grill the peppers until blistered and rub off the skins, then slice off the tops and carefully remove the seeds, taking care not to split the peppers. Keep the tops and stalks. Chop the onion finely and fry in hot oil. Add the meat and cook for 4–5 minutes, stirring all the time. Remove from heat and bind with a beaten egg, season with pepper and salt. Stuff the peppers with this mixture and put them upright into an ovenproof dish. Put on the tops. Combine a rich tomato sauce with a little stock and pour it over the peppers. Cover and cook in a moderate oven, 350° F, gas 4, until done, about 40 minutes.

Cebollas Rellenas a la Catalana
Stuffed Onions

Catalonia

To serve 4

8 fairly large Spanish onions, ½ cup rice, 2 green or red peppers, 2 tablespoons olive oil, 2 cloves garlic, crushed, 2 hard-boiled eggs, approximately ½ litre stock, pepper and salt, 2 tablespoons fresh breadcrumbs.

Peel the onions and cut off their tops about one-third of the way down. Blanch them and plunge them into cold water. Scoop out the centres, leaving behind 2 or 3 layers of flesh. Boil the rice in double its volume of well-seasoned stock and when it has absorbed all the liquid and is nearly cooked (about 15 minutes), mix the chopped centres and tops of the onions and the crushed garlic into it. Wash the peppers, de-seed them, cut them into strips and stew them in oil for 15 minutes. This may be done while the rice is cooking. Add them to the cooked rice. Chop up the hard-boiled eggs finely and add these to the rice. Check the seasoning and stuff the onions with this mixture. Put the stuffed onions into a shallow ovenproof dish and pour in the remaining stock – it should come about halfway up the onions. Cover the dish and bake in a moderate oven, 350° F, gas 4, for about an hour. Fifteen minutes before they are ready remove the lid and sprinkle the onions with fresh breadcrumbs and brown them.

Serve as a separate course or as an accompaniment to a meat dish.

Cebollas Guisadas   *Murcia*
Braised Onions

To serve 4–6

16 medium-sized onions, 4 cloves garlic, 2 tablespoons olive oil, 1 tablespoon vinegar, 1 tablespoon paprika, 1 bay leaf, salt.

Peel the onions and put them into a large shallow ovenproof dish, add the peeled whole garlic cloves and the oil, vinegar, paprika and bay leaf. Sprinkle with salt, cover the dish with foil or grease-proof paper and bake in a slow to moderate oven, 325° F, gas 3, for 2 hours or until the onions are tender. Serve either as an accompaniment to a meat dish or on their own as a separate course.

Guisantes con Cebollitas
Peas with Tiny Onions

To serve 4

1 kg shelled peas, 500 g tiny onions such as pickling onions, 28 g butter, 100 g chopped ham, salt and pepper, a sprig each of thyme, parsley and mint tied in a bunch, $\frac{1}{2}$ litre water, $\frac{1}{2}$ teaspoon sugar.

Peel the onions. Heat the butter in a saucepan and gently fry the onions and chopped ham for a few minutes without browning. Put the peas in and stir well. Add the water and herbs, season with salt and pepper and sugar. Put a lid on the pan and simmer gently for about $\frac{1}{2}$ hour, checking to make sure it does not get too dry. Remove the bunch of herbs and serve. This is a good way of using end-of-season peas.

Cebollitas con Patatas
Tiny Onions with Potatoes

To serve 4

½ kg small evenly sized new potatoes, ½ kg small onions or shallots,
3 tablespoons olive oil, ½ onion, sprig mint, small glass sherry, salt.

Scrape the potatoes and peel the onions. Heat the olive oil in a
saucepan and sauté the ½ onion very finely chopped. When soft
add the sherry. Put in the prepared potatoes and onions and sprig
of mint and about ¼ litre water. Season with salt and simmer very
gently with the lid on for 20 minutes – the vegetables should
cook in the steam. Serve with roast lamb or chicken.

Espinacas a la Catalana   *Catalonia*
Spinach a la Catalan

To serve 4

2 kg spinach, 1 coffee-cup olive oil, 2 tablespoons Malaga raisins, 10 pine-nuts,
2 anchovy fillets, 1 clove garlic, salt and pepper.

Cook and drain the spinach well and cut it up slightly. Put the
oil in a frying-pan and when very hot add the chopped up garlic,
the anchovies cut into pieces, then the spinach, pine-nuts and
raisins cut in half and with their stems removed. Season with salt
and pepper and cook over slow heat for 20 minutes.

Acelgas Guisadas   *Canary Islands*
Stewed Chard

Acelga is a common vegetable in Spain; it resembles spinach but
is coarser in flavour and texture. It is the leafy part of a species of
beetroot, probably originally brought into Spain by the Romans.
In England it is sometimes known as chard; young beet tops or
spinach may be used as a substitute.

To serve 4–6

2 tablespoons raisins, 2 kg chard or spinach, 3 tablespoons olive oil, 4 ripe

tomatoes or a small can of tomatoes, 2 cloves garlic, 1 onion, 2 tablespoons pine-nuts or blanched almonds, salt and pepper.

Soak the raisins in cold water for 2–3 hours. Wash the chard or spinach and cut into very small pieces, then cook it in very little boiling salted water for 15 minutes. Drain thoroughly. Heat the oil in a large saucepan and fry the chopped garlic lightly. Remove and set aside. Then fry the finely chopped onion. When it is half cooked put in the peeled and finely chopped tomatoes, season well and cook for 10 minutes. Add the chard, raisins, nuts and fried garlic and finally about 2 ladles of boiling water, stirring constantly.

Serve as a dish on its own with slices of toast.

Col Hervirdo   *Galicia*
Boiled Cabbage

This bears no resemblance to English boiled cabbage, and is good enough to eat as a separate dish.

To serve 4–6

1 large white cabbage, 4 cloves of garlic, 1 coffee-cup of olive oil, salt.

Wash and shred the cabbage fairly coarsely. Heat the olive oil and the peeled and chopped garlic in a large saucepan. Before the garlic browns add the cabbage, turning it in the oil till it is well coated, then add about 1 cup of water and a little salt. Put the lid on the pan and allow the cabbage to cook rapidly in the steam. Stir occasionally and make sure it does not get dry. Cook for only about 10–15 minutes. Drain off any liquid left and serve immediately, either on its own or as an accompaniment to liver or grilled meat.

Other green leafy vegetables such as spinach, chard, spring greens or kale may be cooked in the same way.

Zanahorias Negras con Butifarrones
Catalonia and the Balearic Islands

Black Carrots with *Butifarrones*

This dish is especially popular in Mallorca and along the Catalan coast where black carrots grow abundantly in early spring. They are not actually black, but a deep purple, showing an attractive pale green pattern inside when cut through. They are slightly tougher than ordinary carrots, and are good used in stews. For this recipe ordinary carrots may be substituted but will of course change the character of the dish.

To serve 4

About 12 black carrots, 12 large Mediterranean spring onions (substitute shallots), 4 *butifarrones*, olive oil, butter, a handful each of pine-nuts and Malaga raisins or muscatels, salt.

Cut the tops off the carrots and very lightly scrape them, just removing the surface bloom (this will stain your fingers black). Cut them into thin rounds. Remove the outside skins from the onions or shallots and cut them into slightly thicker rounds, using most of the green part. Chop the *butifarrones* into similar-sized slices. Heat a mixture of butter and olive oil in a saucepan or earthenware dish, making about 4 tablespoons in all, and stir in the carrots, onions and *butifarrones*. Cook covered on a very low heat for about 10 minutes, stirring often and adding a little more butter or oil if necessary. Throw in the pine-nuts and raisins and season with salt. Cook covered for a further 20 minutes or until the carrots are tender.

This is served as a separate course. If you have used an earthenware dish for the cooking, take it straight in to the table.

Butifarra con Rovellons
Catalonia

Red Pine Mushrooms with *Butifarra*

Rovellons or red pine mushrooms (*Lactarius deliciosus*) grow in the wooded hills of Catalonia and Mallorca. They are rather hard to find as only the tip of the rounded cap pierces the earth and the fact that they are almost the same reddish-brown colour as the soil makes it even harder.

To serve 4

½ kg red pine mushrooms (or substitute large field mushrooms), ½ kg *butifarra* (see page 000), 2 tablespoons lard, 8 tablespoons oil, 2 cloves garlic, parsley, salt and pepper.

Peel the mushrooms and, if very large, cut them into quarters. Crush the garlic and mix it with the oil. Spread a large baking tray with this mixture and put the mushrooms on top. Sprinkle them with oil, seasoning and chopped parsley. Put them into a hot oven, 400° F, gas 6, and bake them for 15 minutes, turning once. Prick the sausages all over and fry them in lard. Mix with the mushrooms and serve very hot with *all-i-oli* sauce (see page 216).

Habas con Butifarrones   *Catalonia and the*
Broad Beans with *Butifarrones*   *Balearic Islands*

In most parts of Catalonia and in Mallorca broad beans are grown extensively. In early spring their black and white flowers are seen blooming on every available patch of ground and between the trees in the almond and olive groves. Since they are to be had in such abundance there are a number of variations in the method of cooking them apart from simply boiling in a little salted water as we do in this country. The following recipe is only for very early tender beans as the whole pod is used.

To serve 4

1 kg very young, freshly picked broad beans, olive oil, a bunch of spring onions, 1 clove garlic, 4 tomatoes, 1 tablespoon paprika, 100 g *tocino* or fat bacon cut in dice, a handful of Malaga raisins or muscatels, 2 *butifarrones*, salt.

Wash the beans and chop them into ½-inch lengths. Heat a little oil in a large earthenware dish and make a *sofrito* of the chopped spring onion, the garlic and the peeled, chopped tomatoes. Add the paprika, *tocino* and raisins, then stir in the beans and sliced *butifarrones*. Add salt and a little water if necessary, cover and cook gently until the beans are tender, about ½ hour. Serve in the same dish as a separate course.

Habas Tiernas Alicantina *Valencia*
Broad Bean Stew from Alicante

To serve 4

2 kg broad beans, 1 lettuce, 4 tablespoons olive oil, 3 cloves garlic, 1 slice bread, 1 tablespoon wine vinegar, 2 teaspoons paprika, ground white pepper and salt.

Wash and cut up the lettuce and shell the beans. Heat the oil in a deep pan and fry the garlic and bread. Remove and set aside. Now put the beans and lettuce into the same oil and stew for a few minutes. Crush the fried garlic and bread in a mortar. Add this mixture to the beans, together with the vinegar and paprika. Put the lid on the pot and cook gently until the beans are tender – it may be necessary to add a little water. When the beans are done season with salt and pepper and serve as a main dish.

Habas de Vitoria *Basque Country*
Broad Beans with Chorizo

To serve 4

2 kg broad beans in pod, 150 g ham, 150 g fat bacon, salt, 200 g *chorizo* in one piece.

Pod the beans and put them in a deep pan, cover with water, put in the ham and the fat bacon whole. Cover the pan, bring to the boil, and cook slowly for about 10 minutes, then add the whole *chorizo*. Season with salt if necessary and continue to cook very gently for a further ½ hour. Strain off the liquid, and keep it as a basis for soup. Scoop out the ham, bacon and *chorizo* and cut it into fairly small pieces. Put the beans into a hot serving dish with the cut-up meats on top. This should be served as a separate course.

Faves a la Catalana   *Catalonia*
Broad Beans a la Catalana

Faves is the Catalan word for broad beans. The word *habas* is used more generally throughout Spain.

To serve 4–6

2 kg broad beans, 150 g pork ribs cut into pieces, a little lard, 1 tablespoon olive oil, a head of young garlic, a bunch of spring onions, a glass of white wine, salt, pepper, 1 tablespoon chopped parsley, 1 tablespoon chopped mint, 200 g *butifarra negra*.

Shell the beans. Fry the pork ribs in a large deep pan in hot oil and lard until golden. Separate the individual cloves of garlic and put them in without peeling them (if more mature larger cloves of garlic are used, peel them first and use only about 4 cloves). Cut the tops off the spring onions and remove the outer skin – put them in whole. Cook for a few minutes and add the beans. Pour in the wine and stir well, add the salt, pepper, parsley and mint and finally the black sausage cut into slices. Cover the pan tightly and cook on a low flame for about 20 minutes. Serve as a first course.

Faves a la Gitana   *Catalonia*
A gipsy way of cooking broad beans.

To serve 4

2 kg broad beans in the pod, 4 bowls Catalan barbecue sauce (see page 220).

Hang the broad beans on a wire by pushing it through the end of the pods. Cook them in the flame of a wood fire until the pod is well charred. Each person shells his own so that they keep hot.

Serve with barbecue sauce in small individual bowls. Young onions (a little bigger than spring onions) may be cooked threaded on wire over the fire in the same way, and eaten dipped in the same sauce.

Faves a la Mallorquina   *Balearic Islands*
Mallorcan Broad Beans

To serve 4–6

2 kg broad beans, 2 tablespoons lard, a coffee-cup olive oil, 1 onion, 1 tomato, herbs – which may include thyme, mint, marjoram and celery, 1 teaspoon ground cinnamon, 1 clove, 1 glass Muscatel wine, 200 g *chorizo*, 100 g *butifarra negra* (see pages 29–30), 100 g lean ham, 1 tablespoon chopped parsley, 1 clove garlic chopped, 2 breakfast-cups stock (ham stock is ideal).

Shell the beans. Heat the oil and lard in a deep casserole with a lid and fry the chopped onion and chopped peeled tomato. Put in all the herbs and spices, except the garlic and parsley, and fry well, stirring continuously, then add the beans and cook for a few more minutes. Pour in the sweet wine, lower the heat and add the sausages and ham cut into pieces and the chopped garlic and parsley. Finally add the stock and season well. Put on the lid tightly and cook over a low heat for 30 minutes. Serve in the same dish, as a main course. It is economical to buy a small knuckle of bacon, boil it and use the meat and stock for this dish.

Alcachofas
Artichokes

Spanish artichokes are usually small and though they are grown virtually throughout the country they are especially abundant in Catalonia, Murcia, the Balearic and the Canary Islands. The general method of preparation is as follows. Trim the base of the artichoke flush with a sharp knife and break off any damaged outer leaves. With scissors trim the points off the rest of the leaves and rub all the cut surfaces with lemon to prevent discoloration. It is best to remove the hairy choke in the centre before cooking. To do this, open out the artichoke and pull out the thistle-like leaves of the inner core – this will reveal the choke at the base. Scrape this out with a spoon, sprinkle with lemon juice and press the artichoke back into shape.

To cook the artichokes bring a large saucepan of well-salted water to the boil and carefully drop in the artichokes one by one.

Bring the water back to the boil and cook briskly, uncovered, for about 15–20 minutes. They are ready when the bases are tender when pricked with a fork. Remove with tongs or a slotted spoon and put them upside down in a colander to drain thoroughly. They may then be served either hot with melted butter or *all-i-oli* sauce, or chilled, with mayonnaise or a vinaigrette dressing (see pages 216, 217 and 219).

Alcachofas Rellenas
Stuffed Artichokes

To serve 4

8 small or 4 large artichokes, 100 g smoked ham, 12 small mushrooms, parsley salt and pepper, 8 thin slices of fat salt pork or bacon rashers, oil for deep frying.

For the sauce: olive oil, 1 onion, 1 glass white wine or dry cider, salt, flour, a little butter, 8 slices of bread.

Follow the instructions for preparing the artichokes (pages 202–3). Meanwhile make a mixture of the finely chopped ham, mushrooms and parsley, salt and a little white pepper. Put some of this mixture into each artichoke and wrap a slice of pork or a bacon rasher round each one and tie up with thread. Fry in deep oil for a few minutes, drain, and set aside.

To make the sauce, heat 3 tablespoons of olive oil in a saucepan and sauté the finely chopped onion. Pour in the wine and allow it to bubble, then add a cup of water and some seasoning and cook for a minute, stirring all the time. Pour this sauce into a large casserole with a lid and put in the artichokes. Cook in a moderate oven, 350° F, gas 4, for ½ hour. Cut the crusts off the slices of bread and fry crisply, remove the threads from the artichokes and put one on each slice of bread and arrange them on a large serving dish. Thicken the sauce in the casserole with a tablespoon of flour and a little butter. Strain and pour over the artichokes.

This is a complete dish on its own.

Berenjenas a la Plancha
Aubergines a la Plancha

Aubergines are cheap and plentiful in Spain. The next few recipes give simple ways of preparing them.

Dip the small whole unpeeled aubergines in water and put them directly on a hotplate or on to hot coals, turning frequently. Tongs are useful for this. Peel the aubergines when cooked, cut them into strips and dip in olive oil seasoned with salt.

Berenjenas Fritas
Fried Aubergines

Cut unpeeled aubergines into thin rounds and sprinkle with salt and leave to drain in a colander for 30 minutes. Dry with a cloth and dip them in flour. Fry in hot oil or butter for a few minutes and serve as a garnish for roast meat.

Berenjenas Asadas   *Catalonia*
Baked Aubergines

To serve 4

4 large aubergines, 2 crushed cloves of garlic, 2 rashers of fat smoked bacon, minced, thyme or marjoram.

Wash the aubergines. Mix the garlic and minced bacon with the herbs. Make a row of small incisions along the aubergines and push a little of the mixture into each with the point of a knife. Put them into a shallow oiled dish and sprinkle with olive oil. Bake in a moderate oven, 350° F, gas 4, for 20 minutes. Serve with meat.

Berenjenas en Batado
Aubergines in Batter

Peel the aubergines and cut them into evenly sized strips. Sprinkle with salt and leave to drain for 30 minutes. Dry them and dip into a light batter made with 2 tablespoons of flour, a little water and the stiffly beaten white of an egg. Fry quickly in hot oil and serve with meat.

Molde de Berenjenas
Aubergine Mould

To serve 4

4 aubergines, salt, 100 g mushrooms, a little butter or olive oil, ¾ litre béchamel sauce, grated nutmeg, white pepper, 2 eggs.

Peel and cut the aubergines into small cubes, sprinkle with salt and leave for 30 minutes to drain. Dry them and fry them in butter or oil with the sliced mushrooms. When they are soft, drain them on kitchen paper.

Make a béchamel, well-seasoned with white pepper and a little grated nutmeg, and stir in the fried aubergines and mushrooms. Remove the pan from the heat and beat the eggs and stir them into the sauce. Thoroughly grease a suitable mould and pour in the mixture; it should not come right up to the top as it will rise a little. Stand it in a bain-marie and bake in a moderate oven, 350° F, gas 4, for 20 minutes, or until set. Turn out or serve in the dish, as you like. Serve at once.

Berenjenas Rellenas
Stuffed Aubergines

To serve 4

4 fairly large straight aubergines, 1 onion, 4 tomatoes, 2 tablespoons olive oil, 200 g finely chopped or minced ham, 100 g very finely chopped *tocino*, 2 tablespoons chopped parsley, salt and pepper, 1 clove garlic, 1 tablespoon roasted crushed almonds, 4 tablespoons fresh breadcrumbs, 4 tablespoons grated cheese.

Cut the aubergines in half lengthways, scoop out and reserve the pulpy centre. Sprinkle the hollowed-out aubergines with salt and leave for 30 minutes. Drain, and simmer them in a little water for

10 minutes. Chop the aubergine pulp finely and mix it with the chopped onion and 2 of the peeled and chopped tomatoes, the parsley, ham, *tocino* and the crushed clove of garlic. Season with salt and pepper. Heat some oil in a frying-pan and sauté this mixture for about 10 minutes, stirring occasionally. Add the grated cheese and roasted crushed almonds and stir until the cheese melts. Fill the aubergines with this mixture and fit them side by side into a shallow well-oiled ovenproof dish. Cover them with breadcrumbs and arrange slices of tomato on the top, sprinkle liberally with olive oil and bake in a moderate oven, 350°F, gas 4, for 30 minutes.

Espárragos Hervirdos
Boiled Asparagus

Asparagus, like most good things, is probably best prepared in the simplest possible manner. It should be tied into not too big bundles and boiled in lightly salted water for between 18 and 20 minutes, certainly no longer. It should then be thoroughly drained and served, minus the string, wrapped in a napkin. Melted butter makes the best sauce to my mind, but vinaigrette dressing or mayonnaise are also good.

Espárragos Andaluz   *Andalusia*
Andalusian Asparagus

Asparagus grows wild in the sandy soil round the Mediterranean coast of Spain and the Balearic Islands. It may be used in much the same way as the cultivated varieties though it is much smaller and slightly bitter. This recipe is suitable for wild asparagus.

To serve 4

½ kg wild asparagus, ¼ litre olive oil, 2 cloves garlic, 1 slice of white bread, ¼ litre chicken stock (a bouillon cube may be used), salt, pepper, 2 teaspoons white vinegar.

Wash the asparagus and cut it into fairly small pieces. Heat the oil in a saucepan and fry the roughly chopped garlic. Remove it and reserve. Crisply fry the slice of bread, remove and set aside. Put in the pieces of asparagus and just sufficient stock to keep it moist. Cover the pan and cook gently for about 15 minutes, making sure it does not dry up – add more stock if necessary. When the asparagus is tender add the salt, pepper and vinegar. Crush the garlic and fried bread in a mortar, moisten with a little stock and add this to the pan. Stir in and cook for 2–3 minutes. Serve with triangles of fried bread.

Adobo de Espárragos   *Catalonia*
Marinated Asparagus

Either wild or cultivated asparagus may be used for this dish.

To serve 4

2 bunches of asparagus, 1 tablespoon white vinegar, 3 tablespoons olive oil, pinch of salt, a little thyme or marjoram.

Boil the asparagus in the usual way. Drain thoroughly and spread out in a shallow dish. Prepare a dressing with the oil, vinegar, salt and herbs and pour over the asparagus. Cover with a plate or foil and chill for several hours. Serve as an hors-d'œuvre or with cold meat or chicken.

Espárragos con Guisantes
Asparagus with Peas

Since asparagus is plentiful in Spain during its season, it is often cooked with other vegetables to make a main dish.

To serve 4

½ kg asparagus or two cans of asparagus tips, salt, 50 g butter, white pepper, 1 teaspoon white sugar, 1 level tablespoon flour, 1 tablespoon chopped mint, 1 kg shelled peas, ¼ litre water, a little milk.

If using fresh asparagus use only the tips and boil them in salted water for 2–3 minutes. Canned asparagus need only be drained.

Melt the butter in a saucepan and stir in the flour, allow it to cool for a few minutes and add the water to make a thin white sauce. Put in the asparagus tips and the shelled peas, the sugar, salt and pepper and the sprig of mint. Add a little milk and allow to simmer very gently for 15–20 minutes, stirring often and adding more milk if necessary. The sauce should be quite thick and the peas tender when done. Serve in little bowls with triangles of bread fried in butter.

Patatas con All-i-Oli   *Catalonia*
Potatoes with *All-i-Oli*

To serve 4

1 kg potatoes, ½ litre *all-i-oli* (see page 216), olive oil or butter, parsley, 2 large tomatoes thinly sliced.

Boil the potatoes in their skins. When cool enough to handle peel them and mash thoroughly. Mix them with the *all-i-oli* sauce and spread evenly in an ovenproof dish. Arrange the thin slices of tomato on top, sprinkle with chopped parsley and a liberal amount of olive oil or pieces of butter. Bake in a moderate oven 350° F, gas 4, for 20 minutes. Serve with meat.

Gachas Malagueñas   *Andalusia*
Potato Pancakes from Malaga

To serve 4

1 coffee-cup olive oil, 4 potatoes, 8 cloves garlic, 6 tablespoons plain flour, 1 cup water, salt, a little lard.

Heat the oil and gently fry the peeled and finely chopped potatoes and garlic until tender. Blend the flour and water to make a thick paste and season with salt. When the potatoes and garlic are ready, drain them and mix with the flour and water. Heat some lard in a small frying-pan and fry a portion of the potato mixture, turning it over like a pancake, and making one for each person.

Patatas Extremeñas   *Extremadura*
Potato Stew

To serve 4

1 kg potatoes, 750 g green beans (runner or French), 1 onion, 2 tomatoes,
2 green or red peppers, 1 clove garlic, olive oil, parsley, 1 bay leaf, salt and
pepper.

Cut the peeled potatoes into chunks, the beans into strips (if
using runner beans first string them), peel and chop the onion
and tomatoes finely, de-seed the peppers and cut into strips,
chop the clove of garlic. Pour a little oil into a casserole with a
well-fitting lid and put in all the vegetables, season with pepper
and salt, and pour over them about 2 tablespoons of olive oil and
half a cup of water. Add a sprig of parsley and a bay leaf. Put on
the lid tightly and cook in a moderate oven for about an hour.
This is a good way to use surplus runner beans during their
season.

Locro de Maíz   *Galicia*
Maize with Tomato Sauce

Maize or corn-on-the-cob is grown extensively in Galicia where
it is sometimes used instead of wheat for bread-making. Dried
maize for human consumption may be hard to find in Britain,
though it is sold in small packets for the making of popcorn.
These are quite suitable for the following recipe.

To serve 4

400 g dried maize.

For the sauce: a little lard, 8 tomatoes or 1 equivalent can of tomatoes,
4 cloves of garlic, 2 teaspoons paprika, salt and pepper, pinch of sugar, a little
water (or use tomato sauce, no. 3, page 225).

Soak the maize in cold water overnight. Next day drain thoroughly and boil in plenty of salted water until tender. The time is variable, but will be approximately 1–2 hours, or more if the maize has been dried a long time – a pressure-cooker is invaluable here.

While the maize is cooking make a tomato sauce as follows: scald, peel and chop the tomatoes if fresh ones are used. Heat the lard in a small saucepan and gently fry the tomatoes and chopped garlic until soft and well blended, about 20 minutes. Add the paprika, salt and pepper, a small pinch of sugar and stir over a low flame, adding just sufficient water to make a thick sauce. When the maize is cooked drain it well and serve at once with the hot tomato sauce poured over it.

Potaje a la Murciana *Murcia*
Red Beans with Rice a la Murciana

To serve 4

250 g red beans, 1 cup rice, 200 g green beans, 1 onion, 2 cloves garlic,
3 tomatoes, oil, salt, freshly ground black pepper.

Soak the red beans overnight, and boil them in 1 litre of water until they are almost done, adding more water if necessary. Add the rice and the washed and sliced green beans. In a frying-pan heat some oil and put in the finely chopped onion and crushed garlic. Peel and chop the tomatoes and add to the pan. Cook gently till the onions are tender and then pour this mixture into the pot, cook for a few more minutes and then add salt and black pepper to taste. The initial cooking of the beans should take 1–2 hours, but a pressure-cooker may be used to save time.

Lentejas y Anchoas   *Catalonia*
Lentils and Anchovies

To serve 4

½ kg brown lentils, 2 large onions, 2 cans anchovy fillets, 4 tablespoons olive oil, 2 or 3 large cloves of garlic, 1 pack of butter (approx. 225 g) – or half margarine may be substituted if it has not too strong a flavour, freshly ground black pepper.

Carefully pick over the lentils to remove any stones. This is most easily done by spreading them out a little at a time on a flat white plate or piece of paper. Many lentils from Spain have various kinds of tiny stones and grit among them, according to the area in which they were grown. Those from Lanzorote in the Canaries (which, incidentally, are by far the nicest, small, hard, greenish and full of flavour) are liberally sprinkled with tiny bits of the black lava on which they are grown. It is worth taking trouble to remove these if you value your teeth.

Wash the lentils and cover them with cold water. Bring them to the boil, remove the pan from the heat and allow to stand for an hour. Roughly chop the peeled onions and put them into the lentils, bring them back to boiling point and simmer for 20–30 minutes, or until the lentils are tender without being mushy. In another saucepan heat the olive oil and put in the peeled and chopped garlic. Let it cook for a few minutes without browning. Strain the lentils. Gradually add the lentils to the hot oil, a ladle at a time, stirring continually, and when they are all in, lower the heat and add the butter cut in pieces and stir until it melts. Pound the anchovies to a paste in a mortar – this is easier if you take them from the tin stuck together in one piece and snip them up with scissors first. Use all the oil from the anchovies. Add this to the lentils and mix very thoroughly.

Serve with lots of ground black pepper and green salad. This is also surprisingly good eaten cold.

Cocida de Lentejas
Lentil Stew

To serve 4

½ kg brown lentils, 1 bay leaf, salt, 2 tablespoons olive oil, 2 cloves of garlic, 1 slice of bread, 1 onion, 1 tablespoon flour, 1 teaspoon paprika, a small piece of *chorizo*.

Pick over the lentils thoroughly to remove stones and grit, and wash them. Cover with cold salted water, add a bay leaf and the sliced *chorizo* and simmer for ¾ hour. Meanwhile fry the chopped garlic and bread in oil and reserve them. Chop the onion finely and fry it in the same oil. When it is tender add a tablespoonful of flour and the paprika. Stir for a few minutes then pour into the lentils. Crush the fried garlic and bread very thoroughly in a mortar and add to the lentils. Taste for seasoning and simmer until the lentils are quite tender and the sauce thick.

Garbanzos Salteados
Chickpea Stew

To serve 4

½ kg chickpeas, or 2 cans of ready-cooked chickpeas, 1 large onion, 2 cloves garlic, 1 coffee-cup olive oil, 4 tomatoes or 1 small can of tomatoes, parsley, 2 tablespoons chopped ham, a small piece of cooking *chorizo*, salt.

The chickpeas should be soaked overnight and boiled in salted water for 2–3 hours, or until tender, unless canned ones are used. Chop up the onion and garlic and stew them in oil until soft, add the chickpeas, the chopped and peeled tomatoes, a small handful of finely chopped parsley and the ham and *chorizo* cut up small. Season with salt, cover the pan and cook gently for 15 minutes. The stew may be eaten hot or cold.

Arroz Empedrat
Rice and Beans

Valencia

To serve 4–6

500 g white beans or dried broad beans, one whole head of garlic, 1 tomato, olive oil, parsley, 200 g of rice, salt.

Soak the beans overnight, put into cold water and bring to the boil. Cook for 1½–2 hours until they are nearly done. In another pan fry the peeled and chopped garlic and tomato, add the rice and cook for 1 minute, then pour in the beans, including their liquid. Put in plenty of roughly chopped parsley and boil gently till the rice is done and has absorbed all the liquid.

This is a dish served to the workers in the *turrón* (see page 239) paste factories; in Jijona it is called *arroz de fabrica*.

Sauces

The best-known Spanish sauce outside Spain is probably *salsa española*, or brown sauce as it is called. Mayonnaise, or *mahonesa* in Spanish, originated in the town of Mahon in Menorca. Some say it was the invention of a French chef who had to make do with olive oil as butter was hard to come by (as was still the case even ten years ago).

On the whole, the Spaniards tend to amalgamate their sauces with the main ingredient of a dish, rather than serve them separately as is the French way, and the *sofrito* (a blend of onions, tomatoes and sometimes peppers and garlic, finely chopped and stewed in oil, page 215) is the starting-point of many dishes. Béchamel sauce and vinaigrette dressing are two standard French sauces which have been adopted by Spain and are used widely in Spanish cooking, and these too are often an integral part of the dish.

Many of the meat and fish *tapas* served everywhere in Spain are cooked in the most delicious sauces, delicately flavoured with herbs – oregano, sage, basil, thyme and especially parsley. Fresh coriander is a herb much used in the Canary Islands for flavouring sauces for fish and for fish dishes. The Moors introduced it to Spain originally, and in Arab countries it is still used in a great many dishes, mostly as a garnish.

Sofrito

A *sofrito* is not a sauce intended to be served as an accompaniment to other things, though it can be used in this way. It is rather a sauce in which other foods are cooked, and is the starting-point of many Spanish dishes. The basic recipe is as follows, but other ingredients such as red and green peppers, parsley and other herbs or a little wine may be added.

To serve 4
½ coffee-cup olive oil, 2 large onions, 2 cloves of garlic, 6 large fresh tomatoes or an equivalent can of tomatoes, salt and pepper.

Gently heat the oil in a frying-pan or a saucepan and add the onions and garlic peeled and chopped fairly finely. Allow them to stew gently in the oil, partially covered, for about 15 minutes or until soft, stirring often for even cooking. Meanwhile scald, peel and chop the tomatoes if using fresh ones. Add the tomatoes and seasoning to the pan, blend well and continue to cook gently uncovered for about 5–10 minutes, adding a little water if it becomes dry. The resulting sauce should be fairly thick, though the consistency may be altered to suit the recipe for which it is to be used.

Salsa Romesco   *Catalonia*
Romesco Sauce

This Catalan sauce takes its name from the small hot red peppers grown in the region. The recipe varies slightly from place to place and tends to be surrounded by an aura of mystique. Here is one version.

To serve 4–6

4 ripe tomatoes, 3 large peeled cloves of garlic, 8 dry red romesco peppers with the seeds removed or 1–2 teaspoons cayenne, 10 blanched almonds, 10 blanched hazelnuts, salt, ¼ litre olive oil, 2 tablespoons wine vinegar. A small glass of dry sherry and some chopped parsley are optional.

Put the whole tomatoes and cloves of garlic on a greased baking sheet and cook in a moderate oven, 350° F, gas 4, for about 20 minutes. Put the peppers and nuts on a separate sheet and put into the oven for about 5 minutes, being careful not to burn them. When the nuts start to turn colour, remove them from the oven with the peppers, and pound them both together in a large mortar. When the tomatoes are cool enough to handle, remove their skins and add them, together with the garlic, to the pepper and nut mixture. Add a little salt and pound this to a paste, and then add the oil drop by drop as for mayonnaise. Add the vinegar at intervals. All this may be done quickly and easily in an electric blender. If you are using sherry, add it last of all together with the very finely chopped parsley. Leave the sauce to stand for a few hours to allow the flavours to blend.

Serve with baked fish and shellfish – such as red mullet, shrimps, prawns, crayfish, mussels or sliced white fish.

This sauce is sometimes added to a fish or chicken dish during cooking.

All-i-Oli   *Catalonia*
Oil and Garlic Sauce

4 or 5 cloves garlic, 1 cup or more of olive oil, salt.

Peel the garlic and pound it in a mortar with ½ level teaspoon of salt. When it becomes a fine paste gradually drip in the olive oil, stirring all the time. If the mixture does not thicken, or starts to separate, add a small piece of bread and pound it into the sauce. A little cold water may be added at the end to dilute it.

This sauce is served with many meat, fish and vegetable dishes in Catalonia, and particularly with barbecued meat.

Salsa Mahonesa   *Balearic Islands*
Mayonnaise Sauce

To serve 4

2 egg yolks, ¼ litre olive oil, salt, the juice of a lemon or 1–2 tablespoons
vinegar.

The first secret of making mayonnaise successfully is to have
everything at room temperature. If you have forgotten to take the
eggs out of the refrigerator well in advance put them (in their
shells) into the bowl in which you intend to make the mayonnaise, together with a wooden spoon, and run some fairly hot
water into it. Allow it to stand for a few minutes, then remove the
eggs and dry thoroughly. Carefully separate the egg yolks from
the whites and put them into the warmed bowl. (The ideal bowl
to use is a large heavy mortar, as this will not revolve as you stir
in the oil.) Stir them round immediately with the wooden spoon
and start to drip the oil in – this is the second secret of good
mayonnaise – it must be literally drop by drop to begin with,
stirring quickly all the time. This is easy if you have an *aceitera* –
otherwise make shift with a small jug or whatever you find easiest
to use. When the eggs and oil have amalgamated they will start
to thicken, and then you can add the oil in a thin stream.

If the mixture curdles (it will look rather like sour milk and
stay runny) it is best to start again in another bowl with more
eggs; the curdled ones may be added carefully once the fresh
mayonnaise is well established. Continue to pour in the oil, adding a few drops of lemon juice or vinegar from time to time (you
can use either or both according to taste) and a pinch of salt. If
the finished mayonnaise is too thick it may be thinned with 1
tablespoon of hot water. The amount of lemon juice or vinegar
may be varied to taste, and herbs may be added if desired.

Salsa Española (1)
Spanish Sauce

There are many versions of Spanish sauce or brown sauce, and it
may include a glass of port or madeira if used with game.

Basically the sauce is composed of a thick brown roux, diluted with a rich stock made with meat or bones, onion, carrot, garlic and herbs all cooked together and strained. Here is one version.

50 g butter, 1 onion, 3 tablespoons flour, 1 carrot, 1 clove garlic, a little raw minced beef or raw game trimmings, 1½ litres stock (bouillon cubes may be used), 1 bay leaf, 1 sprig parsley and 1 sprig thyme, all tied together, black pepper, salt.

Brown the butter in a saucepan and add the very finely chopped onion; cook gently, stirring all the time, until the onion browns. Then add the flour to make a thick brown paste. Put in the raw meat, add a little stock, and then the whole peeled garlic and sliced carrot. Cook a little longer, add the herbs and seasoning and when you have a smooth consistency add the rest of the stock, lower the heat and simmer for 2 hours. Strain and use when needed.

Salsa Española (2)   *New Castile*
Spanish Sauce

2 tablespoons olive oil, 1 heaped tablespoon flour, 1 glass white wine, 1 onion, 1 clove garlic, 1 carrot, 1 sprig parsley, bay leaf, 1 clove, salt and pepper, ½ litre of water, 1 ham bone.

Heat the oil in a saucepan and lightly brown the flour. Add the glass of wine and let it bubble. Put in the sliced onion and carrot, clove of garlic, parsley, bay leaf, clove, salt and pepper, then pour in the water and put in the ham bone. Cover the saucepan and allow it all to cook very gently for 1 hour. Strain the resulting sauce, check for seasoning and it is ready to serve.

Salsa Española (3)

A quick way to make Spanish sauce.

50 g chopped raw ham or bacon, 2 onions, olive oil or butter for frying, 1 clove garlic, 2 tablespoons flour, ½ litre good meat stock, pepper.

Fry the ham, finely chopped onion and crushed garlic in the

butter or oil, stir in the flour and cook until brown. Slowly add the stock, stirring well. Season with pepper and a little salt if necessary and cook for 10 minutes. Strain the sauce before use.

Salsa Vinagreta
Vinaigrette Dressing

Vinaigrette dressing in its standard form is composed of three parts of olive oil to one part of vinegar, with a pinch of salt and finely chopped herbs if desired. Here is a Spanish version using proportionately more oil.

6 tablespoons finest olive oil, 1 tablespoon wine vinegar, a pinch of salt, a pinch of sugar, ¼ teaspoon mustard powder, 1 big clove of garlic.

Make the sauce about an hour before it is required. Pour the oil into a bowl and beat in the vinegar, salt, sugar and mustard. Crush the clove of garlic roughly in its skin so that the skin is broken but it still more or less holds together, and put it into the dressing. Leave for an hour, remove the garlic, beat the dressing again and use as needed. Add finely chopped parsley or thyme, dill or fennel or any other fresh herb available. You can make up a bottle of dressing which should keep for a week or so. Shake it well each time before using.

Salsa Béchamel
Béchamel Sauce

3 tablespoons butter, ¼ litre (1 breakfast-cup) milk, 2 level tablespoons plain flour, ½ teaspoon salt, pinch grated nutmeg, pinch white pepper.

Warm the milk. Melt the butter, remove it from the heat and stir in the sieved flour to form a thick paste. Put the pan over a gentle heat and gradually stir in the milk, taking care to avoid lumps at this stage. When the sauce is well amalgamated add the seasoning and cook very gently for 10 minutes, stirring all the time. The sauce should be of a creamy consistency.

Salsa de Mojo (Rojo) *Canary Islands*
Mojo Sauce (Red)

This sauce is unique to the Canary Islands and is served with
papas arrugadas, in translation wrinkled potatoes – tiny potatoes
boiled in their skins in very little water. A handful of coarse salt
is added to the water, and this forms a crust on the potatoes as the
water evaporates. They are removed from the heat at the critical
moment before they begin to burn. Accompanied by *mojo* sauce
they are often served in bars as a *tapa*. The sauce is also served
with meat or fish and is a great favourite with the Canarians.

To serve 4

2 or 3 large cloves of garlic, 1 teaspoon cumin seed, 1 teaspoon paprika, olive
oil, vinegar, a pinch of thyme.

Peel the garlic and crush it in a mortar together with the cumin
seeds. This takes some time as the garlic should be really finely
pulped. When it is as fine as possible, add the paprika and thyme
and pound a little more. Then slowly add olive oil, stirring well
as for mayonnaise. Add two teaspoons of vinegar and when you
have about half a cup of sauce transfer it from the mortar to
another bowl, and slowly stir in $\frac{1}{2}$ cup of warm water, or more if
you think the sauce is too strong. Allow to cool thoroughly before
serving.

There is another version of this sauce using finely chopped
coriander leaves in place of paprika. This is called *mojo verde* and
is served with fried fish.

Salsa Barbacoa Catalana *Catalonia*
Catalan Barbecue Sauce

To serve 4

4 cloves garlic, 2 sprigs mint, 10 toasted almonds, 10 toasted hazelnuts,
4 peeled tomatoes, salt, black pepper, vinegar, 4 tablespoons olive oil.

Crush the garlic in a mortar with the mint and the toasted nuts,
add the tomatoes, stir together, and add a few drops of vinegar

and salt and pepper to taste. Pour in the olive oil and mix thoroughly.

This sauce is served with meat and vegetables cooked over an open fire, or it is often served with broad beans simply boiled in the usual way.

La Picada Catalana *Catalonia*

2 pinches of saffron, 2 cloves of garlic, 1 pinch of salt, 50 g of mixed toasted peeled hazelnuts and almonds, ½ teaspoon ground cinnamon, parsley, a little sherry, stock.

Pound all the dry ingredients together in a mortar, add the sherry and a little water to make a fine paste. Dilute as needed with fish or meat stock.

This sauce is used in Catalonia to give flavour to many soups or stews. It is added halfway through the cooking and blends well with fish or meat dishes.

Salsa Escarlata *Catalonia*
Scarlet Sauce

To serve 4

1 small can red peppers or 1 large fresh red pepper, 1 clove of garlic, pepper, pinch of paprika, pinch of salt, yolk of a hard-boiled egg, ¼ litre (approx.) olive oil, juice of one lemon or a little wine vinegar.

Drain the peppers if canned ones are used. If you are using a fresh one, put it under a grill or in a hot oven till the skin blackens, allow it to cool a little and rub the skin off. Remove the seeds and cut it into pieces. Pound to a paste in a mortar with garlic. Add the egg yolk, paprika, pepper and salt and blend thoroughly together. Gradually add olive oil, as for mayonnaise, stirring all the time. Add the lemon juice or vinegar to taste as you go along. Serve with grilled fish, or shellfish.

Salsa Verde
Green Sauce a dressing for cold vegetables.

This is delicious with cold cooked cauliflower, green beans, cooked haricot beans, artichokes or any other cold cooked vegetable. It is also used with cold fish and shellfish.

3 or 4 sprigs parsley, 1 stalk celery, ½ slice white bread, 1 small clove garlic, 1 tablespoon wine vinegar, ½ cup olive oil, salt and ground black pepper.

Mince together the parsley and celery, or put through a herb mill. Soak the bread in vinegar and pound all these ingredients together with the peeled garlic to form a paste. Add the oil drop by drop, stirring at the same time to form a thick sauce. Season with salt and pepper and pour over the cold vegetables or fish.

Salsa de Piñones   *Catalonia*
Pine-Nut Sauce

To serve 4

100 g pine-nuts, 1 clove garlic, ½ teaspoon cumin seed, 1 hard-boiled egg yolk, ½ litre chicken stock (bouillon cube may be used).

Crush the cumin seed in a large mortar and add the pine-nuts and the peeled clove of garlic. Add the crumbled egg yolk and reduce it all to a paste with a little of the chicken stock. Transfer it to a saucepan and stir in the rest of the chicken stock, adding seasoning if necessary and simmer for about 10 minutes. Serve with roast chicken.

Pebre
Vinegar Sauce

To serve 4

¼ litre wine vinegar, 1 sprig thyme, 1 bay leaf, 1 small onion or shallot, freshly ground black pepper, salt, pinch of sugar, 1 slice fried bread.

Put the vinegar to heat in a saucepan with the thyme and bay leaf. Finely chop or mince the onion or shallot, and add it to the vinegar, season with plenty of pepper, a little salt and sugar, and simmer for 15 minutes. Crush the fried bread and stir it into the sauce. Simmer gently for a further 10 minutes and serve with meat or fish.

Salsa de Chili
Chilli Sauce

To serve 4

1 small onion, 1 clove garlic, olive oil, salt, ½ teaspoon oregano, 4 tablespoons chilli powder, 1 tablespoon flour.

Chop the onion and garlic finely and fry them in olive oil. Mix the chilli powder with the flour and add it to the pan when the onions are soft. Season with salt and oregano. Add enough water to make a cream-like consistency and boil gently for 20 minutes, stirring often.

This sauce is very hot; if a milder variation is required add a beaten egg after removing it from the heat, or use less chilli. Serve with grilled meat.

Salsa Picante
A Piquant Sauce for Grilled Meat or Fish

2 shallots or spring onions, 2 cloves garlic, 1 teaspoon cayenne pepper, ¼ litre olive oil, 3 tablespoons wine vinegar, salt.

Peel and chop the shallots (or spring onions) and garlic and pound them together in a mortar with the cayenne pepper. When a smooth consistency is obtained add the oil drop by drop as for mayonnaise, adding a little vinegar from time to time. Season with salt.

Escabeche para Carne
A Marinade for Meat

½ cup olive oil, 1 crushed garlic clove, salt, ½ teaspoon powdered cumin, ½ teaspoon oregano, 1 tablespoon vinegar.

Mix together all the ingredients and use to marinate a leg of young lamb, veal steaks or chops.

If the meat is then to be roasted or grilled the marinade may be used for basting.

Salsa de Tomate (1)
Tomato Sauce

1 onion, 2 cloves garlic, olive oil, a handful chopped parsley, 6 large ripe tomatoes or 1 large can tomatoes, ½ teaspoon crushed cumin seed (optional), pepper and salt, 1 tablespoon wine vinegar.

Chop the onion, garlic and parsley finely and fry in oil. Peel and chop up the tomatoes and add them to the pan. Season with pepper, salt and the vinegar, and the crushed cumin seed if desired. Cover the pan and simmer for 10 minutes, then put the sauce through a sieve into another saucepan and cook until the required consistency is obtained. This sauce should keep for a few weeks in a screw-top jar.

Salsa de Tomate (2) – Canaria   *Canary Islands*
Tomato Sauce

½ kg tomatoes, 100 g lard, water, 2 tablespoons olive oil, 1 tablespoon flour, 1 egg yolk, salt.

Melt the lard in a frying-pan and put in the peeled and chopped tomatoes. Lower the heat and allow them to stew slowly, adding about ½ cup of water and stirring from time to time. When the tomatoes are completely cooked and mushy put them through a sieve or food mill into another saucepan. Put 2 tablespoons of olive oil into the first pan and when it is fairly hot add the flour and brown it carefully without burning. Add this to the tomatoes and bring to the boil, seasoning with salt. Remove the sauce from the heat and when it is tepid blend in the raw egg yolk and allow to cool thoroughly.

Salsa de Tomate (3)

A very simple and quick way to make tomato sauce.

1 medium can of tomatoes, approximately 2 tablespoons of tomato paste, 2 tablespoons olive oil, ½ teaspoon sugar, 1 clove garlic, salt and pepper, 1 tablespoon vinegar, and parsley or chives or oregano.

Warm the olive oil in a saucepan, chop up or crush the garlic as finely as possible and stew it in the oil for 5 minutes without letting it brown. Put in the canned tomatoes and the tomato paste, blend thoroughly and add the salt and pepper, sugar, vinegar and whatever herbs you wish to use (these last finely chopped). Cook on a low flame until the sauce has the required consistency. It may be put through a sieve if a completely smooth texture is desired.

Desserts, Cakes and Biscuits

In Spain it is not generally the custom to finish the main meal of the day with a pudding, except on special feast days, although the flan or caramel custard is a universal favourite and is served both in restaurants and at home. Turned from a mould little bigger than a coffee-cup it is more refreshing than sweet.

Cheese is eaten both during and after a meal and is usually a locally made goats' or ewes' milk cheese – a *queso del pais* (cheese of the region), which will vary from place to place. It is often in the form of a flat round cake and is either firm, or very soft with an almost junket-like texture – seldom creamy. A famous exception is *queso tettila* from Galicia, which is made in the shape of a breast. One of Spain's best-known cheeses is the Manchego, which, as its name implies, comes from La Mancha and is made from the milk of the vast flocks of Manchego sheep.

The Spaniard indulges his, or more usually her, sweet tooth in all sorts of sweet jams and pastes, and various kinds of little cakes and biscuits made from almonds, eggs and icings. Originally these were made only in the convents, but now are commercially produced everywhere. Each region has its specialities, *polvorones* and *mantecadas* (very light crumbly shortbread, usually wrapped individually) come from Andalusia and *marzapanes* from Toledo. *Turrón* comes from Jijona and Alicante and is made in several different types, but always with almonds, eggs and sugar or honey as basic ingredients. It used to be eaten only at Christmas, but now it is available all the year round sold in slabs, tightly sealed to prevent the almond oil from seeping out. In this country, it may occasionally be bought in Soho.

There is a very thick, very sweet, drinking chocolate which Spaniards relish particularly for breakfast, taken with *churros* or *ensaimadas*. It has the consistency of custard and the children seem to be brought up on it. With such a start to the day who wants puddings?

A word here about tisanes. Although they hardly qualify as desserts I feel they should be mentioned, as they are a feature of Spanish life. *Manzanilla* is perhaps the most widely drunk tisane and is camomile tea. (The name *manzanilla* means little apple – the plant smells of apples.) The stalks and leaves are used as well as the flowers, and are sold in the markets in tiny bundles for one peseta each – if you buy a dozen you will usually get one free. Supermarkets sell sachets in the form of tea-bags but this way you lose much of the flavour. *Manzanilla* is excellent for the digestion and drunk last thing at night is said to guarantee a good night's sleep.

Other tisanes are *tila* made from the lime tree and used for its calming effects at funerals, *herba Luisa* which has no English translation, and various kinds of mint. *Mate* is occasionally to be seen in the shops, probably for South American expatriates who have become used to it.

Flan de Leche
Caramel Custard

Caramel custard can be ordered in almost any restaurant, though often these days it turns out to be the packet variety. Most Spanish housewives seem to have their own favourite way of making it – here is one method.

To serve 4

½ litre milk, 150 g granulated sugar, 3 eggs, 2 extra yolks, ¼ teaspoon vanilla essence, 100 g sugar for caramel.

Heat the milk and sugar until the sugar dissolves. Remove from the heat. Thoroughly beat the eggs and yolks and add the vanilla essence. Pour the slightly cooled milk on to the eggs and blend well together with a wire whisk or a fork. Prepare the caramel according to the recipe on page 245. Pour a little caramel into 4 wetted moulds or one large one and fill with the custard. Put them into a bain-marie (the water should come about half-way up the sides of the moulds) and bake in a moderate oven, 350° F, gas 4, for about 30 minutes. The custard is cooked when an inserted knife comes out clean. It should be fairly firm. Chill the custards before serving, and turn them out on to plates.

Flan de Naranja
Orange Custard

To serve 4

2 dl orange juice, 200 g sugar, 1 dl cold water, 7 egg yolks, 1 whole egg.

Mix the orange juice with the sugar and heat. When it begins to boil add the cold water. Cook slowly for 10 minutes. Cool. Mix the syrup with the slightly beaten eggs. Strain, and pour into mould or *cocotera*. Cook in a bain-marie in a moderate oven for ½ hour. Leave to cool in the bain-marie. Serve either turned out on to a plate or in the dish in which it was cooked.

Crema de Chocolate
Chocolate Mousse

Basque Country

To serve 4

Approximately 200 g dark chocolate, 3 tablespoons strong black coffee, a walnut-sized knob of butter, a few drops of vanilla essence, 3 eggs, cream and nuts for decoration.

Break up the chocolate and put it to melt with the black coffee over a low flame, stirring all the time. When it is completely melted remove it from the heat and blend in the butter and vanilla. Separate the yolks from the whites of the eggs and beat them one by one into the chocolate. Whisk the egg whites as stiffly as possible and stir these into the chocolate. Pour the mixture into 4 glass bowls and chill for 3–4 hours. Just before serving top with whipped cream and toasted split almonds. A delightfully unsweet sweet.

Marquesa de Chocolate
Rich Chocolate Mousse

Valencia

To serve 4

50 g sugar, 1 tablespoon flour, 4 separated eggs, 4 tablespoons milk, 50 g butter or margarine, 200 g semi-sweet chocolate, 1 teaspoon vanilla essence, grated peel of ½ orange, ¼ litre whipped cream, 100 g hazelnuts.

Combine the sugar, flour and egg yolks. Stir in the milk. Heat, stirring with a wire whisk until the mixture is the consistency of thin mayonnaise. Add the butter a little at a time, stirring after each addition till smooth. Remove from heat. Add the chocolate broken into little pieces, vanilla and orange peel, stirring until the chocolate is melted. Beat the egg whites until stiff and fold into the chocolate mixture. Cool. Pour into a mould and chill for at least 5 hours.

Serve decorated with whipped cream and chopped hazelnuts.

Frangollos
Pancakes

Canary Islands

To serve 4

125 g self-raising flour, pinch salt, 2 tablespoons sugar, ¼ litre milk, 3 eggs, tablespoon brandy, castor sugar for dusting.

Sieve the flour, salt and sugar together into a bowl. Beat the eggs and milk together, adding the brandy at the end. Make a well in the flour and stir in the liquid, mixing until it is quite smooth. Use a whisk if necessary. Heat a very little oil in a small frying-pan and pour in only enough batter to make a thin coating over the bottom of the pan. Cook for a few minutes and then turn. Both sides should be golden-brown. Turn out on to a heated plate and sprinkle with castor sugar. Continue to make pancakes with the rest of the batter, piling them up with a layer of sugar between each.

Pastel de Pascua
Easter Pudding

Balearic Islands

This pudding is eaten by the country people of Mallorca on Easter Monday. It is usually prepared the day before and served cold.

To serve 4

1 litre milk, ¼ kg sugar, grated rind of 1 orange and 2 lemons, 1 stick cinnamon (or 1 teaspoon powdered cinnamon), 4 eggs, about 150 g semi-sweet biscuit crumbs (crushed digestive biscuits are good for this).

Add the sugar, orange and lemon peel and cinnamon to the milk and bring it to the boil in a large saucepan. Allow it to cool while you whisk the eggs until they are light and frothy. When the milk is cool remove the cinnamon stick and fold in the beaten eggs. Carefully stir in the crushed biscuit and pour into a large well-buttered ovenproof dish. Put it into a fairly hot oven, 375° F, gas 5, and bake for about an hour until slightly risen, crusty and golden brown.

Platanos Fritos   *Canary Islands*
Fried Bananas

To serve 4

8 Canary bananas, oil for frying, castor sugar, lemon juice, a little brandy.

Choose bananas on the green side and cut them in half length-ways. Heat plenty of oil in a frying-pan and fry the bananas. Drain them and dust with sugar. Serve hot or cold, sprinkled with lemon juice and brandy.

Buñuelos de Albaricoque
Apricot Fritters

To serve 4

12 ripe fresh apricots, 2 tablespoons brandy or sherry, sugar, 250 g self-raising flour, ¼ litre milk, 2 eggs, pinch of salt, deep oil for frying.

Cut the apricots in half and remove the stones, sprinkle with brandy or sherry and a little sugar. Make a batter with the flour, salt, milk and egg yolks. Beat the egg whites stiffly and fold them into the batter. Coat the apricot halves with batter and fry them in hot oil, drain and dust with castor sugar. Serve immediately.

Manzanas Asadas Asturianas   *Asturias*
Asturian Baked Apples

Apples from Asturias are the best in Spain; this is the region where cider is made.

To serve 4

4 large equal-sized cooking apples, 100 g sugar, a little butter, 1 glass sweet white wine, 2 egg whites, apricot jam, a few drops of dry *anis*.

Wash the apples and remove the cores. Put them into a large shallow ovenproof dish and sprinkle them with a little sugar. Put a nut of butter into each hole and pour the white wine over them. Bake in a moderate oven, 350° F, gas 4, for 10 minutes. Meanwhile whisk the egg whites and the rest of the sugar and a few drops of *anis* until the mixture forms stiff peaks. Remove the apples from the oven. Spread a little apricot jam on each one and top with a spoonful of egg white. Sprinkle with sugar and put them back into the oven for a further 10 minutes, or until the apples are tender and the meringue brown on top.

Guayabas   *Canary Islands*
Guavas

To serve 4
1 kg ripe guavas, juice of 2 lemons, castor sugar.

Fresh guavas must be used for this, as canned ones are too sweet. They may be bought in Soho street stalls.

Peel and slice the guavas thinly. Arrange a layer in the bottom of a glass bowl and sprinkle it with lemon juice and castor sugar. Continue until all the fruit is used up. Chill in a refrigerator for a few hours before serving.

Faramayas   *Galicia*

250 g plain flour, 50 g castor sugar, pinch of salt, 50 g unsalted butter, grated rind of 1 lemon, 1 liqueur glass brandy, 1 tablespoon water, oil for frying, icing sugar.

Sieve the flour and salt and blend in the sugar and lemon rind. Lightly rub in the butter, then add the liquid and knead as little as possible to form a dough. Cover with a damp cloth and leave in a cool place for about 2 hours. Roll out very thinly and cut into squares. Leave on a floured baking tray in a cool place or on a marble top for $\frac{1}{2}$ hour. Fry in hot oil, drain well and dust with plenty of icing sugar. May be eaten hot or cold.

Brazo de Gitano   *Andalusia*
Gipsy's Arm – Cream-filled Roll

To serve 4

Butter, 4 eggs, 150 g sugar, 50 g self-raising flour, whipped cream, jam,
butter-cream or coffee-flavoured custard for filling (see page 244).

Grease a large flat baking tin with butter and dust it with flour.
Whisk the eggs and sugar together thoroughly then fold in the
sieved flour. Pour it into the tin and bake in a fairly hot oven,
375° F, gas 5, for 15 minutes, or until the sponge is cooked. Turn
out on to a large sheet of paper sprinkled with castor or icing
sugar. Cover with another piece of paper and roll it up while it is
still warm. This helps the roll to keep its shape. Leave for a few
minutes, then unroll and fill with whatever filling you care to use.
The outside of the roll may be decorated with butter icing and
sugar flowers.

Buñuelos de Viento   *New Castile*
Airy Doughnuts

To serve 4

¼ litre water, 40 g butter, grated rind of 1 lemon, 1 teaspoon sugar, 200 g
self-raising flour, 6 eggs, oil, whipped cream, artificial cream (see page 244)
or jam for filling, icing sugar.

Put the butter, lemon rind and sugar into the water and bring it
to the boil. Boil for 2 minutes, then add the flour and stir constantly for a further 3 minutes. Remove from the heat and gradually beat in the eggs one at a time (make sure they are at room
temperature, and not straight from the fridge). When you have a
smooth batter, heat an inch or so of oil in a frying-pan and drop
in teaspoons of the batter. Do not allow the oil to get smoking
hot, as this will stop the doughnuts puffing up as they should.
When they are done drain them well and make a slit in one side
with scissors. Push in whatever filling you wish to use – cream is
best. Sprinkle with icing sugar and serve.

Rosquillas de la Mancha   *New Castile*
Doughnuts from La Mancha

¼ kg self-raising flour, ¼ kg castor sugar, 6 egg yolks, ¼ litre olive oil, grated rind and juice of 1 lemon, 1 teaspoon of *anis* seeds, pinch of salt.

Sieve the flour and sugar together, add the oil and beaten egg yolks, lemon and *anis* and a pinch of salt. Knead together thoroughly and form into rings as for doughnuts. Put them on to a greased baking tray and bake in a moderate oven, 350° F, gas 4, for 20 minutes, or until golden. Dust with castor sugar.

Churros (1)

Churros are sausage-shaped doughnuts, crisply fried and eaten hot, coated with sugar and usually dunked in milky coffee, for elevenses, or at almost any other time of the day. They are served in cafés which specialize in them or from little carts in the street, and are very rarely made at home. If you would like to try them, however, here is a recipe.

To make enough for 4
½ litre water, 350 g self-raising flour, 2 teaspoons salt, deep oil for frying, castor sugar.

Bring the salted water to the boil in a large saucepan, remove from the heat, allow to cool a little and stir in the flour. Mix thoroughly until a smooth paste is obtained. Fill a forcing bag with a wide fluted nozzle with the batter and heat the oil for deep-frying until it just starts to smoke. Pipe a long snake of batter in the shape of a coil into the hot oil and fry it to a nice crispness. When ready, cut it into roughly 4-inch lengths with a pair of scissors and drain them thoroughly. Serve at once dredged with castor sugar.

Churros (2)

Here is another richer version.

350 g self-raising flour, an egg, ½ litre milk, salt, oil for frying, castor sugar.

Sieve the flour and salt into a bowl and make a well in the centre. Break into it the egg and stir with a fork, gradually blending it with the flour. When it starts to get too thick pour in half the milk and beat with a rotary whisk until all the lumps have disappeared. Add the rest of the milk and stir until you have a smooth thick creamy batter. Put some into a forcing bag and proceed as above.

Churros make a very popular quick snack for hungry children.

Ensaimadas   *Mallorca*

Anyone who has ever been to Mallorca will surely have tasted *ensaimadas*. These are a kind of very light bun, made in a round flat coiled shape, supposedly to have originated as an imitation of the Moorish turban. The Mallorquins say that nowhere else can *ensaimadas* be made in exactly the right way – due they say, to some magical property of the island air. *Ensaimadas* are made daily in every town and village bakery, to be eaten with breakfast coffee, or as a dessert. On Sundays and feast days they are filled with whipped cream pushed in between the coils. *Ensaimadas* of giant size suitable for whole families are made specially to order, and the baker's shop is usually stacked with round flat boxes of varying sizes in which to carry off these monsters.

People rarely make their own *ensaimadas*, but here is a recipe for those who would like to try.

To serve 4–6

½ kg of plain flour, 50 g of lard, 2 eggs, 3 dl milk, 10 g (1½ teaspoons) dried yeast or 20 g of fresh baker's yeast, 1 teaspoon of salt, 2 teaspoons of castor sugar, icing sugar.

Bring the milk to blood heat, add the yeast, castor sugar and salt, stir until dissolved and leave for 10 minutes or so in a warm place to start the yeast working. Beat the eggs well and stir them into the still warm milk. Sieve the flour into a large bowl, make a well in the centre and pour in the milk and egg mixture. Mix with the hands to form a dough. Set it aside in a warm place to rise, covered with a slightly damp cloth to prevent a skin forming. When it has doubled its size, which will take about an hour, turn it out on to a floured board and knead gently with floured hands. Divide the dough into 10 or 12 pieces and roll each one into a long thin sausage-shape, damp the sides slightly and coil round. Brush each one with plenty of melted lard and set aside in a warm place to rise. When they have doubled their volume again, which will take about $\frac{1}{2}$–$\frac{3}{4}$ hour, carefully transfer them to a greased baking sheet and put them into a hot oven, 400° F, gas 6, for about 20 minutes, or until they are well risen and golden. They may be served hot or cold – dust with icing sugar just before serving.

Tocinillo de Almendra   *Andalusia*
Almond Sweetmeat

To serve 4

250 g castor sugar, 7 tablespoons water, 3 eggs, 4 egg yolks, 150 g grated almonds, 100 g sugar for caramel.

Pour caramel into a wetted ring mould (for caramel see page 245). Melt the castor sugar in the water to make a syrup. Beat the eggs together with the extra yolks, pour in the slightly cooled syrup and stir in the grated almonds. Pour the mixture into the mould and cook in a bain-marie in a moderate oven. Allow to cool and remove from the mould. Serve at once.

Mantecados Sevillanos   *Andalusia*
Shortcakes

400 g castor sugar, 400 g lard, $\frac{1}{2}$ lemon, 500 g plain flour, icing sugar, cinnamon.

Beat the sugar and lard together with the juice of $\frac{1}{2}$ lemon until light textured and smooth. Sieve in the flour and work gently into a dough. If you can do this on a marble work-top so much the better. Roll out very thinly and cut into small rounds, making a little hole in the centre of each. Put on a greased baking tray and bake for 20 minutes in a low oven, 250° F, gas 1, without browning. Dust with icing sugar and cinnamon.

Polvorones   *Andalusia and general*
Shortbread

200 g plain flour, 100 g castor sugar, 100 g lard, 2 pinches powdered cinnamon, 50 g toasted and finely crushed almonds, icing sugar.

Spread the flour on a baking tray and toast it in a hot oven until golden (it only takes a minute or two). Allow it to cool thoroughly. Make a firm dough with the toasted flour, sugar, crushed almonds, cinnamon and lard and roll out to the thickness of a finger. Cut into small rounds or oval shapes about the size of a dessertspoon. Butter a baking tray and carefully put the shapes on to it. Bake in a moderate oven, 350° F, gas 4, for 15 minutes. Cool and dust with icing sugar, and wrap in tissue paper, twisting the ends.

These are sold everywhere in Spain in sweet and cake shops and are not usually made at home.

Pastelitos
Little Cakes

½ kg dried apricots (2¼ cups fruit pulp), 100 g sugar, 250 g shortcrust pastry, 25 g castor sugar, 1 teaspoon cinnamon.

Wash the apricots and soak them overnight. Cook until soft enough to pass through a sieve, or mash well. Add sugar to the pulp and cook again until very thick. Allow to cool. Roll out half the pastry and line a baking sheet. Spread the fruit mixture on this and cover with the rest of the pastry. Press edges together. Sprinkle with mixture of sugar and cinnamon. Mark into small squares before baking and prick each square with a fork. Bake in a hot oven for 20 minutes. Cool and cut as marked. This makes about 25 *pastelitos*.

Pastelitos should be about as thick as the little finger. Any kind of dried fruit or combination of dried fruits can be used. Raisins may be added to the apricot pulp.

Bartolillos *New Castile*
Almond Tarts

250 g puff pastry, 20 g almonds, 150 g castor sugar, 150 g water, 2 egg yolks.

Roll out the puff pastry as thinly as possible and cut it into rounds. Grease a tartlet tray and line the individual moulds with pastry. Blanch and crush the almonds and mix them with the sugar, water and egg yolks. Fill the tartlets and make a criss-cross shape on each with thin strips of pastry. Bake in a hot oven, 400° F, gas 6, for 15–20 minutes.

Bizcocho de Almendras *Andalusia*
Almond Sponge

200 g of butter or margarine, 500 g sugar, 250 g flour, 6 eggs, 250 g toasted, minced or ground almonds, 2 tablespoons brandy, almonds for filling, icing sugar.

Grease two flat cake tins with butter and dust them with flour. Cream the rest of the butter with the sugar and add the beaten eggs gradually, beating all the time. If it curdles add a little of the flour. Add all the rest of the sieved flour, the almonds and the brandy, pour into the two cake tins and bake in a moderate oven, 375° F, gas 5, for 20 minutes. Turn out on to a tray to cool, then stick together with jam and/or cream mixed with chopped toasted almonds. Dust the top with icing sugar.

Rollos de Almendras
Almond Balls

Murcia

500 g plain flour, 500 g sugar, 400 g ground almonds, 3 whole eggs, 2 egg whites and a little milk.

Sieve the flour into a bowl and add the sugar and ground almonds. Blend together thoroughly, then make a well in the centre and pour in the beaten eggs and mix with a fork to make a stiff dough. Add a little milk if necessary. Flour the hands and form the dough into little balls. Put these on a greased baking-tin and brush them with egg white. Bake for ½ hour (or until done) in a low oven, 250° F, gas 1.

Guirlache
Almond Sweets

Valencia

250 g castor sugar, 1 teaspoon lard, a handful of toasted almonds.

Heat the sugar and lard together until it bubbles, add the chopped almonds, and boil for 2 minutes, stirring all the time. Pour out on to an oiled tray, or marble table-top. Roll out fairly thinly and cut into strips before it hardens.

Turrón de Yema
Valencia

Turrón used to be a special Christmas treat and all the larger houses and estates had their own recipes for *turrón* making. Little bags and packets of *turrón* would be distributed to the tenants and servants of the household on Christmas Eve in return for gifts brought for the *dueña* (mistress of the house). Commercially made *turrón* is now available all the year round and it is very good indeed.

This recipe for home-made *turrón* comes from Alicante and it is quite delicious and simple to make, though it differs from the factory-made article.

To serve 4

200 g of whole almonds, 300 g of castor sugar, ¼ litre water, 4 egg yolks,
a little almond oil (if this is not available substitute a bland vegetable oil, not
olive oil), extra sugar for coating.

Have ready suitable moulds for the *turrón*, lined with oiled paper
cut to fit neatly. Special oblong wooden moulds with tightly fitting lids were traditionally used in old Spanish kitchens, but the
ice-tray from a refrigerator would do just as well, or a loaf-tin.
For this recipe use one large or two small ones.

Scald the almonds and remove the skins, grind them to a paste,
preferably in an electric grinder, or put them through a mincer.
In the old days they would have been pounded in a mortar. Put
the sugar and water into a saucepan and boil rapidly for about 7
minutes, or until tiny drops set hard instantly on a cold plate.
Do not let the sugar start to turn colour. Remove from the heat
and carefully stir in the ground almonds until you have a thick
paste which comes away from the bottom of the pan. Blend in the
beaten egg yolks. Press the mixture into the prepared moulds,
place some more oiled paper on top, cover with a piece of card-
board cut to fit and weight it down. Leave it for several hours in
a cool place to set. Turn out and remove the oiled paper. If you
wish to decorate the *turrón* in the traditional way cover the top
with a thin layer of castor sugar and with a very hot skewer
lightly burn criss-cross lines over the surface.

Yemas de Coco
Coconut Balls

250 g sugar, ½ breakfast-cup water, 250 g dessicated coconut, icing sugar.

Put the sugar and water into a saucepan and boil until the sugar
is completely melted. This takes only a few minutes. Remove it
from the heat and allow it to cool slightly, then stir in the dessicated coconut. Make the mixture into small balls (first be sure it
is cool enough), roll them in icing sugar and put them into individual paper cases.

Gofio   *Canary Islands*

Gofio is an ancient Canarian preparation of grain, either wheat or maize. It dates back to the indigenous people of the islands, known as the Guanches, who were virtually vegetarians; *gofio* was their staple diet.

The whole grain is toasted and then finely ground to a flour-like consistency. *Gofio* is still used widely by the Canarians, either mixed with milk as a breakfast cereal or added to soups and stews, or baked in biscuits or cakes.

You can make your own as follows: spread some wheat in the grill-pan and toast it slowly, shaking the pan often. When it cools put it into a coffee-grinder and grind to a fine powder.

Nowadays it is usually bought roasted to either a high or medium degree, but less than fifty years ago it was still made by the peasants in their homes. On the island of Fuerteventura there are a few beautiful old windmills which are still used for grinding *gofio*.

Bizcochitas de Gofio   *Canary Islands*
Gofio Biscuits

To serve 4

50 g *gofio* (see page 241, no substitute), 1 egg, 2 Canary bananas, 50 g
wholemeal flour, 1 teaspoon salt, 100 g sugar, 50 g dried milk, 7 tablespoons
oil.

Beat the egg well and mix in the mashed bananas, which should
be soft and ripe. Blend the dry ingredients together. Add the egg
and banana mixture and the oil to make a stiff batter. Drop
spoonfuls on a lightly-oiled baking-sheet and put it into a hot
oven, 400° F, gas 6, for 15–20 minutes until golden brown.
Remove from the baking-sheet with a spatula while hot, and cool
on a rack.

Quesedillas de Hierro   *Canary Islands*
Cheesecakes from the Island of Hierro

100 g butter or margarine, 100 g sugar, 3 eggs, ¼ kg soft Hierro cheese
(substitute cottage or curd cheese), 100 g crushed blanched almonds,
2 teaspoons blond, i.e. medium roast, *gofio* (see page 241, no substitute, but
may be omitted), juice and rind of 1 lemon, shortcrust pastry.

Cream the butter or margarine and the sugar. Separate the egg
yolks and whites and gradually beat the yolks into the mixture.
When it is light and fluffy blend in the sieved cheese, the *gofio* if
used, the almonds and the juice and rind of the lemon. Whisk the
egg whites stiffly and fold them in. Roll out the pastry as thinly
as possible and use it to line some greased individual moulds or
tartlet tins. Pour in the mixture and bake in a moderate oven,
350° F, gas 4, for ½ hour, or until the filling is set.

Tortas de Aceite   *Murcia*
Oil Cakes

200 g plain flour, 100 g sugar, 1 small glass brandy or rum, 1 egg, ¼ litre
olive oil, 1 teaspoon salt, grated rind of 1 lemon.

Sieve the flour and salt together, add the sugar, make a well in the
centre and add the beaten egg, grated lemon rind, brandy and
olive oil. Knead until a dough is formed. Roll out thinly and cut
into rounds. Dust with sugar and bake in a moderate oven, 350°
F, gas 4, for 15 minutes or until golden. Serve hot.

Pastel a la Gallega   *Galicia*
A Galician Cake

100 g plain flour, 100 g sugar, 1 tablespoon milk, 1 tablespoon baking powder
5 tablespoons oil, 2 eggs, 1 lemon.

Sieve the flour and baking powder together, add the sugar and
stir in the oil, milk, 2 egg yolks and the grated rind and juice of the
lemon. Whip the egg whites until stiff and fold them into the
mixture. Pour it into a buttered loaf-tin and bake for 30 minutes
in a moderate oven, 350° F, gas 4. The oil in this recipe gives the
cake a good keeping quality.

Nata
Home-made Cream

It is sometimes difficult to obtain fresh cream in Spain. Here is a
simple way to make cream if you have an electric blender. It
makes nearly ½ pint of cream.

¼ litre milk – could be dried reconstituted, ½ pack (112 g) unsalted butter,
1 teaspoon powdered gelatine.

Gently heat the milk without letting it boil, and stir in the gelatine until it dissolves. Cut the butter in pieces, add to the milk.
Stir until it melts. Allow the milk to cool slightly and then pour
it into an electric blender. Blend for 1 minute and pour into a jug.
Leave in a cool place for 2 or 3 hours.

Crema para Pasteles
Cream for Filling Cakes

¼ litre milk, 1 vanilla pod, yolks of 2 eggs, 100 g castor sugar, 2 heaped tablespoons cornflour.

Put the milk and the vanilla pod into a saucepan and bring to the boil. Allow it to cool while you beat the egg yolks and sugar together thoroughly. Remove the vanilla pod and pour the egg and sugar mixture into the milk. Blend the cornflour with a little cold milk or water and strain it into the pan with the rest of the ingredients. Cook it over a low heat for 5 mins, stirring constantly. Allow to cool before use.

Pasta de Membrillo
Quince Paste

4 large quinces, 1 kg sugar, 1 litre of water.

Wash the quinces and grate them. Discard the seeds. Boil the sugar and water together to make a syrup and stir in the grated quince. Cook slowly, stirring often until the paste is transparent and fairly stiff. Pour into little pots and use as jam, or press into a shallow oiled rectangular tin, and turn out when cold. This way it may be cut into tiny squares and eaten as sweets.

Cabello de Angel
Angel's Hair

This is a kind of jam, and it is very popular in Spain. It is made basically from the fibrous part of a large mature pumpkin or squash, preferably one kept from the year before.

To make 2 kg of jam

1 kg pumpkin or squash fibres, 1 kg sugar, 1 litre water, 1 lemon, 2 sticks cinnamon.

Choose a large piece of pumpkin or squash weighing about 2 kg. Peel it and cut it up. Cover it with water and boil it for 20 minutes, or until it is quite soft. Drain it and when cool enough separate the fibres, remove all the seeds and drain it thoroughly. Weigh out 1 kg. Simmer the sugar and 1 litre of water with the sliced lemon and the whole cinnamon sticks until it forms a syrup, remove the lemon and cinnamon and put in the squash fibres. Cook slowly, stirring occasionally for 1 hour, then test for jelling by putting a few drops on to a cold plate. If it does not run off when you tilt the plate it is ready. Put it into jars and seal in the usual way.

Caramel for Caramel Custard and Other Dishes

For 4 people

4 tablespoons granulated sugar, 2 tablespoons water.

This is the simplest way to make caramel without having to use a sugar thermometer. Put the dry sugar into a saucepan and heat it over a moderate flame, stirring all the time with a wooden spoon. It will very quickly melt and turn golden, then brown. As soon as it is brown remove it from the heat and put in the 2 tablespoons of water. Be careful, as it will bubble up. Stir it over a low flame until a smooth brown syrup is formed.

The hounds of Ibiza
nuzzled the purple shadows
of Moorish houses
where
the egg plant grew
in secret places
lost in gardens
of Phoenician stones.

PÁDRAIG MACMIADHACHÁIN

Regional Index

Index

MORE ABOUT PENGUINS
AND PELICANS

Penguinews, which appears every month, contains details of all the new books issued by Penguins as they are published. From time to time it is supplemented by *Penguins in Print*, which is our complete list of almost 5,000 titles.

A specimen copy of *Penguinews* will be sent to you free on request. Please write to Dept EP, Penguin Books Ltd, Harmondsworth, Middlesex, for your copy.

In the U.S.A.: For a complete list of books available from Penguins in the United States write to Dept CS, Penguin Books Inc., 7110 Ambassador Road, Baltimore, Maryland 21207.

In Canada: For a complete list of books available from Penguins in Canada write to Penguin Books Canada Ltd, 41 Steelcase Road West, Markham, Ontario.

SOME PENGUIN COOKERY AND WINE HANDBOOKS

THE BEST OF ELIZA ACTON
Edited by Elizabeth Ray

COOKING WITH WINE
Robin McDouall

PENGUIN CORDON BLEU COOKERY
Rosemary Hume and Muriel Downes

FISH COOKERY
Jane Grigson

THE VEGETARIAN EPICURE
Anna Thomas

WHOLE EARTH COOKERY
Sharon Cadwallader and Judi Ohr

LEAVE IT TO COOK
Stella Atterbury

LEFT OVER FOR TOMORROW
Marika Hanbury Tenison

ITALIAN FOOD

Elizabeth David

Exploding once and for all the myth that Italians live
entirely on minestrone, spaghetti, and veal escalopes,
this exciting book demonstrates the enormous and
colourful variety of Italy's regional cooking. Listing well over
four hundred dishes, clearly described and helpfully
classified, the author of *A Book of Mediterranean Food* and
French Country Cooking also enumerates the various herbs
and spices required in many of them, sensibly explaining
where they may be bought, and there are useful chapters
on Italian wines and cheeses. The result is an extremely
readable guide to eating out in Italy which is also a practical
text-book for reproducing the best of Italian food in your
own kitchen.

'I do not remember any other cookery book which has so
impressed me' – Margaret Lane in the *New Statesman*

'Certainly the best book we know dealing not only with the
food but with the wines of Italy' – *Wine and Food*

'Will delight anyone who has the art of cooking and good
living at heart' – *Guardian*

a Penguin Handbook

MEDITERRANEAN FOOD

Elizabeth David

This book is based on a collection of recipes made by the author when she lived in France, Italy, the Greek Islands, and Egypt, doing her own cooking and obtaining her information at first hand. In these pages will be found recipes, and practical ones, evoking all the colour and sun of the Mediterranean; dishes with such exciting and unfamiliar names as the *Soupe au Pistou*, the *Pebronata* of Corsica, or the *Skordaliá* of the Greeks. The book includes recipes from Spain, Provence, Greece, Italy, and the Middle East, making use of ingredients from all over the Mediterranean now available in England. The majority of the dishes however do not require exotic ingredients, being made with everyday vegetables, herbs, fish, and poultry, but treated in unfamiliar ways.

'In *Mediterranean Food* Mrs David proves herself a gastronome of rare integrity . . . She refuses to make ignoble compromises with expediency. And in this, surely, she is very right . . . Above all, she has the happy knack of giving just as much detail as the average cook finds desirable; she presumes neither on our knowledge nor our ignorance' – Elizabeth Nicholas in the *Sunday Times*

a Penguin Handbook

FRENCH PROVINCIAL COOKING

Elizabeth David

Elizabeth David always succeeds in inducing a desire to use each recipe as soon as it is read. Whether she is describing the preparation of a plain green salad, or the marinading of a haunch of wild boar, she writes with the same imaginative directness. Recipes like *pot au feu* are described in all their delicious simplicity, which, it is made clear, means cooking without elaboration and has nothing to do with the higgledy piggledy 'let's hope it's all right' technique. Some excellent advice is included on the choice of the tools that would always be needed in any kitchen.

'It is difficult to think of any home that can do without Elizabeth David's *French Provincial Cooking* . . . One could cook for a lifetime on the book alone' – *Observer*

'If I had my way I would have a copy purchased by public funds and presented to every young wife on her wedding day' – Vivian Rowe in *The Traveller in France*

'Make a beeline for Elizabeth David's new comprehensive study . . . this book will add a new depth of authority to your knowledge' – *Queen*

a Penguin Handbook

PORTUGUESE COOKERY

Ursula Bourne

Portugal is a small country, but it is one of many contrasts, with a distinctive and varied *cuisine*. From the fertile district of Minho in the North, home of *vinhos verdes* and abundant fruit and vegetables, to the sun-drenched Algarve, where rich cakes and sweetmeats betray their Arab origins, the Portuguese share a love of good food.

Portuguese Cookery shows you how to bring the gastronomic delights of Portugal to your own table. Ursula Bourne has assembled the specialities of each region with helpful suggestions on the best way to prepare them at home. All her recipes are both interesting and practicable and together they form an appetizing introduction to a country which attracts more foreign visitors every year.

a Penguin Handbook